India's Nuclear Options
Atomic Diplomacy and Decision Making

India Nuclear Options-Atomic Diplomacy and Decision Making

Brig. (Retd.) S. P. Lohia

Gaurav Book Centre Pvt. Ltd.
NEW DELHI-110002

Publisher
GAURAV BOOK CENTRE PVT LTD
4832/24, Prahlad Lane,S-207 Ansari
Road, Daryaganj, Delhi-110002
Ph.: 43570976, 23278261
Email: gauravbookcentre@gmail.com

Edition: 2019

ISBN: 978-93-83316-35-9

Laser Typesetting
JEE-VEE Graphics, Delhi

Price: $51.95

Printed
Neeta Press, Delhi

Contents

Preface

Indian government statements postulate the future Indian nuclear force as resting on pillars of its long-range Agni missile suite and emerging nuclear-armed submarine force. The first missiles of the Agni suite, the 700-kilometer-range Agni-I and 2,000km-range Agni II, are presently being inducted into the Indian Army. This demonstrates Indian intentions to ensure a credible nuclear threat is retained against Pakistan and posed to China, while signalling its technological military capability as part of its campaign for great power status.

Independent India emerged on the world scene when the world was still reeling under the untold horrors of the nuclear attack on Hiroshima and Nagasaki. The leaders of India who fought the British empire with their bare hands had no fascination for weapons, particularly nuclear weapons. Disarmament became an article of faith for India and we embraced it at a time when we had several other options open. Even though we embarked on a program of developing nuclear energy for peaceful purposes, India consciously abjured nuclear weapons and pleaded for cessation of all nuclear tests and for a non-discriminatory non-proliferation regime.

India should manufacture nuclear weapons not for waging wars against her enemies. Bombs are also to scare away warmongers. Even it we have no ^mention of attacking, there is no harm in keeping ourselves so well prepared and equipped that our enemies fear our strength and dare not risk a war with us.

Nuclear power is normally used as a deterrent. Any country which is not nuclear is at the mercy of those who are nuclear. A country like India who has reached advanced stage of nuclear technology would not like to give up her deterrent power by falling into the traps of "nuclear haves".

This book contains the fundamental and basic information of the subject and useful for teachers, students and researchers.

—*Editor*

1

The Evolution of India's Nuclear Policy

On May 27 th, 1998, the government of the then- prime minister Atal Behari Vajpayee issued a statement to the 12 th Lok Sabha titled the "Evolution of India's Nuclear Policy". This statement came about two weeks after India had successfully completed a total of 5 nuclear tests at the Pokhran range on May 11 th and May 13 th. The monstrousness of these events is reflected most notably in clause 14 of the statement: "India is a nuclear weapon state. This is a reality that cannot be denied." However, in the same clause it is also established that India shall refrain from using "these weapons to commit aggression or to mount threats against any country" and in clause 24 (the final one) it is stated that although "India stands at a defining moment of [her] history" the "rationale for the Government's decision is based on the same policy tenets that have guided the country for five decades".

Thus it is authorise that Vajpayee's government attempted to convince both the Indian and the international public that the nuclear tests would not alter the basics of India's foreign policy while at the same time admitting that indeed a watershed event had occurred.

The question now is whether this argumentation can be seen as reasonable or not. Basically, there are two problems: 1) Can the nuclear tests be seen as being concordant with India's foreign and nuclear policies until then? Were they even a somewhat logical product of these policies? 2) Once the tests had been carried out, would it be possible or even expedient for any future Indian government to keep following traditional policy fundamentals? Understandably, these problems have been addressed by different scholars in deviant ways, depending on their respective backgrounds.

The Indian physicist T. Jayamaran argues that the nuclear tests "signalled the initiation of a sudden and dramatic policy turn on nuclear issues by India's Bharatiya Janata Party-led government" as "the new policy abandoned India's earlier position in favour of using atomic energy only for peaceful purposes and it opened the door for the nuclear weapons option".

Consequently, he criticises the government for having conducted the tests without an underlying vision of future policies. Instead, according to him, the government tried to portray the tests as mainly a heroic scientific achievement.

The Vice-Chancellor of the University of Jammu, Prof. Amitabh Mattoo, claims in his key note address presented at the inauguration ceremony of the Think Tank on Defence and Foreign Policy of the University of Kerala's V.K. Krishna Menon Study Centre for International Relations in Trivandrum on April 12 th, 2008, that the nuclear tests of 1998 marked the "beginning of [...] a new phase of realism in India's foreign policy".

The tests made India's small strategic elite realise that a fundamental shift had occurred globally from moral, idealistic foreign policies towards *realpolitik,* a development which had started with the end of the Cold War in the beginning of the 1990s. Thus, while Jayaraman focuses more on official government policies Mattoo concentrates on what was going on behind the scenes where, according to him, indeed a new strategic thinking had begun.

The new realism among India's strategic elite has also been noted by Ashley J. Tellis, today a Senior Associate at the Carnegie Endowment for International Peace, who cites two articles from *The Hindu* and *The Indian Express* in which the authors hail the nuclear tests for ending both ambiguity and hypocrisy in India's foreign and nuclear policies. Tellis himself however emphasises the difference between nuclear testing and achieving a true nuclear capability.

According to him, India remained at a crossroad after the tests; and in trying to determine whether nuclear capability, i.e. a sophisticated nuclear weapons program, should be pursued or not India would probably move "in a direction quite different from that which most previous nuclear weapon states have taken". In Tellis' opinion India's further nuclearization process would rather be slow, gradual and distinctive "thanks to a number of factors—including India's traditional and highly publicized commitment to disarmament; its continuing economic and developmental constraints; its susceptibility to pressures emanating both from existing nuclear weapon states and from the global non-proliferation regime in general; its singular view of nuclear weapons as "pure deterrents" rather than as war-fighting instruments; its unique civil military system, which has few parallels in the Third World; and, finally, the fact that its adversaries' coercive capabilities, while significant, can be countered by a minimal, albeit perhaps not a token, deterrent". As distinguished as these accounts are they nevertheless have in common that indeed they view the nuclear tests of 1998 as a watershed event with far- reaching consequences.

Can we therefore dismiss Vajpayee's statement to the Lok Sabha as pure politics? Although it seems conceivable that the then- government of India had no clear vision or no sound conception about the consequences of the nuclear tests and how to deal with them it nevertheless cannot be denied that those responsible realised that the world had changed for India. An example for a new approach is the India- US nuclear deal which will be discussed later. What remains to be examined at this point is whether the nuclear tests are a result of a continuous foreign and nuclear policy or mark an abrupt break.

NUCLEAR PROGRAMME AND PROLIFERATION

Usually analysts proffer four arguments about proliferation. These are: (i) security concerns, (ii) prestige, (iii) technological imperatives, and (iv) domestic politics. Let us go through each briefly. The security or the realist argument posits that security concerns directly related to a state's physical security and survival ultimately drive a state to acquire nuclear weapons. Thus, a state operating under an anarchic international system and facing serious security pressures might go for the nuclear option. The second position informs us that nuclear weapons are a symbol of prestige. States acquire great power status or international recognition by developing a nuclear arsenal. The third view proposes that a state's decision to go for nuclear weapons is an inevitable outcome of the technological momentum created by nuclear research and development programmes. The final argument is that intra-bureaucratic politics as well as politicians' drive to score domestic political points may lead a state down the nuclear path. In other words, bureaucrats acting on the basis of their own individual policy preferences or bureaucracies carrying out their specific institutional interests may propel a country towards nuclear weapons.

India went for nuclear weapons has followers of all schools vying with each other to explain India's actions. For George Perkovich, domestic factors and prestige issues play the most important role in India's actions. He points out that India's quest for nuclear weapons capabilities began before a Chinese threat emerged and was driven not by military or national security experts but rather by bureaucrats like Homi Bhabha. It was also a reflection of India's moral norms and post colonial identity manifested through Nehru's recognition that India could gain international power, standing and a measure of security if she went for nuclear weapons.

Others like C. Raja Mohan and Bhumitra Chakma argue that it was mainly security concerns that led to India's decision to acquire nuclear weapons. Chakma convincingly writes that given India's pressing economic problems it is very difficult to imagine that she would invest such huge resources in a nuclear programme merely to satisfy the need for recognition and prestige. Similarly, India's decision to persist with the nuclear programme was not strongly influenced by technological imperatives or domestic pressures. If such were the case, then India would not have abstained from going nuclear in the 1960s and Indira Gandhi and other prime ministers would have chosen to carry out the tests when their domestic popularity was plummeting. While prestige, technology and domestic factors might have played some role, it was the emergence of China as a nuclear weapon state and later on, the development of the Pakistani nuclear bomb, which led India to acquire a nuclear arsenal. Raja Mohan argues in a similar vein. He mentions the same reasons as Chakma, but adds that in the 1990s the demise of the Soviet Union and the removal of a security back-up, the emergence of the US as the sole superpower, China's rise and international pressure to adhere to the NPT and CTBT" all aggravated India's security concerns and pushed New Delhi inexorably towards the nuclear option. Sumit Ganguly also places emphasis on the realist rationales while conceding that prestige and technological imperatives also had roles to play.

While the role played by prestige, technological and bureaucratic factors in India's nuclear programme must be acknowledged, the arguments made by Chakma, Raja Mohan and Ganguly – regarding the importance of realism in deciphering India's nuclear posture – appear to be the most convincing. At the same time, this 'realism' is strictly an Indian understanding of realism, and a study of Indian strategic culture is necessary to unearth the peculiar ways in which Indians have viewed security. Some argue that realism and culturalist explanations of international events are two distinct approaches. They then consider whether the culturalist explanations might yield superior insight. Stuart Poore, for his part, sees strategic culture protagonists as posing a direct challenge to the hegemony of realist thinking. However, there are, and can be, no uncultured realists. As argued above, India's approach to nuclear weapons – including the means of their development, the rationale for them, and India's stance on global efforts to stem proliferation – reflects a distinctive Indian way of thinking and acting. The use of *moralpolitik* is a good example of such behaviour.

Indian Strategic Culture and Administering

The Indian strategic culture, even one dealing with nuclear weapons, must start by understanding the role of history in the development of Indian strategic culture. Why is history so important? Because the movers and shakers behind India's nuclear journey were men and women who were conditioned by the way they understood Indian history.

Writing about the first atomic bombs, constructed by refugee scientists in the United States, John Lukacs reminds us that the "causes" of the atom bomb are historical (and ultimately, personal); they are scientific and technical only on a secondary level of "causes." The main reasons for the development of the bomb included Hitler, the Second World War and the persecution of Jews in Germany. Lukacs contends that the bomb was made at a particular time and for a specific purpose, not merely because at a certain phase of scientific development a certain stage of technological know-how was attained. He argues that it was actually because at a certain point in history, certain scientists began to fear that other scientists might be building an atom bomb for Hitler.

Although important scientific and technological breakthroughs had taken place between 1938 and 1945, these ought not to obscure the principal reasons behind the bomb's creation, which as in every historical act, were formed by personal choices, through historical thinking and historical consciousness, and conditioned by the political, racial, national, religious and ideological inclinations of responsible individuals. In the same way, one can see how Nehru's understanding as well as the general Indian perspective of Indian history influenced opinions about the building of the bomb.

The fact that India has been constantly subjected to foreign invasions and subjugation is ever present in the Indian mind, and Nehru was a serious student of Indian history who knew the feeling of insecurity it generated. This insecurity was premised, in part, on the belief that the Europeans had been able to intervene in India because of Indian divisiveness, and that Britain's ability to play off the Indian powers against one another had been particularly successful. But the overarching feeling was that this conquest was made easier, if not possible, because of superior Western technology.

Nehru himself was no exception to this conviction. Speaking on the occasion of the introduction of the Atomic Energy Bill, he noted that in the past few hundred years of human history the world had developed a new source of power, i.e. steam, and that this had subsequently ushered in the industrial age. India, Nehru pointed out, did not develop steam power and it became a backward country for that reason. The message of the speech is that India was colonised because of her lack of technological sophistication. This understanding of technological backwardness and its disastrous consequences for India's security has been a powerful rationale in Indian thinking about the nuclear bomb.

But there is another dimension to this need for countries like India. Technological backwardness not only meant a danger to her security, making her vulnerable to colonial and neo-colonial powers, but also implied social backwardness. Lacking in technological skills, and unable to master elementary, let alone complex, scientific and technological knowledge – this was how the civilisations of India, China and Africa were identified by European conquerors and colonisers and were thus deemed unfit to be counted as equals. Michael Adas writes that underlying all attempts to 'transform' non-Western societies was the assumption that Europeans were best suited to rule African and Asian societies because they represented the most progressive and advanced civilisations ever known.

The ultimate proof of this assumption lay in Europe's unrivalled scientific and technological achievements. European superiority manifested through technological advancements gradually but surely attained racial connotations. But even in the 19th century, when racist theories relating to non-Western people found wide acceptance among the articulate classes of Europe, many thinkers gave credence to scientific and technological proofs of Western superiority while rejecting those based on racist arguments. Racism should therefore be viewed as a subordinate rather than dominant theme in the European intellectual discourse on non-Western peoples. For newly independent India's leader, the attainment of technological and scientific prowess through the mastery of nuclear science was an objective that would not only ensure security, but also serve as a proof of the ability of Indians to compete with Western powers.

Thus, India's strategic culture was influenced by the need to destroy the myth of Western technical (also read military) superiority that has become the symbol of the Western claim to racial superiority. And any attempt to prevent such a policy is seen as perpetuating the inferior status of India and Indians as experienced during colonial rule. The terms India has used to justify her nuclear programme – apartheid, racism, equal treatment, etc. – have been reiterated a number of times. They are wielded either to endorse India's progress in developing a nuclear arsenal, or to explain India's position at various conferences on nuclear proliferation. This characteristic of Indian strategic culture was not limited to people like Nehru, who had spent most of his life under colonial rule, but can also be seen in recent times. Jaswant Singh's article and his position have already been mentioned. And Perkovich points out that when a Western researcher reported that India had sought material help from China for her nuclear programme, the then IAEC Chairman Raja Ramanna lashed out by saying that Indians are used to "white" people having a low opinion of them and that the researcher's remark indicated envy at India's achievement of total independence in her nuclear requirements. Raja Ramanna's behaviour, according to Perkovich, highlighted the recurrent and vitally important issue of racist colonialism prevalent, as India sees it, in the international nuclear arena.

Given the waves of foreign invaders that came to India, it is only natural that Indians should be concerned about any foreign intervention in South Asia. The Indian desire for nuclear weapons must be seen in this light. It has already been shown how the *Enterprise* exercise of 1971 led India to believe that a superpower's nuclear arsenal could also be used to thwart Indian objectives and threaten India herself. The fear of (Western) intervention with its obvious security connotations for India has been a part of Indian strategic culture due to Western forays and the subsequent conquest by Britain in the eighteenth century, reinforced by the experience of 1971.

The importance of seeking a nuclear capability to ward off the probability of any such event occurring again cannot be emphasised enough. India has always been sensitive to any nuclear threat made by Western powers against non-nuclear states, and Rajiv Gandhi was in tune with this position when he made known that he was very concerned by the nuclear threats implied during the Gulf crisis of 1990-91. A similar concern and uneasiness engulfed Indian policy makers and analysts when the North Atlantic Treaty Organization (NATO) decided to intervene in the crisis surrounding the former Yugoslavia in 1999. Such an act was perceived by Indians, suffering from their own separatist conflicts, as a harbinger of more unilateral actions by the United States and thus justified India's acquisition of nuclear weapons. Indian history, in short, is an important source for understanding Indian strategic culture with regard to nuclear weapons.

The role of religion in understanding the nature of Indian strategic culture is also significant for "religion is a particularly useful device for sacralizing violence and thus legitimizing it." Not only does religion play a cathartic influence on the way societies see war, it also influences the way societies act in times of war and peace and their approach to the use of force. Looking for the traits of a community's strategic culture in religion might not be a common practice in contemporary social sciences, but in a country like India, where the influence of Hinduism is so powerful and pervades all aspects of life, it would be a most serious error to ignore it.

The Indian quest for nuclear weapons has been justified by some analysts as having its roots in Hinduism's sacred texts. In the *Vedas*, the *Epics* and the *Puranas*, citations can be found which might be said to describe ancient weapons of mass destruction, perhaps even nuclear weapons. Indeed some analysts identify the most terrible weapon described in the *Mahabharata* (one of the *Epics*), the *Brahmastra*, as the ultimate weapon, the modern version of which is the nuclear bomb. While the modern mind will rightly find this claim incredible, given the powerful impact such religious texts have on the Indian mind, it would be wise not to ignore them totally. A devoted admirer of science and technology like Nehru identified the tendency to cite the presence of WMD in the ancient texts as nothing more than traditional stories of magical exploits. But elsewhere Nehru quotes Goethe's observation on Roman myths ("if the Romans were great enough to invent things like that, we at least should be great enough to believe them") and suggests that Hindu epics and stories should be believed. It is clear that nuclear weapons were not totally unacceptable to the Indian mind, at least from a religious point of view.

It has already been pointed out that *moralpolitik* has been a significant, if not the most important, characteristic of the Indian strategic culture insofar as the issue of nuclear weapons is concerned. This *moralpolitik* trait also finds its justification and practice in Hindu religious texts. A study of the two epics, *Ramayana* and *Mahabharata,* provides a better understanding of the Indian propensity to take a high moral position publicly but to secretly and deviously act in a completely different manner. This chapter proposes that Indian strategic culture has two traits, both derived from the central characters of *Ramayana* and *Mahabharata,* i.e., Rama and Krishna respectively. Both Rama and Krishna's features operate concurrently in the Indian strategic mind.

Let us briefly identify these two features. The central character of the *Ramayana* is Rama, a prince forced into exile through the evil machinations of his stepmother. The *Ramayana* is all about the adventures of Rama as he endures his exile and finally reclaims the throne. Rama is an incarnation of Vishnu (one of the three main gods who rule the Hindu pantheon of gods) and is the very embodiment of goodness. He is virtuous, truthful, and mighty but always on the side of the right, a fierce warrior but seldom moved by anger, kind and helpful. There were only a few minor lapses in his impeccable conduct. Rama displayed a fatalistic nature through his acceptance of suffering. He would not fight for his rights. He accepts his fate or karma and will not struggle against it. The main character of *Mahabharata* is somewhat difficult to pin down as the epic contains quite a few great heroes. The story centres on an apocalyptic battle pitting two sides (kinsmen) and ends with the defeat of Kauravas and the victory of Pandavas. The Pandavas are helped in this titanic battle by Krishna, another incarnation of Vishnu. But unlike Rama, Krishna is not bound by any ethical considerations. It was Krishna's crafty and resourceful ways that led to the extermination of the Kauravas. Deception, subterfuge, a relentlessly offensive posture and the use of cunning methods were Krishna's forte. It is Krishna who urges Arjuna, the great warrior hero of the Pandavas, immobilised by the prospect of fratricidal war, to show no pity or remorse, but to do his duty (*dharma*) and kill his enemies even if they were Arjuna's cousins, teachers, mentors and kinsmen.

Indian strategic culture sees an interaction between both these traits. Thus India talks about morality, virtue and victimhood – the Rama of world politics. At the same time India will resort to whatever means are necessary to attain her objective – the Indian Krishna. Therefore, the *moralpolitik* trait of Indian strategic culture embodies both these values within itself. But it has to be remembered that though the *Ramayana* and the *Mahabharata* are immensely popular epics, it is the *Mahabharata* that really captures the Indian mind. In other words Rama is the Indian ideal, Krishna the Indian reality. India will adhere simultaneously to both postures, as *moralpolitik* stipulates, without any contradiction. After all, are not Krishna and Rama incarnations of one entity, Vishnu?

The importance of religious beliefs influencing Indian strategic culture must also take into account that most familiar feature of Hindu religion – the caste system. In an interesting model developed by Anirudha Gupta, one sees independent India formulating a foreign policy in South Asia based on a "caste" system. Thus, India is the Brahmin of the region and other states fall into various castes according to their capabilities. The same framework can be applied to the world system which is perceived to be rigidly hierarchical. As per the stipulations of the caste system, the Brahmin is at the top of the social hierarchy and India's quest for nuclear weapons can be identified as a means by which a 'Brahmin' India seeks to be in the top rank of the world hierarchy. And as no one can deny the Brahmin his divine right to be at the top, any proliferation measure intended to prevent India from attaining her rightful status is to be ignored. Therefore, the reasoning behind India's nuclear programme and her behaviour with regard to such weapons must be approached with an understanding of the religious beliefs and characteristics of Indian society. Such an understanding will help explain why India's realist, i.e. *moralpolitik,* approach to nuclear weapons is so uniquely Indian. While religious texts and beliefs help shed light on the use of *moralpolitik,* one must also note that India's actions have their origins in the teachings of traditional Indian strategic thinking.

The most important source of such thinking is the *Arthashastra* written by Kautilya. It was with the help of Kautilya that Chandragupta Maurya laid the foundations of a truly great Indian empire in 320 B.C. For understanding India's adherence to *moralpolitik* policies, it should be noted that Kautilya advocated the use of deceit to attain one's objective and such methods as wearing a mask of moral probity, religious righteousness or citing moral righteousness to mask one's intentions, all fall under this category. Nehru was strongly influenced by Kautilya's theories, and it is important to consider how Indian strategic culture has been influenced by Kautilya's teachings. Indian strategic culture and its impact on the nuclear programme must take India's geographical realities into consideration.

George Tanham in his seminal essay on Indian strategic thinking identified geography as having profoundly affected Indian history and culture and therefore her strategic thinking. A history of invasion along India's north-western routes has traditionally oriented defence planners to pay special attention to that region. The arrival of the Europeans from the sea and their naval superiority made India aware of the need for a powerful navy. When one thinks of India's nuclear programme, geography is seldom mentioned.

But it has profound implications. Even though India is placed in the South Asian region by analysts, India's security thinking takes into consideration the fact that China, too, is an actor in the South Asian strategic framework. China and India share a long border and China has a geographical advantage through her control over the Tibetan plateau overlooking the plains of India. There is also the reality of China's military and nuclear connection with

Pakistan. Most Western analysts are unable to include an 'outside' country in their neatly compartmentalised artificial geographical units, but the fact is that China is included by the Indians in any nuclear calculation in South Asia.

Expression of Indian Strategic Culture

The exclusion of the armed forces from the nuclear programme decision-making process has been made clear by George Perkovich in his study. The absence of the armed forces from the decision-making loop on the nuclear issue resulted in one army chief, General K. Sundarji, depicting the frustration of the service chiefs through a novel titled *The Blind Men of Hindustan*. On the other hand, various other actors such as the political parties, the Indian Parliament, the bureaucracy and even public opinion, have had little or no impact on decisions relating to the nuclear programme. The real debate on nuclear weapons has been carried on by followers of Mahatma Gandhi who stressed the principles of nonviolence and morality in India's actions. While this paper has argued that Gandhi himself was not against violence when it came to pursuing India's interests, the truth is that some segments of the Indian population came to adhere rigidly to such a concept, as a result of misreading the subtle nature of the thoughts and actions of Gandhi and Nehru. Nevertheless, in the 1970s the seemingly contradictory approaches were merged through a clever synthesis, resulting in a now widely accepted formula. Known as the Subrahmanyam formula, it reinforced the broad strategic culture under which the nuclear programme is located. It stipulated that India would acquire nuclear weapons in order to pressure the nuclear 'haves' to disarm, and to protect itself against nuclear blackmail. Thus, by combining idealism with self-interest, the thunder of the no-bomb lobby – which had a negligible impact, if at all, on the programme – was taken away.

But while in the previous years the armed services had very little to do with nuclear weapons, this now seems to be changing. Further, Indian strategic culture should not be perceived to be static. With the development of an Indian triad, it is undergoing a slow but substantive change, and this is taking place in the balance between the political and operational aspects of deterrence.

The once overwhelming political understanding of nuclear weapons manifested through the total absence of the armed forces from the nuclear arena is slowly giving way to a more operational conception of nuclear weapons.

The development of various delivery systems – including long range missiles and weapons platform systems like nuclear submarines – is pushing the erstwhile practice of deterrence, which remained restricted to broad declarations on doctrine and the development of limited capabilities, towards more pressing operational questions about the quantity and quality of weapons and the infrastructure surrounding them.

The journey India has taken from the writing of the letter in 1944 by Bhabha to the Tata Foundation, to the nuclear tests of 1998, has been a long and arduous one.

As this chapter has tried to show, realist security considerations played the most important role in propelling India towards nuclear weapons. But this realist thinking has been Indian in nature. The motivations for such thinking and behaviour are influenced by what India thinks about herself. Thus, one notices how history, religion and geography have all interacted and produced a distinctively Indian approach to nuclear weapons.

While all the nuclear states of the world have travelled more or less the same path towards developing nuclear weapons, the rationales and the way they went about doing it differed. Strategic culture helps explain these different pathways and styles. In India's case a distinctive style, that of *moralpolitik*, epitomises the Indian way of approaching the nuclear issue. This *moralpolitik* has been brought about by India's history, geography, religious and strategic thinking. It is important to recognize that this culture is not transhistorical, either in the sense that it can be traced back to some 'authentic' pre-colonial tradition or that it is timeless, immutable and unchanging. It is a strategic culture influenced by events, experiences past and present and modified as and when thought necessary. As the world awakens to the growing importance of India, an understanding of Indian strategic culture as discerned from her nuclear policy will certainly help make sense of the way India sees the world.

NUCLEAR POLICY AND POWER

It is believed that in recent time's nuclear weapons have played major roles in the strategic considerations of both major and regional powers. The frequency with which nuclear weapons have been brought into play to manage strategic interests is a pointer to a dangerous and disturbing trend. South East Asia has witnessed a military crisis since 1999.

The Kargil conflict occurred within months of the two countries going overtly nuclear. India's strategy was to limit its operation to recapture its which Pakistan had occupied and India's restrain in the scale of its military operations obtained international support and put Pakistan on notice about taking recourse to military means against India.

According to some defense analysts Pakistan leadership assessed that nuclear weapons had deterred India from widening the Kargil conflict. After the December 13, 2001 terrorist futile attack on India's parliament, India lunched "Operation Pakistan" and moved the army to the borders with Pakistan. The air force and navy were also moved into a state of operational readiness. There were statements from the military leadership of Pakistan indicating their readiness to use nuclear weapons if necessary. The threat of war from India made the major powers to pressurize Pakistan to end its terrorism policy against India. It is believed that threat of nuclear war was the main reason behind the involvement of the major powers.

But India's stand on the role of nuclear weapons is quite clear. India has emphasized at the conference of disarmament that Pakistan has been involved in nuclear blackmail and the south Asian region is confronted with aggressive nuclear positioning and irresponsible threat of use of nuclear weapons by irresponsible military leadership. It is evident that India is not in race with any other nuclear power. India has exercised its nuclear option without violating any international obligations in order to the threats that world have compromised its national security. India has its own nuclear doctrine which affirms its commitment to no-first-use of nuclear weapons and not using these weapons against non-nuclear weapon states. The defensive nuclear doctrine has a command and control system under certain political authority. Land marks of India's nuclear doctrine are-

- Building and maintaining a credible minimum deterrent.
- A posture of no-first-use: nuclear weapons will only be used in retaliation against a nuclear attack on Indian Territory or on Indian forces elsewhere.
- Nuclear retaliation to a first strike will be massive and designed to inflict unacceptable damage.
- Nuclear retaliatory attack can be authorized by a certain political leadership only through NCA.
- No-use of nuclear weapons against non-nuclear weapon state.
- In the event of a major attack against India or Indian forces anywhere by biological or chemical weapons. India will retain the option of retaliating with nuclear weapons.
- Continuance of strict control on export of nuclear and missile related materials and technology, participation in the fissile material cut off treaty negotiations and continued observance of the moratorium on nuclear tests.
- Continued commitment to the goal of a nuclear-free world through global verifiable and no discriminatory nuclear disarmament.

Then the three pillars of India's nuclear doctrine are: All other components of the doctrine survivability strategic trend, punitive retaliation in rapid response and shift from peace time deployment to fully employable forces in the shortest possible time are all strict mathematical derivations of the above three basic principles.

No-first–use

The nuclear doctrine states that India is committed to a no-first-use of nuclear weapons. The theory of deterrence and no-first-use go together. The first aggressive use of a nuclear weapon will be a confession that deterrence has failed and use of nuclear weapons was the only recourse left. It is globally recognized that nuclear war between two nuclear powers would not lead to any meaningful military decision beyond appalling losses to both sides. In these circumstances no-first-use is the most appropriate policy.

Credible Minimum Deterrent

The concept of minimum nuclear deterrent will include sufficient survivable and operationally prepared nuclear forces, a robust command and control system, effective intelligence and early warning capability and comprehensive planning and training for operations in line with the strategy and the will to employ nuclear forces and weapons.

The nuclear doctrine envisages a deterrent that has the capability of inflicting destruction and punishment to the aggressor. The principles of credibility, effectiveness and survivability will be central to India's nuclear deterrent. The nuclear doctrine does not quantify the minimum deterrent. It calls for highly effective military capability. The nuclear doctrine stresses upon effective, enduring diverse forces which are based upon a nuclear tread of air-craft, mobile land-based missiles and sea-based assets.

Nuclear Command Authority (NCA)

On January 4, 2003 India revealed a three tire nuclear command authority (NCA) to manage its nuclear weapons. This board frame work was approved ion the nuclear doctrine prepared by the national security board set up after the may 1998 nuclear tests. The NCA comprises of (a) political council, (b) executive council and (c) strategic forces command. Political council is headed by the prime minister. It is the body which authorizes the use of nuclear weapons. Executive council is headed by the national security adviser to the prime minister. Its function is to provide inputs for decision making by the NCA and to execute the directives given to it by the political council.

The executive council may comprise of the chiefs of defense services, the IIC chairman, the convener of the NSAB, the cabinet secretaries, heads of intelligence agencies and secretaries of ministers represented in the cabinet committed of security (CCS). The strategic force command (SFC) would be responsible for the administration of the nuclear forces and will be actually tasked with the firing of nuclear weapons. SFC is the second tri-service command after the first one in Andaman and Nicobar Islands was established in 2001.

Indian's nuclear doctrine is the most responsible doctrine which aims at providing minimum credible deterrent. It is a consensus document which does not limit the country in any way in exercising its nuclear weapon options. It provides complete elasticity in deciding; the number of nuclear weapons India should possess and classifies the emphasis on the survivability of the deterrent. Establishment of the NCA will add credibility to India's nuclear posture. The NCA stands out in its firm commitment to deterrent stability through civilian control over nuclear weapons. Most significant aspect of India's nuclear doctrine is that it is intimately tied up with continued commitment to total nuclear disarmament. The five major nuclear powers are reluctant to give up their monopoly over production and deployment of nuclear weapons while denying a similar privilege to other countries.

In contrast with India's nuclear doctrine there are ambiguous, questions about nuclear capability, precise doctrine and delivery systems of Pakistan. There is a fundamental difference between the nuclear policies of India and Pakistan. Whereas no-first-use of nuclear weapons remains the key element of India's nuclear policy Pakistan maintains the first strike option in its nuclear doctrine and has refused to sign an agreement no-first-use. With India's over-whelming superiority over Pakistan in conventional forces, Pakistan looks towards nuclear weapons as a Safe bet to overcome its disadvantages in a conventional view. In its first ever meeting the nuclear command authority under the chairmanship of the prime minister reviewed the arrangements in place for the strategic forces programmed. In a significant departure from the earlier stand the government warned that India would retain the option of retaliating with nuclear weapons if attacked with chemical or biological weapons by even non-nuclear adversaries. It also said that WMD attack on Indian forces outside Indian Territory would result in a nuclear response.

CONTEMPLATIONS ON INDIA'S NUCLEAR POLICY DURING THE NEHRU ERA

One of the most outstanding statesmen of the twentieth century, Jawaharlal Nehru has left his indelible imprint on all aspects of modern India. An intense nationalist, a romantic revolutionary, a charismatic leader committed to social justice and individual freedom, Nehru was also an internationalist, conscious of the cross currents of global politics and India's emerging role in the world scene. The two major strands of nationalism and internationalism blended beautifully into an ideal mould in this unique, yet humane, personality. It is very difficult to fit Jawaharlal Nehru into any ideological framework. He was a product of evolution, of the stresses and strains as much as hopes and aspirations, which characterized the prolonged nationalist struggle. As his daughter, Indira Gandhi, has brilliantly summed up:

He drew much from the thought of the East and the West and from philosophies of the past and the present. Never religious in the formal sense, yet he had a deep love for the culture and traditions of his own land. Never a rigid Marxist, yet he was deeply influenced by that theory and was profoundly influenced by what he saw in the Soviet Union on his first visit in 1927. However, he realized that the world was too complex, and man had too many facets, to be encompassed by any single or total explanation. He himself was a socialist with an abhorrence for regimentation and a democrat who was anxious to reconcile his faith in civil liberty with the necessity of mitigating economic and social backwardness.

His struggles, both within himself and the outside world, to adjust such seeming contradictions are what make his life and work significant and fascinating. To put the subject in proper perspective it is necessary to keep in mind certain salient features of the international system. The first and foremost question does the possession of nuclear weapons give additional leverage to a nuclear weapons state in the pursuit of its foreign policy goals. During the last days of the Second World War, when the United States was the only nuclear power, it was able to decisively turn the fortunes of the war to its side by dropping the atom bombs in Hiroshima and Nagasaki. But with the emergence of the bi - polar world from the early 1950's and with Soviet Union acquiring nuclear weapons, the value of the bomb was only to deter the enemy. What is more, the massive nuclear arsenal in the hands of

Moscow and Washington did not enable them to win victories in the battle fields of Vietnam or in Afghanistan. The two major powers suffered humiliating defeats in these two costly battles. Equally relevant, the argument put forward by Indian strategic specialists like K. Subrahmanyam and General Sundarji that if India and Pakistan went nuclear, there would be certain amount of sanity in their foreign and strategic policies has also been belied. As is well known, the conflict in Kargil in June 1999 took place after the two countries went nuclear. In fact if India had not exercised the nuclear option in May 1998 New Delhi could have embarked on a full scale conventional war against Pakistan to put an end to the Pakistani military incursion making use of its conventional military superiority. The lesson is clear, for dealing with Pakistan and China India requires both conventional and nuclear power.

Nuclear Non-Proliferation Treaty

Equally relevant, the Nuclear Non-Proliferation Treaty (NPT) which was signed in July 1968 divided the world into two, the nuclear haves and the nuclear have nots. The objective of the Treaty was to prevent nuclear proliferation. By the mid-1960's, as Jawaharlal Nehru has pointed out, India had made commendable progress in the field of nuclear research, what is more, Prime Minister Lal Bahadur Shastri had given instructions to Homi Bhabha after Lop Nor to work toward reducing the time needed to develop nuclear explosives. If India had exploded a nuclear device before July 1968, however crude it might have been, it would have brought about a fundamental transformation in the international nuclear scene. There were powerful bomb walahs in India at that time, which included highly influential specialists like Homi Bhabha, KC Pant, K. Subrahmaniam, Prof. Subramaniam Swamy, Inder Malhotra, Prof. JD Sethi, Prof. Raj Krishna and Prof. Sisir Gupta. The author has not come across any convincing explanation why this policy option was not seriously considered in the corridors of power at that time.

The success of foreign policy depends upon correctly understanding the likely trends in international relations and using them to one's advantage. To Jawaharlal Nehru's credit, it must be pointed out that more than any other political leader, except perhaps VK Krishna Menon, he was conscious of the Sino-Soviet differences and its possible benign fallout for India. Nehru was the first statesman to foresee the emergence of more liberal trends in the Soviet Union. In his book, *The New Dimensions of Peace,* Ambassador Chester Bowles has mentioned that Nehru told him in early 1950's that Sino-Soviet convergence of interests was unlikely to last for more than few years. In September 1959, in a speech in Parliament, Nehru referred to the statement in *TASS* on September 9 and how it indicated that Soviet Union was taking a calm, objective and dispassionate view of the Sino-Indian border situation.

The *TASS* statement, as is well known, was the first indication of the Sino-Soviet differences being aired in the public. Nehru was, unlike the opposition and the military brass, sensitive to the widening schism between the two communist giants. He knew of the sharp exchanges that took place between Kruschev and Chen Yi in Bucharest in June 1960, the Chinese anger at the Soviet Union for selling MIG planes to India, the withdrawal of Soviet technicians from China and skirmishes in the Sino-Soviet border in 1960. Nehru delinked China's policy from communist ideology and characterized it as an outcome of what he called "Chinese expansionism". Such a stance enabled India to take advantage of the Sino-Soviet dispute and get considerable Soviet support in the years to come. It is interesting to note that while large number of countries expressed their sympathy and support to India in the India-China War, only two countries supported China, namely North Vietnam and Albania. North Vietnam's policy was dictated by its dependence on China during those years and Anwar Hoxa's policy must be viewed in the background of Albania's support to China in the ideological conflict with the Soviet Union. At the same time, it must be mentioned that Nehru miserably failed to understand that Beijing will have no hesitation to use force to buttress its territorial claims. And China had used force not only against India, but also against Soviet Union and Vietnam in later years.

In order to focus attention on ramifications of the subject under discussion, it is necessary to highlight the thinking of three influential figures who dominated the Indian scene, namely, Homi J. Bhabha, Jawaharlal Nehru and VK Krishna Menon. .Homi Jehangir Bhabha was undoubtedly the father of Indian nuclear research and the architect of India's nuclear strategy and diplomacy. In the 1930's, Bhabha studied with the eminent nuclear scientist Lord Ernest Rutherford. He also associated himself with other great experts in the field like Niels Bohr, James Franck, Erico Fermi and WB Lewis. On his return to India, Bhabha convinced the Tatas to finance the establishment of a centre for research to study nuclear physics. Thus India's nuclear progamme predates the dawn of independence. The Tata Institute of Fundamental Research (TIFR) was established in Bombay on 19 December 1945, four months after Hiroshima and months before India became independent Bhabha was already in command of India's nuclear future. He dominated the Indian nuclear scene till his unfortunate demise in an air crash twenty years later.

Bhabha was a personal friend of Jawaharlal Nehru, having met him in his voyage home in 1939. Bhabha addressed the Prime Minister even in official correspondence as "Bhai" and Nehru addressed him as "My dear Homi". When Nehru became the Prime Minister, he entrusted Bhabha with complete authority over all nuclear related matters. Not only functional autonomy was given, it was also above parliamentary and administrative scrutiny. At Bhabha's request the Atomic Energy Act was passed by the Constituent Assembly, creating the Atomic Energy Commission. With remarkable prescience, Bhabha wrote very early in life, "When nuclear energy has been successfully applied to power production, in say, a couple of decades from now, India will not have to look abroad for its experts but will find them ready at hand". As a scientist, familiar with *realpolitik*, Bhabha was convinced that India's voice will be heard in international gatherings only if India became powerful and had nuclear weapons. Bhabha told Raja Ramanna, "We must have the capability. We should first prove ourselves and then talk of (Mahatma) Gandhi, non-violence and a world without nuclear weapons".

During the early years of independence, India pursued what Nehru called "a peaceful nuclear programme", implying that the programme was developed not to manufacture nuclear weapons, but instead to provide energy to the people. But certain important figures in the Indian nuclear establishment, including Homi Bhabha, thought differently.

Prof. Sumit Ganguly refers to a conversation between Homi Bhabha and the British Physicist Lord PMS Blackett about his interest in acquiring nuclear weapons. In a paper delivered in the 12th Pugwash Conference in January-February 1964, Bhabha elaborated his views as follows: "Nuclear weapons coupled with an adequate delivery system can enable a state to destroy more or less totally the cities, industry and all important targets in another state.

It is then largely irrelevant whether the state so attacked has greater destructive power at its command. With the help of nuclear weapons, therefore, a state can acquire what we may call a position of absolute deterrence even against another having a many times greater destructive power under its control". Homi Bhabha was able to influence not only stalwarts in the scientific community, but also political leaders to his way of thinking. SS Khera, former Cabinet Secretary, is of the view: "Those who knew Dr. Homi Bhabha and worked with him were aware of his urge to work towards having everything ready for the bomb".

Bhabha's colleagues in the Atomic Energy Establishment had the same passionate commitment to make the nuclear bomb at the earliest so that India could become a great power. According to Raja Ramanna, "There was never a discussion among us over whether we should'nt make the bomb. How to do it was more important. For us it was a matter of prestige that would justify our ancient past. The question of deterrence came much later. Also, as Indian scientists we were keen to show our western counterparts, who thought little of us those days, that we too could do it". Let us turn now to the thinking and policies of Jawaharlal Nehru. Nehru was one man foreign office, controlled both foreign office and Department of Atomic Energy. What is more, as mentioned earlier, he emphasized the importance of secrecy in nuclear matters and immunized himself and his colleagues from public scrutiny. Brought up in Gandhian traditions of non-violence, and given his abhorrence of violent conflicts and commitment to peaceful resolution of international disputes, it was but natural for Jawaharlal Nehru to openly oppose the manufacture of nuclear weapons. What is more, one of the major aspects of India's foreign policy was its strong advocacy of universal nuclear disarmament. On November 13, 1945, Jawaharlal Nehru declared, "The revolution caused by discoveries having to do with atomic energy can either destroy human civilization, or take it up to unheard of levels". The peaceful use of nuclear energy was the official policy of the Government of India. This point was highlighted in bilateral agreements with Canada, UK, USA and USSR.

A careful reading of Nehru's speeches and policy declarations clearly reveal that he did not foreclose the nuclear option for ever. It goes to the credit of Jawaharlal Nehru that he laid the strong foundations of atomic research, so that when the country decided to exercise the nuclear option, it could do so without much difficulty. As is well known, given his scientific temper, he wanted to channelise science for developmental purposes. But the nuclear energy was dual technology, it could be used for constructive and destructive purposes. On June 26, 1946, Nehru declared, "As long as the world is constituted as it is, every country will have to devise and use the latest scientific devices for its protection. I have no doubt that India will develop its scientific researches and I hope the Indian scientists will use the atomic force for constructive purposes. *But if India is threatened she will inevitably try to defend herself by all means at her disposal* (Emphasis added). I hope India in common with other countries will prevent the use of atomic bombs".. In January 1956, Nehru announced in Parliament that if adequate resources were delivered, an Indian bomb could be made in three or four years. In 1961, when the Zerlina reactor went critical, Nehru stated that although India could make the bomb in two years, it chose not to do so. In December 1959 speaking before the Parliamentary Committee on Atomic Affairs, Homi Bhabha declared that India has progressed to such a stage where, if a political directive was received, a bomb could be made without external assistance. The time period, however, was not specified.).

What sort of interaction took place between Homi Bhabha and Jawaharlal Nehru? Who influenced whom? We do not have any exact information, because all the important documents are kept behind the stone walls of official secrecy. Prof. Ashok Kapur, the well known authority on India's nuclear policy, has written that India could have proceeded into nuclear weaponisation at any time after 1957, but it did not. Recently I came across a purported conversation that took place between Homi Bhabha and Jawaharlal Nehru in mid-1958. The quotation given below is attributed to Kenneth D. Nichols, an American military engineer. Nehru asked Homi Bhabha, "Can you develop an atomic bomb? Bhabha assured him that he could and in reply to Nehru's next question about time, he estimated that he would need a year to do it...He concluded by saying to Bhabha, "Well, don't do it until I tell you" I am skeptical about this conversation, because it is very unlikely that high ups in the Indian Government would have discussed such matters with American Generals in the late 1950's.

ISSUE OF NUCLEAR WEAPONS IN NEHRU ERA

Unlike Jawaharlal Nehru, who adopted an ambivalent stand on the issue of nuclear weapons, VK Krishna Menon was dogmatic to the core. Menon was spokesman for the Government of India in all negotiations relating to disarmament. He emphatically maintained that India should not manufacture nuclear weapons, come what may. Menon was not a pacifist, he justified the use of violence in Jammu and Kashmir and forced Nehru's hands in Goa. As Michael Brecher puts it, Menon was "emotional to the extreme" and his image of nuclear weapons was "fuzzy". Menon was emphatic that if India manufactured nuclear weapons, India's image would suffer considerably for India played a big role in the finalization of Partial Test Ban Treaty. The nuclear bomb, Menon asserted is not "a weapon of war or a weapon of defence; it is a weapon of mass destruction ... The bomb has no value; it has not even a deterrent value. This is quite apart from the futility of weapons of annihilation and all the consequences of atomic war". The conversation with Michael Brecher took place when Menon was in political eclipse; in fact, he could not influence the policies of wither the Government or the Congress party after his resignation from the Cabinet following India's humiliating defeat in the India-China War in October-November 1962.

A study of the contrasting styles of Homi Bhabha, Jawaharlal Nehru and VK Krishna Menon on the issue of India's nuclear policy highlights the fact that the Indian political system was resilient and provided space for dissenting views. The role played by the three great nationalist leaders are today being subjected to close scrutiny, but despite their inadequacies and imperfections, there is no denying the fact that the three leaders made yeoman contributions to the building of modern India.

NUCLEAR COMMAND AND CONTROL IN INDIA

Command and control can be defined as the exercise of authority and direction of a properly designated commander over assigned forces in the accomplishment of a mission. The command and control for nuclear operations depends on the functions it must perform and the information it must collect, which determine the facilities, personnel, and equipment required to support the operations and the hostile threat that inhibits this performance.

Because India is an established democracy with a long-standing tradition of strict civilian control over the military, there was little doubt that the control of the Indian nuclear button would rest in civilian hands. The decision to declare the establishment of the NCA, therefore, seems to have been intended to reassure the international community about India's civil command over the nation's nuclear assets. Also, by setting up the NCA under civilian control to institutionalize the command structure in the public domain, India might have been pitching for a better public relations game compared with Pakistan's military-dominated NCA that came into being in February 2000.

In sharp contrast to the Indian nuclear command and control structure, which is dominated by the civilian authority under the leadership of the prime minister, Pakistan's nuclear command system was initially placed under the control of a military-dominated NCA headed by President Pervez Musharraf who was also army chief then. It was only recently when concerns started growing about Musharraf 's ability to control the nation's nuclear assets, and the United States seemed ready to seize Pakistan's nuclear arsenal that Musharraf, who had become a civilian president, decided to formally assume control and legally define the functions and command of the NCA. However, of all the major nuclear states in world, Pakistan is the only country where the nuclear button is in the hands of the military.

The evolution of the Indian nuclear option has been characterized by extreme secrecy and without the involvement of the armed forces. An effective command and control system is not possible without the participation of the armed forces. The Indian armed forces have made their displeasure at this practice clear to the government, arguing that it might prove counterproductive.

After keeping the Indian military out of nuclear policymaking since the very beginning, it is a considerable challenge for India to ensure that the military is fully integrated in nuclear decision making and fully functional operationally for an effective deterrent, because the armed forces will be the ones that will have to use the nuclear weapons, if ever required. To effectively deter its adversaries, India needs a system that it is ready to use and people trained to do so at the appropriate time.

The establishment of the NCA seems to have been aimed at addressing this issue. The executive council is the arm of the NCA that will provide inputs to the political council and execute the directives given. This council is well represented by the armed forces, including the Defence Intelligence Agency. Also, with the setting up of the SFC, India seems to have gone a long way in "militarizing" its nuclear posture.

A proper command has been established with the flow of command from the prime minister to the NSA to the chairman of the COSC to the commander in chief of the SFC. The SFC would work out plans and targets in the event of a nuclear attack and also the numbers required to form a "credible minimum deterrent." The SFC is responsible for managing and administering the nation's consolidated nuclear force as well as for operating the directives of the NCA under the leadership of the commander in chief. India expects to spend about $2 billion a year over the next decade to establish the SFC infrastructure.

The absence of an integrated triservice approach in decision making is also a major problem in the Indian context. There has been persistent criticisms of the "turf war" between the three services on issues related to the control of nuclear assets, budgetary support, and encroachment on their "core competence" by the other services. The new SFC brings much-needed coordination on nuclear matters, and it is hoped that it would end the turf wars among the armed services. However, while the command and control of the country's nuclear assets will move to the SFC, the three services will not be transferring their entire nuclear assets. The training in nuclear weapons and their delivery system as well as their servicing would remain the task of individual services. The SFC, on its part, is yet to get possession of weapon delivery systems, adequate manpower, or even a permanent headquarters, showing a lackadaisical attitude on the part of the government in strengthening the institution of SFC. The government has also tried to rectify the problem of the lack of integrated decision making in armed forces by setting up the Integrated Defence Staff (IDS), a triservice body, to integrate the higher echelons of the armed forces. This has led to some real movement in the integration of the three services. The work on a joint doctrine for all three services has commenced.

It is believed that the nation's three triservice commands, the IDS, the SFC, and the Andaman and Nicobar Command, will be making decision making in the armed forces more integrated. But despite some of these steps taken by the government in recent years, it is not clear if the turf wars among the three services would actually diminish. It is instructive to note the dominance of the Indian air force in the present arrangements, because the delivery systems available to India—fighter-bombers, long-range aircraft, and medium-range missiles—are under its control. Not surprisingly, both commander in chiefs of the SFC so far have been air force officers.

It is in this context that the Indian government's promise to establish the post of a chief of Defence Staff (CDS) who will administer the nation's nuclear arsenal and provide a "single point" of military advice to the government acquires new salience. But so far there has been little movement on this promise. The need for a CDS is a subject that refuses to go away from the public discourse in India. The post of a CDS is viewed as essential in providing an institutional link between the political leadership and the armed forces in terms of higher direction of war as well as agency for institutionalized contingency planning on behalf of the country.

Several chiefs of the Indian army have raised this issue, including General J. N. Chaudhuri in the 1960s and General Krishna Rao in 1982. The Indian army would like to have the post of a CDS as the most powerful of the three services, and it is confident that it would get the post, thereby giving it greater influence in the central policymaking process.

But there is a lot of resistance not only from the civilian leadership and bureaucracy but also from the navy and the air force. The underlying reason for this resistance has always been the suspicion of the civilian leadership in India of the Indian armed forces, and any increase in its power is not seen in the interests of the civilians. It has been noted by some that the civilian leadership continues to pursue the strategy of divide and rule that was devised by Krishna Menon in the 1960s, thereby making sure that the united armed forces never pose a threat to the political leadership. The result has been a complete lack of any centralized institutional arrangement for higher strategic decision making in defence issues.

Because of India's NFU posture, survivability of India's command and control after first strike remains a major concern, because in the absence of command or control, the nuclear arsenal, even if it survives the first strike, will be rendered useless. An aerial nuclear command is difficult to target by any adversary. But there is an absence of a reliably fast aircraft platform equipped with secured communication and command and control infrastructure to act as an effective aerial nuclear command.

The current Indian second-strike capability is based on a dyad of short- to medium-range bombers and missiles. It is believed that the strategic depth of India as well as the dispersal-disbursement of weapon components would ensure the survival of a credible deterrence after a Pakistani first strike. The threat is greater from a Chinese first strike. The Indian navy's planned acquisition through the lease-purchase of two Akula (Bars)-class Type 1971 nuclear-powered submarines (SSNs) and the indigenous development of an Advanced Technology Vehicle (ATV) is expected to be an effective deterrent for a Chinese first strike.

The Indian navy has also revised its doctrine to one that emphasizes the need for a submarine-based credible minimum nuclear deterrent capability. India plans to launch its first indigenous nuclear submarine by 2009. However, deployment of nuclear submarines remains a long-term project even though, with the indigenously built Air Defence Ship and the Admiral Gorshkov aircraft carrier deal with Russia, India hopes to have two aircraft carriers by 2011.

In the meanwhile, the induction of the Dhanush sea-based, surfacelaunched ballistic missile (a naval variant of Prithvi) is expected to ensure a sea-based deterrence, though many problems remain with the performance of the Dhanush. Also, the range of the Dhanush is only 350 kilometers, making it necessary to position the missile close to the enemy shores to be able to reach targets on land. This makes the Dhanush highly vulnerable to detection and counterstrike. The survival chances of the Indian arsenal, however, increase with its missile launchers being road and rail mobile. With an effective plan of deception, concealment, random movement, and relocation of missile launchers judiciously mixed with that of dummy launchers, the chances of any first strike completely degrading the Indian deterrent receded. While relying on the short-ranged Prithvi may require predelegation of launch authority because of tactical limitations of the weapon systems and its proximity to the Pakistani border, India's move towards Agni missiles of various configurations is aimed at alleviating some of these concerns.

India is also gradually moving towards some kind of a ballistic missile defence arrangement. The cooperation with Israel, the acquisition of the Green Pine Radar System, the request for technical information on Patriot missiles from the United States, the proposed deal for the Arrow missile, and the participation in the development of the U.S. missile shield programme are pointers to India exploring its options with regard to strengthening its defences from the missiles of its adversaries. India also expects its indigenous anti-ballistic missile system to be ready for military use by 2010.

Significant investments are also being made in protecting the Indian communications network from any electromagnetic pulse (EMP) attack. The air-based command and control infrastructure is being strengthened with the replacement of old turboprop Avros with the Brazilian Embraer jets. These jets would be adequately protected against airborne or ground-based missile attack. Finally, India's defensive nuclear posture implies that in the event deterrence fails, the country's nuclear weapon systems must have the survivability and effectiveness for a rapid punitive response.

This raises the obvious question: what is the alternative chain of command to conduct a retaliatory strike in the event that a first strike wipes out the civilian/political leadership? The Cabinet Committee on Security is said to have approved the arrangements for alternative chains of command for retaliatory strikes but has chosen to remain silent about what they are or how they will work. While secrecy does confer some advantages, it is also arguable that a clear and publicly stated succession of command strengthens the credibility of deterrence and increases public confidence in a world that is increasingly wary of nuclear decisions being taken without proper authority and nuclear weapons falling into the wrong hands.

As a result, the enunciation of the nuclear doctrine and the establishment of the NCA have given rise to a range of issues that impinge on the future trajectory of civil-military relations in India.

IMPLICATIONS FOR CIVIL-MILITARY RELATIONS

India has had, as noted above, a sustained tradition of strict civilian control over the military since its independence in 1947. This has been even more pronounced in the realm of nuclear weapons policy, where institutions and procedures have not been evolved that would allow the military to substantially participate in the decision-making processes. The Indian military has traditionally not been involved in decisions concerning nuclear testing, design, or even command and control. Stephen Rosen, in his study of the impact of societal structures on the military effectiveness of a state, argues that the separation of the Indian military from the Indian society, while preserving the coherence of the Indian army, has led to a reduction in the effective military power of the Indian state. This has led to civil-military tensions affecting the command and control of nuclear weapons in India. The civilian leadership tightly controls nuclear weapons and has denied the military any control over nuclear weapons in peacetime, thereby demonstrating a lack of confidence in its military with regard to nuclear weapons. George Perkovich has argued that "fear of military usurpation of democratic political authority" has been a major factor in preventing Indian deployment of nuclear weapons.

But with India's emergence as a nuclear weapon state in 1998, the need for improved mechanisms for civil-military coordination became more pronounced. It is only with the recent enunciation of an Indian nuclear weapons doctrine and command structure that the issue of changing civil-military relations with respect to the management of nuclear weapons has been given some serious attention. The NSAB that was set up after the nuclear tests of 1998 to come up with nuclear doctrine included five former military officials. Interestingly, the Defence Planning Staff at the Ministry of Defence had also drafted a "doctrine" at the same time NSAB came out with its own version. It has been claimed that there were many similarities between the two and, as such, the NSAB version won the "unstinted support of the military." Indeed, if the Indian armed forces remain dissatisfied with the present doctrine, they have certainly kept it to themselves.

The civilian leadership, for its part, has continued to maintain a strict control over the nuclear decision making with little space to the armed forces for inputs. The former Indian naval chief, Admiral Vishnu Bhagwat, was sacked in 1998 when he pointed out that the nuclear submarine project of India, one leg of India's planned nuclear triad, was not being well managed and the cost overruns had got out of control. The Indian government construed this as an attempt to pressure it, and it was alleged that Bhagwat had leaked information pertaining to a state secret. The civilian leadership's lack of tolerance for any foray of the armed forces into the policy realm was once again on display in 2002 at the height of Operation Parakram, when the then Indian army chief, General S. Padmanabhan, remarked that India would severely punish anyone who dared to launch a nuclear strike against it. While these remarks merely implied that India would retaliate to any nuclear attack, a stated Indian policy, the army chief was publicly reprimanded by the Indian defence minister within hours of his statement.

This reluctance by the Indian civilian leadership to involve the armed forces in nuclear policy might have been understandable when India was in the process of developing its nuclear weapons capability. But now when Indian leaders want India to be acknowledged as a nuclear weapon state, India would have to "adapt existing strategic and tactical doctrines to meet a possible future situation where its leaders and the government decide that nuclear weapons may actually have to be used to win a war." As a consequence, the Indian armed forces will inevitably have to be brought into the decision-making loop. India has reiterated its commitment to what it terms a "credible, minimum deterrent" posture for its nuclear arsenal. Though it remains a matter if debate, what this means in practical terms is that it is clear that India has made this choice for a number of strategic and economic reasons. In the foreseeable future, India's nuclear arsenal will remain fairly small in size and diversity, and as a consequence, it will be easy for India to have a tight civilian control over it. Conversely, to make its deterrent more credible, India might have to go in for an assumed capability to shift from peacetime deployment to fully employable forces in the shortest possible time.

This might suggest an alert deployment that might force India to relinquish some civilian control and give the military more authority vis-à-vis the use of nuclear weapons. This is the dilemma that a state with a relatively small nuclear arsenal like India trying to enhance its credibility as a nuclear weapons state is bound to face, producing concomitant complications for the civil-military relations in so far as the management of nuclear weapons is concerned. As the size and complexity of India's nuclear arsenal increases, different kinds of complications will emerge, because absolute civilian control would be difficult to maintain and the military would seek greater operational autonomy.

While India seems settled on a small number of warheads in the near term, it is going ahead with procuring an array of delivery systems, mainly to enhance the credibility of its deterrent. The credibility of the Indian nuclear doctrine that is defensive in nature and scope only hinges around the ability of the Indian nuclear force to survive a first attack in sufficient numbers to inflict unacceptable damage in response. This has led India to accelerate the development of the Agni medium-range missiles, to consider the acquisition of new long-range bombers, and to induct a leased nuclear powered submarine, which will form India's nuclear triad. As the complexity of nuclear arsenal will increase, centralized control will become more difficult to sustain and decentralization and delegation would be the preferred mode of operation, giving the military greater autonomy.

India's doctrine of NFU entails that India will use nuclear weapons only in retaliation against an attack by nuclear, chemical, or biological weapons on the Indian territory or on Indian forces anywhere. This reliance on late use of nuclear weapons by India makes it easier to assert tighter civilian control, because India will have to take certain steps in order to support its NFU commitment like demating of warheads and delivery systems. Though many have argued against India's adoption of a purely retaliatory nuclear policy, a firstuse policy would force India to go in for decentralization of the control of nuclear forces to theater commanders in the armed forces. This would dilute the civilian control over the nuclear arsenal, and the Indian civilian leadership seems wary of such a dilution at least in the immediate future.

A NFU doctrine as reflected in the demating of warheads and delivery systems also increases the time available to decision makers to respond to crisis situations, thereby preventing risky undertakings and enhancing stability. As a consequence, such a posture would be supported by the civilians, because this gives them greater control over the situation. Given the dominance of civilians in the nuclear decision-making loop in India, it is not surprising that such a posture is preferred.

Military doctrines, however, are a function of the strategic environment a state faces, technological changes, and domestic factors. This is also true of India's nuclear doctrine. As and when, because of the changes in any of the above-mentioned factors, India decides to shed its NFU posture and adopts an early-use nuclear doctrine, it will be forced to dramatically alter the structure of civil-military relations vis-à-vis nuclear weapons. Tight civilian control will become impossible to maintain, and the military will have to be given greater operational control of the atomic arsenal than is the case today. As of now, however, this does not seem a near-term possibility.

To enhance the survivability of its small nuclear arsenal, India might also disperse its assets widely and more frequently, thereby increasing the number of targets that need to be destroyed by its adversary to take out its deterrent. However, the security risks increase tremendously with frequent movement of nuclear assets. Not only this, but the civilian authorities would also find it hard to monitor the nuclear assets of the country closely when the delivery systems and warheads are distributed separately throughout a large number of locations. And the military establishment, which in all likelihood would be responsible for the dispersal, would gain an upper hand in the management of nuclear assets.

One of the major problems that states face in establishing the command and control of their nuclear weapons is how to resolve what has been termed as the "always/never dilemma." States want to make sure that their nuclear arsenals always work "efficiently" when they are needed, that is, when authorized by the duly established command, nuclear weapons actually explode in the manner desired. However, because of the high stakes involved, states want to make sure that their nuclear arsenals never go off when their use is not authorized by the established command.

Duly tested nuclear warheads and delivery systems with a reliable C4I (command, control, communication, computers, and intelligence) and a well-established chain of command is needed to ensure that the nuclear arsenal remains reliable enough to operate as and when authorized by the civilian leadership.

The explication of the Indian nuclear doctrine and the establishment of the NCA are the steps in this direction taken by India to take care of the "always" part of the "always/never" dilemma. Enhancing the credibility and reliability of its nuclear arsenal made it imperative for India to militarize its nuclear posture by involving the military in the nuclear decision-making process, something that the Indian civilian leadership had tried to avoid doing so far, much to the chagrin of the Indian military.

However, attempts by states to take care of the "never" part of the dilemma generally encounter serious obstacles in the accomplishment of their objectives. The threat of accidental and unauthorized launches and third-party use of nuclear weapons is always a real one, especially for the nascent nuclear state like India. Attempts to prevent such threats would invariably imply greater civilian control and oversight. The absence of a sophisticated, dedicated, and reliable early-warning system and intelligence setup could be a problem area in the fog of war.

The flight time of missiles and bombers between India and Pakistan or India and China is a few minutes. The reaction time available for launching a counterstrike is as low as two-to-three minutes in the case of Pakistan and around ten minutes in the case of China. Missiles and bombers can generally carry conventional as well as nuclear payloads. Faulty warning, or absence of proper intelligence, could accidentally trigger a nuclear response to a non-existent threat. In the absence of a robust C4I, an accidental nuclear war can easily be triggered.

This would be a major issue, however, if India adopts a second strike option that is based on a launch-on-warning doctrine that presupposes that a first strike may result in a significant degradation in the capability to punt a retaliatory second strike. Thus, as soon as there is a confirmation of the launch of weapons against it, the nation should launch its own strike. This doctrine thus calls for weapons to maintain high levels of alert and dispersion, and proper delegation to the field commanders.

But the Indian nuclear posture is not based on launch-on-warning. Rather, it seems to be modeled more or less along the lines of "force in being," as suggested by Ashley Tellis. This refers to a nuclear deterrent that consists of available, but dispersed components: unassembled nuclear warheads, with their components stored separately under strict civilian control and dedicated delivery systems kept either in storage or in readiness away from their operational areas—all of which can be brought together as rapidly as required to create a usable deterrent force during a supreme emergency.

There are suggestions that this is the posture that has been adopted by the Indian government. While the fissile core is under the control of the Department of Atomic Energy, the triggering device and weapon assemblies are in the custody of the Defence Research and Development Organization, which is also entrusted with the task of configuring and mating the warheads with the missiles and bombers. The delivery platforms are in the custody of the armed forces. The weapons can be reconstituted rapidly during an emergency or national crisis. Since the weapons are not configured and mated to the delivery platforms, they are in a state of de-alert. The time to bring together all these components and launch a second strike is reported to be few hours. This gives sufficient time to the Indian leadership to verify and confirm the first strike before launching a counterstrike. A clear escalating ladder of steps has thereby been devised to eliminate any chance of a mischievous or accidental detonation of nuclear weapons.

In this context, it is interesting to note that India has gone for such a nuclear posture despite suggestions that new nuclear nations that encounter capable regional adversaries would not prefer rendering their arsenals vulnerable to a disarming first strike by keeping their weapons in an unassembled state. On the whole, while the "always/never" dilemma implies that the greater the assurance of "always," the lesser the assurance of "never," and vice versa, in the case of India, the small size of its current nuclear arsenal and an adoption of a posture of "force-in-being" has helped India to resolve this dilemma in the short run. As the Indian nuclear arsenal undergoes qualitative and quantitative transformation in the coming years, the "always/never" dilemma and the concomitant civil-military tensions will get more pronounced, unless handled with care. As it is, the recent increase in the threat of terrorism and the nuclear proliferation concerns emanating from Pakistan has given rise to new complications, with some even suggesting that both India and Pakistan should be provided with Permissive Action Links (PAL) to secure their nuclear arsenals.

The civilian establishment in India even today remains wary of giving too much power to the military. This is clearly evident in the realm of nuclear weapons, where the government has found it difficult to come to any decision on the crucial post of a CDS. There have been some serious objections, both from within and outside the government, which a CDS might end up wielding too great a power vis-à-vis the civilian government. Also, the lack of decision on CDS is also partly the result of interservice rivalry, because the army maintains the bulk of the resources and prestige in the Indian security apparatus and is reluctant to relinquish it. The three service chiefs also see a CDS as usurping their power regarding defence management. As a consequence, the fledgling IDS not only remains rudderless, but the objective of promoting "jointness" in operational planning among the armed forces also suffers from a lack of strategic guidance.

The historical dominance of the civilian establishment has made it possible for civilians to command extraordinary control over the nuclear weapons policy. It has been argued that the command and control system will tend to be more delegative if the civil-military relations are more stable. In the case of India, however, despite remarkably stable civil-military relations, the civilians have not desired to delegate significant power to the military in the realm of nuclear weapons. How this will affect India's nuclear weapons policy at the operational level will only become clear in the coming years.

2

India's Nuclear Diplomatic Policy

In 1966 India's diplomatic policy towards nuclear weapons made a fateful shift. While international interest in non-proliferation, focusing on restricting the spread of nuclear weapons to *any* additional states, India's Nehruvian policy of broadly opposing nuclear arms developed a pointed new emphasis. Indian negotiator V.C. Trivedi adopted the stance advocating non-proliferation and nuclear disarmament as long as it was universal - that no club of permanent nuclear powers should be permitted. As long as existing nuclear powers resisted disarmament, they left other nations no choice but to pursue the same option as they saw necessary. The quid pro quo was clear - India would not eschew nuclear arms unless the existing nuclear states did also. This fundamental logic led to India refusing to sign the Nuclear Non-Proliferation Treaty and voting against it on 12 June 1968, and has informed Indian nuclear diplomacy ever since.

The new and inexperienced prime minister's views on the nuclear option were unfocused and tentative, but she tended to follow along with Sarabhai's view that nuclear weapons were useless unless part of a comprehensive and hugely expensive defense system, far beyond India's means. Over the next few years, as she grew more savvy and confident, her views on the PNE program shifted. Whether or not it was due to an explicit change in government policy, late in 1967 the new effort to develop nuclear explosives got underway at BARC, an effort that would continue uninterrupted until it culminated in a successful nuclear test less than seven years later.

STRATEGIC CULTURE AND INDIAN NUCLEAR POLICY

Indian strategic culture – defined as a set pattern of thought and behaviour – with respect to nuclear weapons may be described as nuclear minimalism. Its chief characteristics are:

Low level of importance accorded to nuclear weapons. Nuclear weapons are viewed as dangerous and deeply problematic, and hence not central to the attainment of national security. Though potential nuclear threats have existed since China, soon after its war with India, became a nuclear power in 1964, there has never been a sense of urgency in India's nuclearization. The fact that India did not build an arsenal after the 1974 test and the absence of deployment after 1998 show that India remains a reluctant nuclearizer.

A political rather than a military approach to nuclear weapons. Such a view treats nuclear weapons as political instruments that are unusable for purposes other than deterrence, as opposed to an operational view, which would tend to regard them as extensions of conventional weapons. There is little interest in the concept of nuclear warfighting, even among military officers. Defence strategy as a whole, and nuclear strategy in particular, are completely civilian-dominated.

Emphasis on minimum deterrence. This involves the conviction that it does not take large numbers or a high degree of sophistication to deter an adversary. Immediately after the 1998 tests, the Indian government, backed by its nuclear scientists, announced that more tests were not needed. Moreover, from this standpoint, nuclear balances are of no consequence. Hence, India need not worry about China's far larger nuclear arsenal. This precludes arms racing, which is both costly and risky. It restrains unnecessary spending on a nuclear build-up and prevents the diversion of resources from the more pressing needs of economic development.

Strong commitment to arms control. This is a logical extension of the long-held apprehension that nuclear weapons are as much a source of insecurity as of security. India's preference is for comprehensive, non-discriminatory and multilateral disarmament, but the earlier unrealistic expectations of its feasibility have been toned down. Today, bilateral as well as multilateral (non-discriminatory) arms control is considered acceptable. India has agreed on a number of pre-nuclear confidence building measures (CBMs) with China and Pakistan. In contrast with the United States and the Soviet Union, India and Pakistan agreed on a nuclear CBM even *before* they officially declared their nuclear weapons status when they signed in December 1988 an agreement not to attack each other's nuclear facilities. In the wake of the 1998 tests, the Lahore Memorandum of Understanding (February 1999) provided for mutual notification of impending missile tests. Currently, follow-up negotiations with Pakistan are being taken up.

However, there are some problems that appear to be inadequately resolved. Two significant ones – a failure to comprehend fully the relationship between different levels of conflict, and a lack of doctrinal clarity – are discussed below.

The Nuclear-Sub nuclear Linkage

A major problem with Indian thinking about nuclear weapons is its lack of clarity in relating the different levels of armed conflict, i.e., the relationships between subconventional, conventional and nuclear conflict. Initially, the advent of nuclear deterrence was regarded as having brought to an end *all* forms of physical conflict between India and its adversaries. Notably, it was expected by the leadership that Pakistan could no longer attempt to pursue its long-standing objective of obtaining full control over the disputed state of Jammu and Kashmir through military means.

Once India and Pakistan had established mutual deterrence, prudence would be the order of the day. Pakistan could no longer risk a conflict in Kashmir, the strategic status quo would be permanently frozen, and India would be able to deal with its Kashmir insurgency as an internal problem. This crucial error in Indian strategic thinking was exposed by the Kargil conflict of 1999. Accompanied by insurgents, Pakistani forces dressed in civilian garb occupied territory on the Indian side of the mutually agreed Line of Control (LoC) in Kashmir. The aim was to create a crisis without officially crossing the LoC, i.e., to obtain a military advantage while retaining official deniability. This would evoke a general fear of escalation from subconventional to conventional to nuclear conflict and thereby induce international intervention, compelling India to negotiate.

The attempt backfired for two reasons. First, India was able to use massive conventional firepower and throw out the occupying forces, whereas Pakistan could not overtly cross into Indian territory in response for fear of raising the conflict to a full-scale conventional war. Second, Pakistan's actions evoked a strongly critical international response, particularly from the United States, forcing it to announce a humiliating withdrawal of its campaign. However, the Kargil conflict did demonstrate to Indian leaders the problem of the "stability-instability paradox": that the standoff between nuclear rivals permits lowintensity or subconventional conflicts to occur between them. The working of the stability-instability paradox imposed on India a kind of strategic paralysis which Indian leaders found frustrating in the extreme. Though Kargil had failed, Pakistan was able to sustain its low-cost strategy of backing terrorist groups such as the Hizbul Mujahideen, the Lashkar-e-Taiba, and the Jaish-e-Muhammad in striking at will within India. Indian leaders struggled to devise a suitable response. The discourse among policy makers steadily shifted away from a search for political solutions to a quest for appropriate modes of force projection against Pakistan.

The options aired included hot pursuit of terrorists into Pakistani territory, limited strikes or special operations missions against terrorist camps in Pakistan, and a vague and undefined conception of "limited war." In January 2000, Defence Minister George Fernandes asserted that nuclear weapons "can deter only the use of nuclear weapons, but not all and any war," and that Kargil had demonstrated that Indian forces "can fight and win a limited war, at a time and place chosen by the aggressor." While admitting that under the nuclear shadow, there were "definite limitations if escalation across the nuclear threshold was to be avoided," Fernandes claimed that conventional war "has not been made obsolete by nuclear weapons." However, the likelihood that a resort to armed conflict might invite an adverse international response prevented action.

The terrorist attacks of September 11, 2001 in the US altered the situation. The American intervention in Afghanistan created a favourable climate for a strong Indian response to Pakistan's support for cross-border terrorism. Furthermore, major terrorist attacks on the Jammu and Kashmir legislature in October, and on the Indian Parliament in December, sharply increased pressure on the Indian government to act. Indian leaders sought to break out of their straitjacket of inaction and turn the stability-instability paradox against Pakistan through the exercise of coercive diplomacy. They initiated a massive conventional build-up along the Pakistan border and threatened to launch an unspecified form of limited war unless Pakistan stopped abetting terrorism in India. Though nuclear weapons did not enter the picture directly (there is no evidence so far of nuclear weapons being readied by either side), the mobilization did have a strong nuclear-strategic component. India's strategy was a two-pronged one. It attempted *direct compellence* in pressurizing Pakistan to back off in the face of a looming full-scale conventional and possibly nuclear conflict. It simultaneously attempted *indirect compellence* by causing the United States, fearful of a regional holocaust, to pressurize Pakistan to reverse its strategy of supporting cross-border terrorism.

Thus, a linkage was established between subconventional and nuclear conflict through conventional mobilization. India warned that if Pakistan chose to bring nuclear weapons into the fray, it (Pakistan) would suffer far more than India. On December 29, 2001, Fernandes warned:

Pakistan can't think of using nuclear weapons despite the fact that they are not committed to the doctrine of no first use like we are. We could take a strike, survive, and then hit back. Pakistan would be finished. I do not really fear that the nuclear issue would figure in a conflict.

In effect, what the Minister was saying was that nuclear balances do matter. This was in direct contravention of his government's doctrine of minimum deterrence, which rests on the belief that they do not. Besides, the idea that India could tolerate some damage from nuclear weapons seriously undercut its deterrence philosophy.

In the end, the whole exercise was fruitless. Despite considerable US pressure, Pakistan's promises to end support for terrorists operating in Kashmir were tactical and temporary, and, in the face of Pakistani counter-mobilization, India had to withdraw its forces in October 2002 after a ten-month-long deployment. It could not take the risk of treating a smaller quantum of nuclear damage as acceptable in practice, as opposed to its rhetorical argument. Deterrence overrode compellence. While the Indian government has not abandoned the possibility of other forms of limited conventional action, it is evident that the experience has taught a lesson. The episode revealed the difficulty involved in attempting to create strategic space for limited armed conflict in a nuclear environment. This explains the BJP-led government's October 2003 decision to resume negotiations with Pakistan.

Lack of Clarity on Minimum Deterrence

Where does India stand today? The picture is not yet clear. Its doctrine of "credible minimum deterrence" has yet to be articulated fully, and has undergone significant changes between 1999 and 2003. After the 1998 tests, Prime Minister Vajpayee made a brief announcement in Parliament on the elements of his government's nuclear doctrine. He stated that further testing was not necessary for credibility, affirmed India's commitment to the principle of no first use (NFU), and declared that arms control and disarmament remained central to the national agenda. But he said nothing about the sources of threat, the nature of deployment, the types and number of weapons desired, targeting, and other details which are normally considered the primary components of a deterrence strategy. Much of the public understanding of India's minimum deterrence doctrine till recently was based on the Draft Nuclear Doctrine (DND) released by the National Security Advisory Board (NSAB) in August 1999. The DND envisages "credible minimum deterrence" based on a capacity for "punitive retaliation with nuclear weapons to inflict damage unacceptable to the [nuclear] aggressor." For this, the requirements are "sufficient, survivable and operationally prepared nuclear forces" and the organization and will to employ nuclear weapons in the event deterrence fails. It proclaims NFU as well as non-use against countries which are not nuclear and are not allied with nuclear powers. It also calls for robust conventional forces in order to raise the nuclear threshold.

The DND supports a triad of air, land and sea-based delivery systems whose "survivability will be enhanced by a combination of multiple redundant systems, mobility, dispersion and deception." It distinguishes between an unspecified mode of "peacetime deployment" and a shift to "fully employable forces" in the event of a conflict arising. There is an emphasis on credibility – "any adversary must know that India can and will retaliate" – and on effectiveness based on "reliability, timeliness, accuracy and weight of attack." The document goes on to outline the requirements for command and control, security and safety, and research and development, and concludes by focusing on disarmament and arms control. The DND has been criticized for its lack of clarity and its open-endedness. Its call for a triad of delivery systems, and its emphasis on effectiveness and survivability go against the grain of a minimum deterrence posture since they reflect the typical Cold War approach used by the United States and the Soviet Union, both of which built needlessly large forces on the basis of such arguments. In short, the DND reveals a distinct preference for the operational rather than the political aspect of deterrence.

However, as Minister of External Affairs Jaswant Singh told an interviewer subsequently, the report was released in order to generate a national debate and was "not a policy document of the Government of India." Singh's interview provides a much more political exposition of Indian nuclear thinking. There are, certainly, a number of common elements in the DND and the interview. Both declare that India will not be the first to use nuclear weapons; that its retaliation-only posture will be based on the mobility and dispersal of assets as well as on an unspecified level of redundancy;

that a distinction has to be made between peacetime and active deployment, implying the possibility of a normally de-mated disposition of warheads and launch vehicles; and that ultimate authority over the arsenal must be civilian.

But Singh's enunciation of nuclear doctrine differs from the DND in important respects. While noting that nuclear assets must be survivable, he does not endorse the DND's stress on India's need for "multiple redundant systems" as necessary for survivability. The latter implies a discomfort with imbalance and a penchant for arms racing because its points of reference are the operational characteristics of an adversary's inventory.

Singh explicitly states that "parity is not essential for deterrence," that India will not engage in arms racing, and that minimum deterrence is only a question of "adequacy," not specific numbers – a point not made clear in the DND. Singh also makes the crucial point that retaliation need not be instantaneous. The implication for stability is clear: there is no need for Indian nuclear forces to be on high alert status, ready for instant retaliation.

This facilitates a relatively stable nuclear posture. This is a question that is not addressed in the DND. Further, whereas the DND does not focus on the question of targeting, Singh observes that "we have discarded the Cold War reference frame of nuclear war fighting," and that "we do not see nuclear weapons as weapons of war fighting," which is an unambiguous rejection of counterforce doctrine.

Another difference is with regard to the development of a nuclear triad. While the DND calls for a triad, Singh's position is that though development of diverse capabilities will go on, it is "premature" to talk of a triad and, more important, that a triad is not a "pre-requisite for credibility." The overall effect of the interview is to convey a relatively strong sense of commitment to nuclear minimalism based on a restrained posture with few weapons. In this respect, Singh is more reassuring than the DND. His delineation of nuclear doctrine is in keeping with a pattern of strategic preferences that treats nuclear weapons with circumspection. This helps explain the early initiative taken by Prime Minister Vajpayee in February 1999 (less than a year after the nuclear tests of 1998) to travel to Lahore in an attempt to establish regional strategic stability.

The brief announcement on nuclear doctrine and on the establishment of a National Command Authority (NCA) in January 2003 added something to our understanding of official Indian thinking. Its main points on doctrine were:

1. Reaffirmation of "credible" minimum deterrence;
2. Reiteration of NFU;
3. The threat of "massive" retaliation in response to a first strike against Indian forces anywhere;
4. Non-use of nuclear weapons against non-nuclear weapon states;
5. The option to retaliate with nuclear weapons against a chemical or biological attack;
6. Adherence to strict export controls; and
7. Renewed commitment to arms control through participation in the Fissile Material Cutoff Treaty (FMCT) negotiations, continued observance of the national moratorium on testing, and sustained commitment to universal disarmament.

Though these commitments do tell us something about India's deterrence posture, none of them has a direct bearing on the central character of *minimum* deterrence. NFU is a promise rather than a guarantee, and adversaries are unlikely to take it seriously in their calculations of risk. Besides, in comparison with earlier statements, it is diluted by the exceptions made with regard to chemical and biological weapons.

Massive retaliation is a threat that will in any case be expected by an adversary, for nuclear weapons, inevitably, are conducive to worst-case assumptions. Perhaps the pronouncement nearest to conveying a commitment to minimum deterrence is the pledge not to test, since a sophisticated arsenal of diverse and "reliable" weapons would require testing. The critical aspects of minimum deterrence are *not* mentioned in the announcement: the perception that deterrence can be achieved with a small number of weapons, with weapons of relatively little variety and sophistication, and with weapons that are not deployed or even assembled. If these aspects of minimum deterrence were to be spelt out, then a truly minimalist doctrine would have been articulated. That they have not been officially declared does not mean that a minimum deterrence doctrine does not exist. Quite clearly, it does. That is evident in its practice. However, the continuing search for diverse capabilities – land, air and sea-based – shows that the concept of minimum deterrence is not consistent. The only argument in favour of a triad is that it will reduce vulnerability, which is a standard Cold War argument. Sufficiency has to be defined in terms of the risk of retaliation faced by the adversary in contemplating the use of nuclear weapons, not one's own risk in being devastated by a first strike.

This brief review shows the lack of clarity and consistency in India's understanding of minimum deterrence. If ambivalence is allowed to persist, the possibility of nuclear thinking and practice drifting toward an open-ended operational conception of deterrence will increase. As India's nuclear infrastructure grows and takes shape, operational pressures led by military personnel, whose job, after all, is to treat nuclear weapons as usable weapons, will also grow.

Questions about vulnerability and reliability – and above all "credibility" – will be raised in the quest for more and "better" weapons. Unless minimum deterrence is clearly and thoroughly understood, there is always the possibility that some combination of intellectual drift, organizational pressures, and sustained threats will push doctrine toward open-ended expansion.

DREAMING INDIA'S NUCLEAR FUTURE

The manner and timing of its unveiling has been attacked in Opposition political circles and criticised in the press, but this must be recognised as being entirely in character. The dIND is a worthy follow-up to the authoritarian decision made by the Ras htriya Swayamsevak Sangh(RSS)-BJP high command to explode five nuclear devices in Pokhran on May 11 and May 13, 1998 and to weaponise the nuclear option, a decision made pre-emptively, in the utmost secrecy, in the name of 'national security' - targeting especially Pakistan and China - and 'shakti', without any objective review or democratic decision, in clear violation of the promises made in the National Agenda for Governance, in utter disregard for both the consequences for the region and the basic interests of the Indian people. It is significant that the only reference to the nuclear issue made in the 1999 manifesto of the National Democratic Alliance (NDA) is the promise that the recently established National Security Council will advise the gov ernment on "the establishment of a credible nuclear deterrent". However, as part of a motivated post-Kargil, pre-election exercise to boost Prime Minister Atal Behari Vajpayee's image as a great leader in war and peace, the Prime Minister's Office has pu t out a draft that was not preceded by the long-promised "strategic review" and was not discussed by the Cabinet. The adverse reaction the NSAB document has drawn in the Indian press, from Opposition parties, and internationally has made the Vajpayee gov ernment go instantly on the defensive. It has claimed that the dIND does not signal any real change in the nuclear weaponisation policy in place and, in any case, is meant to be debated before a final 'consensus' national decision is arrived at after the general elections.

A CLOSE study of the hawkish document reveals first its pretentious, confused character: this is unmistakably the work of amateurs (mostly self-proclaimed strategic affairs specialists) playing nuclear games and a bit of star wars as well, not anything t hat reflects professional military, or serious security, thinking. The exercise involves an attempt to cover all bases and, in aggressiveness, goes well beyond the doctrine of 'credible minimum nuclear deterrence' presented in outline by Prime Minister V ajpayee in his statement of December 15, 1998 in the Rajya Sabha. In that statement, Vajpayee indicated that the main features of the weaponising nuclear policy were as follows: (a) India will deploy its nuclear deterrent; (b) India's nuclear doctrine in cludes a policy of 'No-First-Use' and 'Non-use against non-nuclear weapons states'; (c) a policy of 'No-First-Use' with a minimum nuclear deterrent "implies deployment of assets in a manner that ensures survivability and capacity of an adequate response, " in other words the development and deployment of a deterrent with a second-strike capability; (d) by way of meeting the concerns of the

United States and its allies, India was willing to join the Comprehensive Test Ban Treaty (CTBT) and the Fissile Mat erial Cutoff Treaty (FMCT)-to-come and to make its export control laws relating to "sensitive technologies" more stringent; and (e) India will continue its missile development programme and not accept "any restraints on the development of India's R&D cap abilities".

The dIND is an attempt to seize the high ground of militarism in the Indian nuclear weaponisation debate. This is why it has assumed a significantly more aggressive posture than that indicated in Vajpayee's somewhat defensive statement made eight months earlier. The apologia of India's nuclear weapons programme being a minimal exercise in the development of instruments of self-defence forced by an insensitive world on a reluctant, peace-loving nation has been dispensed with. While paying lip-service to the formulation that "India shall pursue a doctrine of credible minimum nuclear deterrence", the dIND prescribes an open-ended, far-reaching programme of nuclear weaponisation with capabilities that will push the limits of the minimum. The preambular section attempts to set out the context in which BJP-led India made its security-led choice: the continued reliance of the nuclear weapons states on their large nuclear arsenals; their proclaimed willingness to use nuclear weapons "even in a non-nuclear context"; their virtual abandonment of nuclear disarmament goals; and "the very existence of offensive doctrines pertaining to the first use of nuclear weapons and the insistence of some nuclear weapon states on the legitimacy of their use even against non-nuclear weapon countries." Out of such international threats to "peace, stability and sovereignty of states" sprang India's nuclear weaponisation. The job of the dIND, the Preamble explains, is to outline the broad principles for "the d evelopment, deployment and employment of India's nuclear forces".

The Objectives section leads off with the assertion that "India's *strategic* interests" (emphasis added) require in consequence "effective, credible nuclear deterrence and adequate retaliatory capability should deterrence fail" and it is even conte nded that the U.N. Charter allows such a course by sanctioning "the right of self-defence". Two things about this formulation are worth noting. The first is the reference to strategic - and not security - interests, a distinction that is of some importan ce. More important, it becomes clear that the grand inspiration for the dIND is deterrence theory.

The new-found official fascination with the logic of deterrence marks a low point in the history of India's nuclear policy and indeed in the country's politics and international relations. It represents an abject acceptance of the cast-off intellectual r ags of western nuclear weapons establishments at a time when the theory has been shown to be dangerously flawed and indeed false and when it has begun to be questioned by those (like Robert McNamara and General Lee Butler) who once held leadership roles in its practice. The lowest point perhaps came when Prime Minister Vajpayee, replying on March 15, 1999 to the Lok Sabha debate on the motion of thanks to the President, came up with his famous statement: "The nuclear weapon is not an offensive weapon. I t is a weapon of self-defence. It is the kind of weapon that helps in preserving the peace. If in the days of the Cold War there was no use of force, it was because of the balance of terror." Not surprisingly, the dIND stands or falls by the theology of nuclear deterrence.

THE principal source of confusion in this document, its most damning failure, is the inability to answer in any rational, meaningful or logical fashion the questions: deterrence against whom? "Credible" or "minimum" or "effective" against whom? Driven pa rtly by the reluctance to admit openly that the major preoccupation of the pro-nuclear weapons lobby is with Pakistan and China and driven partly by delusions of thermonuclear superpower status, the document presents the absurd proposition that India's n uclear weapons are directed against *all* possessors of nuclear weapons. To quote para 2.4 of the dIND: "The fundamental purpose of Indian nuclear weapons is to deter the use and threat of use of nuclear weapons by any State or entity against India and its forces."

The heart of the dIND is para 2.2, which is worth quoting in full: "The requirements of deterrence should be carefully weighed in the design of Indian nuclear forces and in the strategy to provide for a level of capability consistent with maximum credibi lity, survivability, effectiveness, safety and security." Although subsequently it is pleaded that the basic doctrine is one of "credible minimum nuclear deterrence" and "retaliation only", it is clear that the whole exercise is to raise the nuclear stak es by introducing the principle of maximising so-called minimum deterrence by emphasising second-strike (or even third-strike) capability and "survivability". It is this maximum and "dynamic" version of "credible minimum deterrence" directed against all nuclear weapons states (and their military allies), read along with the justification of the Indian misadventure in terms of a global rationale, that animates the open-ended, adventurist and unlimited programme of nuclear weaponisation recommended by the NSAB.

It is worth noting that the Objectives section of the dIND, while asserting the validity of the doctrine of deterrence, adds to the irrationality by emphasing the principle of "punitive retaliation to inflict damage unacceptable to the aggressor". The no tion of unacceptable damage has often been promoted in the debate among Indian strategic affairs hawks, notably by K. Subrahmanyam, the conceptual father of the dIND, as a more rational basis for determining the size of India's nuclear arsenal than the p rinciple of assured destruction. However, on closer examination, the principle of "unacceptable damage" turns out to be as nebulous as the notion of deterrence itself. In the first instance, just as in any other form of deterrence, the notion of unaccept able damage involves determining the state of mind of the adversary, a virtually impossible task as the history of nuclear deterrence shows. Secondly, the assertion that "the actual size, components, deployment and employment of nuclear forces", that is the nuclear force structure, will be aimed at "convincing any potential aggressor that... India... shall inflict damage unacceptable to the aggressor" sounds as absurdly non-credible as the boast made (in a May 17, 1998 press conference) by Dr. A.P.J. Ab dul Kalam, Scientific Adviser to the Defence Minister and the key figure behind India's ballistic missile programme, that with Pokhran-II India had acquired the "capacity to vacate" any nuclear threat to itself. Does this mean that India will build a nuc lear force able to retaliate and do unacceptable damage to the United States after a U.S. nuclear attack on India, as worst case analysis suggests? Since the threshold of unacceptable damage varies considerably between, say, Pakistan and the United State s and given the all-embracing nature of the target of Indian nuclear deterrence, the notion of unacceptable damage to "any potential aggressor" is virtually useless. What is worse, this means that the *minimum* in the "credible minimum nuclear deterrent" has less and less meaning.

IN India, democratic and secular public opinion has always regarded nuclear weapons with horror, as weapons of mass destruction of a genocidal character. The hawks of the NSAB are quite aware that their doctrine, which seeks to legitimise and even glorify nuclear weapons as acceptable means of achieving strategic goals, runs directly into conflict with this sentiment. The dIND has no inhibition in identifying the building blocks of Indian nuclear deterrence: "sufficient, survivable and operationally pre pared" nuclear forces; a "robust" command and control system; effective intelligence and early warning capabilities; comprehensive planning and training for "operations in line with the strategy"; and, perhaps most important, the politico-military "will to employ nuclear forces and weapons". In other words, no moral qualms, no squeamishness, no falling back on Gandhian or Nehruvian values, no peace-oriented value system that has underpinned the country's foreign and nuclear policies since Independence c an be allowed to come in the way of fulfilling this madcap vision.

Underlining the dIND's militarist vision of India's future is the formulation in para 2.7 that requires the maintenance of a high level of conventional capabilities. The claim that this will raise "the threshold of... threat (of use) or use of nuclear we apons" is demonstrably false. In fact, the opposite is true, as Munir Akram, Pakistan's Ambassador at the Conference on Disarmament in Geneva, pointed out recently: "Thus, although the Indian document states the purpose of a conventional arms build-up is to raise the nuclear threshold, in fact the conventional build-up will further lower the nuclear threshold and bring closer the danger of nuclear use in the sub-continent." At any rate, if this is the adversary's perception, it is clear that Indian dete rrence thinking has got it hopelessly wrong.

The dIND deal with nuclear forces, credibility and survivability, and command and control. In this hawkish vision, "minimum" virtually fades away and "credible", "effective", "enduring", "diverse", "flexible" and "responsive" take over in a way that suggests that no real limit will be placed on the Indian nuclear programme in quantity, scope and quality. Thus Indian nuclear forces, according to para 3.1, will be based on "a triad of aircraft, mobile land-based missiles and sea-bas ed assets in keeping with the objectives outlined..." Although nuclear-powered submarines as carriers of nuclear-tipped missiles are not mentioned, this is primarily because official Indian policy is not to talk about India's supposedly secret nuclear su bmarine programme; the whole dIND approach makes it clear that submarine-based assets, considered the least vulnerable but the most complex and expensive, are envisaged. Survivability of all these forces will be "enhanced" by a combination of "multiple r edundant systems, mobility, dispersion and deception". Clearly, this encourages the adversary (who may be different at different points of time) to target Indian nuclear and other strategic assets in a far more comprehensive fashion. In the sub-continent al nuclear standoff that is bound to follow should the dIND be accepted by the government, the elements of mobility, dispersion and deception will add substantially to the risk of an actual nuclear exchange.

A notably irresponsible and dangerous feature of the recommended doctrine is that it will push what is claimed to be a 'No-First-Use' policy towards "launch-on-warning" or "launch-under-attack". Para 3.2 of the dIND envisages "*assured capability*" (emphasis added) to "shift from peacetime deployment to fully employable forces in the *shortest possible* time" (emphasis added). Timeliness of response is re-emphasised in para 4.2 that speaks about the need to maximise the efficacy of India's nuc lear deterrent "through synergy among all elements involving reliability, timeliness, accuracy and weight of the attack." The matter is clarified further in para 4.3(i), which, addressing the issue of survivability, states that "India's nuclear forces an d their command and control shall be organised for very high survivability against surprise attacks and for *rapid punitive response*" (emphasis added). Precisely how rapid is the response to be? It is here that the ambiguity and confusion begin. Fu ture interpretations of this formulation may extend to the position that Indian nuclear forces should launch either on warning or under attack. The building of such a capability will mean that India must undertake a nuclear weapons programme with all the associated assets that will approach the levels of the advanced nuclear powers. While all this may seem as grandiose and unreal as it is irresponsible and dangerous, it is very much the dream of the hawks of the NSAB, who will not let us forget for a mo ment that India must be ready to "effectively employ nuclear weapons".

The dIND vision is unmarred by any acknowledgement of the realities of Indian nuclear capabilities or of Indian S&T in general. Nuclear forces and command and control need to survive even "repetitive attrition attempts", meaning more than one strike [par a 4.3(i)], demanding a capability that it is not clear even the advanced nuclear weapon powers possess in practice. The emphasis on timeliness of response will inevitably lead to India's nuclear weapons being on alert status of increasingly high levels. The option of India keeping the fissile material for its weapons separate from delivery systems, a possibility suggested by Jaswant Singh in his last round of talks with Strobe Talbott, is clearly at odds with the prescriptions of the dIND. The NSAB is e ither unaware of, or not bothered by, assessments that Indian nuclear weapons are not adequately safety-tested given the limited range of tests conducted at Pokhran-II. The only way that the 'safety' of Indian nuclear weapons can be ensured with current technical capabilities is to keep the fissile material separate from the warhead assembly and the delivery systems.

In keeping with its complete freedom from humanitarian concern, its total insensitivity to issues of economic, developmental and human security, the dIND does not even attempt a token discussion of a civil defence programme commensurate with the scale of nuclear weaponisation recommended. Nor has any economic cost consideration entered its ken. Earlier ballpark estimates by economists, notably the work of C. Rammanohar Reddy, suggested that the cost of India's "credible minimum nuclear deterrent" might run to Rs.50,000 crores over a ten year period.

The open-ended, 'maximal' version of the nuclear deterrent proposed by the NSAB will render such numbers tremendous underestimates.

Indisputably, the dIND has caused deep anxiety and unease among India's neighbours and a tit-for-tat response from Pakistan seems guaranteed. In their enthusiasm for nuclear weapons, the confused luminaries of the NSAB have even amended official commitme nts, made for instance in the Prime Minister's December 15, 1998 statement in the Rajya Sabha, on non-use of India's nuclear weapons against "non-nuclear weapon states". The dIND, in a disturbingly ambiguous formulation, recommends that "India will not r esort to the use or threat of use of nuclear weapons against States which do not possess nuclear weapons, *or are not aligned with nuclear weapon powers*" (emphasis added). As Admiral L. Ramdas, former Chief of the Naval Staff, puts it, what the dIN D has done, for transparently partisan reasons, is to open "a Pandora's box to frighten the entire neighbourhood".

All this does not necessarily mean that the prescriptions of the dIND will remain unchanged when a new government takes over after the general elections. Nor does it follow that official nuclear policy has returned to a path of defiant independence. The essence of the strategy of the Hindu Right is to try and hang on to *de facto* nuclear weaponisation at any cost. Among other things, this will mean abandonment of the global nuclear disarmament agenda and all principled opposition to the discrimina tory global nuclear order. As External Affairs Minister Jaswant Singh told Arun Shourie in a remark quoted proudly by the latter in the Rajya Sabha debate of December 15, 1998: "Look at it as a crowded railway compartment. When you are trying to come int o it, your perspective is one. When you are in it, you want the rules that will keep you in and keep the others out." From a democratic standpoint, the pursuit of nuclear weaponisation while surrendering to the CTBT and the FMCT that is being negotiated and being co-opted into the discriminatory global nuclear order as a minor partner must be recognised as the worst possible course for India's nuclear policy. Meanwhile, the hawkishness that has underlain Pokhran-II, the subsequent articulations of offic ial policy relating to nuclear weaponisation, the test-firing of the extended range Agni II intermediate range ballistic missile and the explicit linking of this to nuclear weaponisation is likely to be modulated in accordance with perceived short-term p olitical exigencies and the twists and turns of the evolving regional and international situation. Everything except *de facto* nuclear weaponisation is bargainable; the limits of acceptance/non-acceptance by the United States and its allies can be probed and tested. The aggressive posture signalled by the dIND must be understood only in this context.

NUCLEAR PROLIFERATION POLICIES DURING THE COLD WAR

In the South Asian context, a conflictual bipolar security complex, India and Pakistan's transformational process of emerging as opaque nuclear powers was an example of different motivations, aspirations and ambitions for obtaining nuclear status. While the dominance of *realpolitik* trends over states' nuclear decision-making process is not an entirely surprising phenomena, the evolution of India's approach to the nuclear option is interesting from philosophical and strategic viewpoints. The genesis of the Indian nuclear policy from a categorical opposition to nuclear weapons in the Nehru era to Pokhran I, India's first so-called Peaceful Nuclear Explosion (PNE) in 1974, signified a discontinuity in New Delhi's post-1947 strategic thinking. What caused this discontinuity? What factor(s) led the country of Mohandas Gandhi, who once labelled nuclear weapons as 'diabolic', to obtaining potential nuclear power status under Indira Gandhi? Do the same factors suffice in explaining Pakistan's motives for developing its own nuclear capabilities in the mid-1980s? While some political scientists emphasised national security considerations in locating the roots of India and Pakistan proliferation policy, others have used an alternative theoretical approach with a greater level of structural balance between domestic, military security and symbolic motives. The latter multi-causal approach, summarised by Scott D. Sagan, is particularly useful in providing an inclusive analysis of nuclear proliferation causes. In this context and through the application of Sagan's explanatory models, the essay attempts to analyse the layers in India and Pakistan's 'nuclear thinking' leading to the development of military nuclear technology. The alternative multi-causal explanation constitutes a practically efficient theoretical framework for the comprehensive understanding of states' hybrid logic for nuclear proliferation.

Opposing the neorealist mono-causal security-oriented analysis (i.e. "the security model"), Sagan's approach considers the domestic and norms aspects as effective factors in triggering military nuclear proliferation, thus offering two additional explanations: "the domestic politics model" and "the norms model." According to Sagan, security model states (either weak or strong) perceive nuclear weapons as an enormously powerful means of deterrence to secure their national security in an anarchic international system, if their regional or trans-regional rival(s) acquire nuclear capability. Strong resourceful states develop their own bomb, while weak states, incapable of proliferation, are obliged to join a balancing alliance with a nuclear power to maintain their security and sovereignty with the promise of nuclear retaliation.

In contrast, the domestic politics model reflects the influence of three main domestic actors on governments' nuclear proliferation policies: first, states' nuclear energy establishments (consisting of scientific institutions and civil companies); second, the military elites (especially in the Air Force branch) as domestic bureaucratic actors; and third, politicians who tend to profit from the nuclear weapons discourse for political parties or individual standing regarding pro-proliferation public opinion.

Therefore, these pro-proliferation actors gain additional influence if nuclear weapons are a positive symbol in states' domestic debates – thus the states proliferate in accordance with the influence of one or more of the aforementioned actors. Finally, in the norms model, states' nuclear policies are pro-proliferation due to 'nuclear symbolism' and the 'nuclear myth': states observe military organisation and advanced weaponry as essential elements in their image as modern and sovereign states. The 'nuclear myth', or symbolic implications of nuclear proliferation (e.g. technological advancement, military might, projection of grandeur, etc), are perceived as a means of forming states' modern identity and enhancing their international prestige. While there seems to be an analytical overlap and theoretical interference between the domestic and symbolic models, Sagan's three models offer an efficient toolbox for examining the deciding factors in India and Pakistan's nuclear policies.

The security-model analysis of Indian nuclear policy prior to Pokhran I can be conducted by analysing India's threat perception at the regional and trans-regional levels. The trans-regional level analysis confirms the gravity of Sino-centrism in India's trans-regional threat perception sphere, and the validity of Sagan's security-model explanation. The dynamics of post-1962 Sino-Indian bilateral relations is the fundamental factor in India's horizontal proliferation policy in the security model.

While the Sino-Indian protracted conflict began in 1953 over territorial claims, the 1962 Sino-Indian war and its disastrous consequences for the non-aligned India moved the Chinese threat factor from the periphery of New Delhi's threat perception circle to its centre, triggering incremental yet significant changes in Indian defence policy and military strategy. The subsequent Indian military reorientation towards re-equipment and operational reinforcement (e.g. the creation of ten mountain divisions designed for warfare in the Himalayas and increasing the Army's manpower ceiling to 825,000) confirms the demise of Nehru's *moralpolitik*-type policies regarding China.

However, the fundamental shift in India's nuclear weapons position occurred when Beijing shocked New Delhi with the detonation of its first nuclear device in October 1964. New Delhi's subsequent reaction to China's nuclear capability demonstrated a paradigm shift in India's previously Nehruvian anti-proliferation policy towards what then Prime Minister Lal Bahadur Shastri reluctantly phrased as India considering "nuclear explosion for peaceful purposes".

Compatible with the security-model's two policy scenarios, India's inability to develop its own nuclear weapons forced New Delhi to secure nuclear deterrence by joining a balancing alliance with a nuclear power. Accordingly, when India's request to the United States, the Soviet Union and the United Kingdom for nuclear guarantee was refused, India's only option for deterring a nuclear China and maintaining its national security was to obtain horizontal proliferation on its own, leading to the 1974 PNE.

Similarly, the regional-level analysis indicates the significance of nuclear weapons in India's quest for regional hegemony and security in the South Asian region, although against the much less significant threat of Pakistan.

A quick glance at pro-Indian political scientists' analysis of the motivation of India's quest for regional security through nuclear weapons reveals New Delhi's mindset regarding Pakistani conventional threat as well as India's strategic policy manoeuvre to achieve several objectives at once. In the bipolar South Asian security complex, Pakistan was (and is) India's major regional security and strategic concern.

In spite of its conventional inferiority to India, Pakistan attacked its greater and more militarily powerful neighbour in 1948, 1965 and 1971. While India's decisive military victory in the 1971 war, and the subsequent disintegration of Pakistan through the independence of Bangladesh, considerably weakened Pakistan, it managed to retain most of its military infrastructures.

The series of Indo-Pakistani military conflicts convinced Indian strategists that Pakistan could use the period of Indian domestic political instability to launch other military attacks on India. In the light of alarming Sino-Pakistani cordial relations, and the presumption of Pakistani will to attack India, India's nuclear proliferation became instrumental in maintaining Indian regional security as well as establishing Indian regional hegemony through deterring Pakistan from future attacks. As Saira Khan formulates, the most efficient war-avoidance strategy for India in such conflictual regional settings was 'deterrence by possession of nuclear weapons.'

Similar to the Indian behavioural pattern for proliferation, but in contrast to India's multi-layered threat perception, the application of the security-model framework on Pakistan's nuclear policy produces a mono-causal explanation: Pakistan's nuclear proliferation was a linear reactionary policy to India's 1974 nuclear detonation. In addition to Indo-Pakistani territorial, ideological and ethnic elements of conflict that have formed the essentials of the South Asian security complex since 1947, the 1971 war and dismemberment of Pakistan reinforced Indo-centrism in Pakistan's threat perception.

The war crippled Pakistan's economy and displayed the perceived unreliability of Pakistan's allies (i.e. the United States and China) in the time of crisis. Realising its conventional military inferiority to India, in 1972 President Zulfiquar Ali Bhutto initiated a nuclear policy in pursuit of nuclear weapons. Islamabad's nuclear program, however, gained a critical boost by India's 1974 PNE. Closely resembling the pattern of India's reaction to the 1964 Chinese nuclear test, Pakistan's nuclear policy was decisively directed towards inevitable nuclear proliferation after India's 1974 PNE. Against India's combined conventional military superiority and nuclear weapons capability, Pakistan had to obtain its own nuclear weapons as soon as possible to provide deterrence against the gravest threat to its national security. In this context, with Islamabad's failure to obtain security guarantees from the nuclear powers against a nuclear India, Pakistan had no other option other than to embark on its own nuclear proliferation program.

Applying the domestic-model of analysis on the Indian case clearly exhibits the decisive influence of two of the three domestic actors outlined by the model on India's nuclear decision for horizontal proliferation: nuclear energy establishments (consisting of pro-proliferation scientists and defence laboratories) and politicians eager to enhance their respective parties or/and individual standing in public opinion. Due to the pattern of the civil-military relationship in India where the former utterly dominates the latter, military elites as bureaucratic domestic actors had practically no influence over New Delhi's process of nuclear decision-making. After the Chinese 1964 nuclear test, Homi Bhabba, the head of India's Atomic Energy Commission (AEC), tenaciously lobbied for the allocation of required resources for developing nuclear weapons. Eventually, the AEC leadership's lobbying for proliferation along with pro-nuclear Congress party pressure on the government forced the reluctant Shastri to order the initiation of a classified project to develop technical ability to design and detonate a PNE within a certain timeframe. In spite of Bhabba's successor, Vikram Sarabhai's fierce opposition to any form of nuclear proliferation, the AEC developed an alliance with defence laboratories for lobbying the new Prime Minister Indira Gandhi. In a meaningful coincidence, the dynamics of Indian domestic politics in the early 1970s were defined in terms of economic recession, large-scale riots in various regions and the internal conflict in the ruling Congress party, thus an all-time low domestic support for Gandhi's government. In such dire circumstances, with the Prime Minister acknowledging that a theatrical nuclear explosion could have been a decisive 'political ace' for increasing her standing in public opinion, Gandhi's approval of 1974 PNE is hardly surprising. In a later interview, in spite of her initial denial, Gandhi admitted that the PNE "would have been useful for election". As the result, immediately after the detonation, public support for Gandhi's government and the ruling Congress party increased by one-third, both being "restored to the nation's confidence." Considering the pre-PNE Indian domestic politics dynamics, the influence of AEC, the Prime Minister and the ruling party on nuclear proliferation is evident.

Domestic-model Framework

In contrast, the application of the domestic-model framework on the Pakistani case constitutes the presence of non-political domestic dynamics and a higher level of military influence on the process of Pakistan's pursuit of nuclear weapons. As mentioned earlier, a year after the 1971 war and two years before Pokhran I, Pakistan's former leader Bhutto instructed the country's top scientists to concentrate on the development of nuclear weapons. Yet, such policies could not be pursued without the involvement of the military institution in the process. Decades of military rule has promoted the Pakistani military as the strongest bureaucratic institution in the country, setting the pattern of the country's civil-military relationship in favour of military control. However, in spite of the military's vast influence in Pakistan's polity, nuclear decisions were made within a coordinated policy framework consisting of Prime Minister Bhutto, the chiefs of the armed forces, the Foreign Minister and the chief of joint services headquarters.

The pro-bomb direction of Pakistani organic nuclear decision-making machinery was maintained even after the fall of Bhutto in 1977. The policy momentum and continuity in the country's pursuit for nuclear weapons in the post-Bhutto era confirms the absence of a domestic politics perspective in favour of the strong presence of a national security perspective: all Pakistani political leaders with different attitudes and policy perspectives maintained the essentials of Bhutto's nuclear policy. As for the nuclear establishment agency's influence, however, a division in the scholarly literature is detectable: while Kapur introduces I. H. Usmani, chairman of Pakistan Atomic Energy Commission (PAEC) as the most important figure in Pakistan's nuclear decision-making during 1970s, Khan maintains that the scientific institutions' influence was largely barred by the institutionalised military, limiting their range of influence to the lobbying of politicians and military elites in favour of proliferation. Yet, in spite of Kapur's exaggerated emphasis on Usmani's influence, the dominance of the security discourse over Pakistan's nuclear policy process is to such a degree that the domestic model's dynamics echoes the trends of the security model.

Finally, analysis of India's Cold War period nuclear proliferation policy signifies the link between India's quest for obtaining international prestige as a mean of gaining 'great power' status and its pursuit of the absolute weapon. From India's perspective, a direct link between nuclear proliferation and international prestige existed: countries in possession of nuclear weapons enhanced their standing in the international system's power pyramid. Nuclear states, developed or underdeveloped, were (and continue to do so) taken seriously by other members of the international community because of the practical implications of possessing the ultimate weapon. India's perspective regarding nuclear symbolism was formed by observing the impact of China's 1964 nuclear explosion on Beijing's power status and international recognition of Chinese power which followed. In addition, China obtained its seat in the United Nations which had previously been denied. The United States' recognition of China's power demonstrated to India the symbolic importance of nuclear weapons in establishing a state's prestige. Remembering the existence of rivalry between the two states, the Chinese model of enhancing prestige propelled India to embark on a quest for horizontal nuclear proliferation to enhance its prestige, not only in the international context, but in regard to its territorial quarrel with China.

In contrast to India, and in spite of the 'Islamic bomb' rhetoric, Pakistan's nuclear proliferation program did not focus on enhancing the country's international prestige nor did it perceive nuclear weapons as a means of promoting a sense of Islamic nationalism. Reviewing the views of Pakistani scholars, strategists and officials regarding the country's motivations for nuclear proliferation clarifies the symbolic-model inefficiency for explaining the rubric of Pakistani proliferation policy. In an interview with Khan, former Pakistani Foreign Minister Agha Shahi rejected the existence of any considerations of symbolic type in Pakistan's military nuclear program. Similarly, the strategist Ross Masud, the Chairman and Director General of the Islamabad's Institute of Strategic Studies confirmed Shahi's view that the projection of Pakistani grandeur by nuclear weapons "has never been a factor in Pakistan's decision-makers' minds", contributing any enhancement in Pakistani prestige to an unintended "spillover effect". In this context, Pakistan's nuclear policy was fundamentally less concerned about the notion of prestige enhancement than national security. However, as mentioned by Masud, while the Pakistani horizontal nuclear proliferation could produce the prestige dimension, such an outcome could not be regarded as the cause of proliferation but as its secondary consequence. In addition, the much referred notion of the 'Islamic bomb' was in fact more of a rhetorical strategy to attract financial support from wealthy Arab states than a symbol of the Muslim states' international prestige. Therefore, the application of a symbolic-model framework on Pakistan's proliferation policy does not demonstrate the symbolic motive as a primary factor in the country's nuclear weapons development.

After outlining the general theoretical frameworks and their policy implication, the essay discussed India and Pakistan's motivations for horizontal nuclear proliferation according to the security model, the domestic politics model and the symbolic model, respectively. Analysing India's motivations through the security-model framework introduces nuclear China as primary incentive for India's nuclear proliferation and India's thrive for regional hegemony in the South Asia through deterring Pakistan as the secondary motivation. In contrast, the same model shows that Pakistan's sole concern for deterring India as its primary motivation for nuclear proliferation. In the domestic level, while India's nuclear policy was heavily influenced by leaders' political motivations and nuclear energy establishments lobbying – Pakistan's proliferation policy, witnessing a high level of military influence, lacked a domestic politics perspective and was mostly concerned with security perspective. Finally, while the application of symbolic model on India's nuclear policy confirms the significance of nuclear symbolism in India's quest for international prestige through nuclear proliferation, it demonstrates prestige angle as secondary to security-centric Pakistani proliferation policy.

DEMOCRACY AND DEFENCE POLICY

Democracy influences both the process and the content of defence policy. Thus, in a democratic set-up, defence policy is based on a consultative process. Its goals and objectives, as well as many finer details, are often debated in Parliament, the media, by think-tanks and during election campaigns. This process ensures a more participative, inclusive and transparent defence policy. This indeed is the case in India and other democracies. An important outcome of this process is that democratic governments cannot concentrate on militarisation alone.

They have to balance the needs of other sectors like the economy, health and education, with the requirements of defence. This ensures that there is no emphasis on militarisation and on an aggressive defence policy. It is well known that democracies do not go to war with each other. The reason for this is that ordinary people want peace and prosperity and democratic governments have to reflect this aspiration in their defence policy. On the other hand, dictatorial regimes have compulsions to spend large amounts on military to take care of both domestic instability and regime survival against external intervention. History is replete with such instances in the past and there are many contemporary examples today. This indeed is the case with democratic India's defence policy which has always focused on its own defence and has never contemplated aggression, even against its smallest neighbour. India's defence expenditure in early years of its independence was below two per cent of GDP.

Even now, it is less than 2.5 per cent, despite many real threats it has to face. Compare this to the amounts that some of our neighbours spend on military! Another important outcome of defence policy making through a democratic process is that such a process enables nations to develop comprehensive national strength. The concept of comprehensive national strength includes economic strength, technological strength, infrastructure and other important aspects that help to build up a nation's power. A country cannot be defended by its military power alone. Recent history shows that even great powers with huge militaries can face serious difficulties in achieving their goals and can even disintegrate due to the weight of their own internal contradictions. In India, we have been able to develop comprehensive national strength and, today we are counted amongst the world's most important powers. This is not only on account of our military but also due to our economy, our science and technology, our knowledge power, our sunrise industries and our democracy. Given its vigilant citizens with a stake in the security of the nation, the genuine requirements of defence are taken care of in democracies.

Thus, despite the fact that India has been peace-loving, it has always made an effort to keep pace with the latest defence technologies. In its initial years, India had opposed nuclear weapons tooth and nail and favoured complete disarmament. But, when the powerful nations of the world did not give up nuclear weapons and when our neighbours developed their own nuclear weapons, the Indian democracy showed enough dynamism and flexibility to change its policy and develop nuclear deterrence. However, our nuclear doctrine affirms that India will not resort to first strike and never use nuclear weapons against non-nuclear weapon states. Thus, even India's nuclear doctrine has a purely defensive orientation. India's nuclear policy has evolved over time and is based on its essentially consensual approach in matters of national security. India's defence policy is flexible enough to respond to changes in the international strategic environment.

The primary task of the Indian Armed Forces has been to provide security for our citizens and to defend our vital interests at home and abroad. Democratic India also wishes to play a friendly and responsible role in the international arena. India has always been in the forefront of UN peace-keeping missions. It has been an important actor in international fora, particularly the United Nations. In accordance with its growing profile and role, it deserves a place in the United Nations Security Council. India also seeks to provide an adequate military capability for operations to promote international stability, and humanitarian missions after natural or other disasters, providing assistance to the civil authorities at home, and maintenance of essential national services. India has worked for regional peace and stability and rendered exemplary service to provide relief in times of disaster. A recent example is that of relief operations following the Tsunami disaster. We are also ready to cooperate with the nations of the region to provide maritime security and participate in disaster management and disaster forecasting mechanisms.

In its external dimension, India has always sought a cooperative relationship with all nations. It has also made continuous efforts towards peace at the international level. It was in this background that in the Cold War era, India had refused to side with one bloc or another. India led the Non-Aligned Movement to mitigate tensions at the international level and to play a positive role in resolving conflicts. However, its proximity to the Soviet bloc for defence supplies was misinterpreted. Due to the configuration of the Cold War era, India and some western nations were unable to come together and form a strong partnership. Now that the Cold War has ended and India is rapidly integrating with a globalising world, it has entered into either a strategic partnership or a strategic dialogue with all important powers of the world. Our growing friendship with United States, Russia, European Union and Japan is a testimony to this positive development. India and China have set aside their boundary dispute to come together in the area of economic cooperation. Earnest efforts are also being made by the two sides to resolve the boundary issue but this does not allow our growing cooperation to be affected. We are trying to develop close and cooperative relationship with all our neighbours, including Pakistan. Our future vision of South Asia is a region which is stable, at peace with each other and cooperating to accelerate economic growth and prosperity of its people. We want our neighbours to take full advantage of our growing market and a rapidly globalising economy.

India has suffered from terrorism for many decades and has been able to cope with the problem effectively. In doing so, it has respected human rights. It is an important player in the war against terrorism which is seen as an assault on our secular, inclusive and democratic polity. Countries which are undemocratic in their orientation are often a heaven for terrorists and even pursue terrorism as a part of state policy. This is an important distinction between the defence and security policies of democracies and autocratic rulers. Because democracies do not favour draconian measures and respect the rule of law, they are some times perceived to be soft or weak. The process of debate and consultation also can be a stretched out process at time. However, democracies are inherently strong and tend to promote defence policies which are conducive to the welfare of their own people and to peace and stability in the world.

What is Wrong with India's Defence Industrial Policy?

Defence industrial policy in the initial years after independence was guided by the simple phrase called 'self sufficiency'. This was subsequently modified to 'self reliance' in defence production and has become a matter of varied interpretation. While for some it means the ultimate objective of complete non-dependence on imports for defence hardware, for others it means selective self-sufficiency in certain critical technologies. And for some others it is a simple reduction in the ratio of imports to indigenous sources of supply to the armed forces.

However, one can say that India's defence industrial policy broadly consists of three components: (i) maximisation of indigenous manufacturing and production (ii) License production of what could be obtained from abroad and (iii) direct purchase of those equipment not covered by the other two categories but considered essential for ensuring security. Another important unspoken element was that everything, whether indigenous production, license production or direct purchase, was done within the government set-up in line with the general industrial policy. The recent policy change, of course, demonstrates the intention to involve the private sector in defence R&D and production through licensing and the indirect opening of the defence industrial sector to foreign companies through equity participation and the offset arrangement.

The moot question is: was there something wrong with the past policy objectives? On the face of it, the policy components and objectives appear quite sound and logical for a country like India. In simple terms, it means that indigenous production should be maximised; what could not be produced indigenously should be produced under license arrangement; and those that could not be obtained through these two routes should be acquired by direct purchase. A sound policy indeed. But the soundness of a policy has to be judged from tangible outcomes. Arguably, the problems might not have been in the contents of the policy per se. It is due to the nature defence technology and limitations of vision as embedded in the policy.

The policy objective was essentially to substitute imported equipment with indigenous production in the hope of attaining 'self-sufficiency' or 'self reliance'. Unfortunately, the security imperatives of a country translated into defence equipment are like 'moving targets'. Neither the technological capability of the defence sector nor its policy instrument as highlighted above was able to catch up with the targets.

The increasing quantum of defence imports from year to year, the country's inability to upgrade the imported equipment held for significant period under license production, and, indirectly, insignificant defence exports amply testify to this situation. The general industrial policy wherein defence items and their productions were kept strictly within the government set-up further compounded the problem. In this context, two aspects of the policy – indigenous production and license production, merit detailed analysis.

Maximising indigenous production would imply more than one thing. It would mean meeting the quantitative requirements in terms of the existing demands of the armed forces for equipment or items at any point of time. It would also mean increasing the varieties of items and equipment required by them. Most importantly, it would mean the ability to meet the challenges of supplying their ever-changing demands of technology specific equipment and items. India's defence industrial policy has conspicuously failed in this respect. In fact, the implication of this policy is that the country should be able to indigenously produce the challenging demands made by the armed forces. Its logical extension is that defence research and development efforts have to be strengthened through policy focused research and development and adequate resources allocations thereto. It is a known fact that the defence research and development organisation has 50-odd laboratories and establishments. However, its lack of focused research and development is equally well known, though of late it has been able to achieve break-throughs in certain strategic technologies. Moreover, its budgetary allocation has been quite modest even within the overall defence budget and until recently it was part of 'Army Demand'. In fact, the Parliamentary Standing committee on Defence recommended that defence R&D budgetary allocation should be at least 14 to 15 per cent of the total defence budget so that indigenous production to imports in the ratio of 70:30 could be achieved. This recommendation was in line with the projected target of the report of the self-reliance committee entitled '10 year plan for self reliance in Defence systems'. But the fact remains that there is no evidence of adequate policy back-up to attain this desirable but difficult goal. The DRDO does not seem to be suffering from lack of funds per se since only 8 to 10 per cent of its total budget is reported to be spent on fundamental research. Perhaps, the solution to this issue lies somewhere else.

How about production under license, another important pillar of the policy? The normal assumption is that production under license would enable the country not only to acquire the capability to produce a particular equipment or product but also help it gain the technical know-how for subsequent upgradation and further technological innovations. For the last fifty-odd years, India has been producing a number of defence equipment under license. Good examples in this regard are the Vijayanta tank and the MIG series of fighter aircraft. But this does not seem to have helped in the development of the Arjun Main Battle Tank and the Light Combat Aircraft. Moreover, India has not even been able to upgrade certain fighter aircraft held and operated for a long time by its armed forces. Thus, the above assumption is definitely not correct.

A closer examination of license production arrangements reveals certain interesting features. License production arrangements are more of an 'institutional framework' under which various types of contractual agreements could be entered into between the supplier and the buyer. It is not necessarily a proven mechanism of technology transfer as such. It may envisage the setting up of a simple production line or facilities in the buyer country for assembly of the finished parts and components for the final finished product. In such cases, hardly any technology transfer takes place and the supplier does not part with any technical know-how. In fact, the supplier agrees to sacrifice only a small portion of his economic interest. It is also not possible to discern under these circumstances whether the supplier has compensated itself for this marginal loss by way of increasing the cost of the technology or equipment and components thereof. On the other hand, there could be a situation where license production involves an intensive process of technology transfer within and beyond the physical production of the equipment in the host county. This is rare rather than routine. The truth of the matter is that since technology is know-how, it is the function of human understanding. The focus of active mechanisms, implicitly or explicitly, is people. However, the truth is that no foolproof prescription could be given for the effectiveness of technology transfer. It all depends on the nature of technology to be acquired. Perhaps, India has learnt it by the hard way the limitations of licence production for attaining the objective of self-sufficiency or self-reliance in defence production.

The fact that defence technology needs long term investment, its obsolescence is high and economies of scale are difficult to attain unlike in other areas of civilian technology are well known. This is essentially because higher capability tends to drive downward the scales of production. In the context of a limited number of customers, this trend is more regressive. On top of this, contrary to logical expectation, the production of the next generation of an equipment or of a different variant does not bring down the cost of the equipment. It has been the British experience that a new generation could cost between one and a half times to four times of the previous variant. This is due to the fact that production of the next generation is not a simple straight line trajectory work but involves the integration of various systems, which sometimes may involve a number of companies and agencies, that were not partners earlier.

This leads to the conclusion that the policy of maximising indigenous production without a strong R&D policy back-up would not bring tangible results. License production is more of an economic compromise between the supplier and the buyer, and it does not and cannot bring about significant technology transfer without an inbuilt specific and suitable mechanism. Every country at one point of time or the other will attain a saturation level when it comes to supplying certain categories of equipment for its armed forces. Therefore, the ultimate defence industrial policy goal must be to foster defence exports without which it is difficult to sustain the economic base of a country's defence industry.

India's defence industrial policy seems to be lacking in all these important ingredients. Since the industrial base has to be sustained for technological and economic reasons, exports are an essential element of defence industrial policy. This is why many countries and their companies are aggressively competing in the global defence market for exports under different arrangements including license production. It is reported that way back in 1995, the United States government spent more than $7.6 billion in subsidy to help export defence equipment to sustain the economic base of its defence industry. It is a matter of fact that strategic depth in defence production can be increased only by aiming at being 'internationally competitive' through the policy objective of defence exports. In the absence of such an approach, India's defence industrial policy is unlikely to take off in the foreseeable future.

Is India on the Path to Vibrant Defence Industry?

Every major power aspires to build a vibrant defence industrial base. This status is however not easily attainable. Apart from the United States and to some extent Russia and France, all other countries are in the state of struggling to arrive at such a defence industrial position. Certain countries like the United Kingdom may be able to attain this, but due to strategic or economic preferences may deliberately choose not to consider the enormous costs involved as against the perceived security requirements. India's aspiration for this is well documented wherein it has publicly pronounced its goal of 'self sufficiency' soon after political independence and now graduating it to 'self-reliance'. The unfortunate part is that India is still far from nearing that level even after fifty years of this laudable policy. One of the identified ongoing policy drawbacks is its weak linkage with the civilian sector of industry.

The thrust of the new policy initiative therefore is participation of the private sector in defence industry for both research and development as well as production purposes. It has also opened up the defence sector to foreign equity participation up to 26 per cent, with the government recently expressing its willingness to consider even up to 49 per cent on case-to-case basis. Together with this is the initiation of the 'offset policy' for major foreign procurement of defence equipment of Rs.300 crores and above. The big question is: will all these initiatives contribute to the growth of a vibrant defence industry in India?

The immediate effect of these initiatives is that significant numbers of licenses have been applied for and issued to major Indian companies for production of varied components and systems. In fact, according to CII sources alone, as of date, more than 140 companies are involved in about 345 defence items/products. Complete systems/platforms/weapons systems constitute the majority of the licenses issued, which demands higher financial investments and technical capability. This reflects the ambition and confidence of the private sector in their new ventures. On the other hand, there is a flurry of partnership agreements/collaborative ventures by these industrial companies with major global defence industrial giants from the United States, Western Europe and Israel. This is of course not to ignore the existing and ongoing collaborative projects of Defence Public Sector Undertakings (DPSUs) and Ordnance Factories (OFs) with companies from these countries at the governmental level. An analysis would reveal that India's defence industrial scene now is moving on two distinct parallel lines. The first is equipment and technology emanating from Russia and Eastern Europe, which represent approximately 70 per cent of the country's defence industrial set-up. The new addition is Western technology or modified/upgraded technology through private sector companies that are poised to enter India's defence market. The moot question is: Will these different technologies eventually strengthen India's defence industrial base or add further complexities through highly mixed inventories?

In this emerging situation, a few logical things are bound to happen. First, due to the emerging competition from Western technology largely through the private sector, the Russians or other traditional suppliers are likely to at least scale down their often-repeated business behaviour of project delays, delay in supply of spares and parts, and unwillingness to transfer technology. Moreover, the tendency to jack up costs midway while implementing agreements may also get tempered with the arrival of new competitors. However, the fact remains that the domination of Russian origin technologies and their grip on the Indian military establishment will sustain for quite some years to come particularly given that they are largely embedded through the defence public sector undertakings and other government agencies. The major positive impact of the new situation is, however, that the government agencies/DPSUs are likely to wake up from their slumber at least in those areas where they are producing items of common use, which can be easily produced at a competitive level by the private sector. This will be the immediate benefit brought in by the private sector.

While the above may be the likely positive impact, it is unlikely that Western technology will be able to easily challenge the existing market structure through the private sector. This is due to the peculiarity of defence technology and its market structure. First, given that control of technology is the essence of the growth and expansion of MNCs, the global Western defence giants may not easily part with high-end technology, whereas the Indian establishment would be looking for sophisticated weapons and equipment to supplement what has already been acquired from existing sources. The private sector's ability to enter the market will depend on its capability to supply the components, parts and sub-systems of the new equipment in the initial period. Secondly, opportunities for the private sector would largely depend on the government decision to opt for higher and complete major systems of Western origin technologies such as the MMRCA. If such a decision goes in favour of any of the fighter aircraft of western origin, the private sector would definitely have significant scope to capture the market through the offset channel or through normal business dealings. Thirdly, the ability and willingness of Western technology to supplement the defence technology requirements of the armed forces would be the decisive factor. As of now, the armed forces are already in possession of a certain level of defence technology. What they are looking for is conceptually of a higher level, which would be supplementary in nature to bridge perceived security gaps. Will the western powers through their MNCs be willing to part with this level of technology to fill the gap, which, though may be lower than the high-end strategic technology that they possess? If the answer is in the affirmative, the prospects of their capturing the Indian market are very bright. So is also the market potential for the myriad private domestic defence companies in the next five to ten years.

The challenge for Indian industry as a whole would be the will and ability to integrate the two major technology streams in the coming years. This demands the need for dedicated and focused research leading to the capability to integrate existing systems with incoming systems. While the major platforms may continue to be of Russian/Soviet origin, the genius of Indian industry would be tested in its capability to build armaments and other sub-systems and integrating them at higher levels. This is the core challenge and the capability to do it would eventually make the defence industry genuinely vibrant. This will usher in the 'Indian brand of defence technology' even for export purposes free from possible objections on accounts of violations of intellectual property rights. The role of the Government of India as patron and principal customer shall be very crucial for success in achieving the above objective.

INDIAN DEFENSE POLICY IN MAJOR TRANSITION

Recently the US journal Defense News reported that the Indian government is working on a program whereby Israel would replace Russia as India's largest supplier of weapons and defense equipment by 2008.

Since Russia now supplies some 70 percent of India's weapons imports, this report, if true, would mark a major transformation in Indian defense policy. Under the terms of the program, India would identify the products it wants and ask the Israeli government to negotiate with domestic firms on its behalf as Jerusalem does with regard to its own weapons.

Israel is already the second-largest supplier of military systems to India, so this program could effect a major transformation in India's security relationships. The potential repercussions of this project, which would clearly show a serious break with Moscow's arms salesmen, are immense. Given the deep ties between the US and Israeli defense industries, if this program does materialize it will also probably enhance the United States' competitive position in the Indian defense market and result in further substantial increases in the already rising amount of US arms sales and security cooperation with India. Those sales could either be bilateral or brokered through Israel, such as weapons made jointly by Israel and the United States, including missile defense systems that India reportedly is interested in acquiring.

This program would then also strengthen the developing tripartite relationship among Israel, India, and the US in regard to defense sales. We can see this already occurring, because the United States has brushed aside Pakistan's objections to India's receiving the Israeli Phalcon radar, made with US technology and thus subject to US veto on its transfer to a third party.

Realization of the projected Indo-Israeli project would also simultaneously symbolize and express India's rising continental Asian status as a great power with interests and capabilities across the continent, allowing it to break free of its confining chains as merely a major South Asian power if not the regional leader, something that both Indian and foreign observers have labeled as a prerequisite for a full partnership with the United States.

Not only would those trends strengthen Indo-Israeli ties, they would provide fuel to the oft-reported desire on the part of at least some US elites to create a tripartite alliance with India and Israel against terrorism (if not for other, broader objectives that would emerge later). Joint Indo-Israeli defense collaboration on a scale envisaged above would also, or so these advocates hope, tie into the US alliance and Israeli partnership with Turkey, creating a kind of pan-Asian bloc. The new program grows out of India's difficulty in negotiating a US$10 billion multi-year defense acquisition program with Russia. Three areas in particular seem to have caused some anxiety in New Delhi.

In March 2002, The Times of India reported that the Parliamentary Standing Committee had urged the government to avoid overdependence on Russia for armaments and spare parts. The committee reportedly acknowledged Russia's previous contributions and reliability as a provider of defense equipment to India but cautioned that the current dependence on Moscow for almost 80 percent of its arms imports is unhealthy. It also observed that Russia was not providing military hardware on the same beneficial financial terms that it had during the Soviet era. Therefore the committee also urged the Indian government to cease making advance payments for weapons acquisitions from Russia, and that in the future it seek to put more defense contracts up for competitive tender. Russia also has come under criticism because of India's difficulty in obtaining and negotiating speedy delivery of spare parts for these weapons systems. At the same time it became clear that given its worsening relations with Pakistan, India is seeking to diversify its foreign purchases and use foreign partners to develop its own defense industrial capability, eg by conditioning purchases on obtaining offsets from the sellers to develop its own indigenous capability.

The alliance, if it were to materialize, would build on the already greatly improved Indo-Israeli relationship that has led to large-scale military sales from Israel and to India's rapprochement with the United States as well. As the Phalcon deal suggests, it could become possible to envisage tripartite collaboration among these states on missile defense, especially if India's great goal of securing the end to all US sanctions on the transfer of both civil and military technology is realized.

Moreover, the broadening of India's ties and reach in political-military terms through the acquisition of top-quality defense systems would enable it to play the kind of role that analysts in both India and the US postulate as being essential to any serious strategic partnership with the United States. And that role also accords very much with some of the deepest aspirations of India's foreign and defense policy elites, thus highlighting a congruence of visions concerning India's future international position.

In effect India's aspiration to play a major role "from Socotra to Sumatra" would have been both realized and blessed by the United States, as Secretary of State Colin Powell implicitly suggested in 2001. India would then become not just a South or even Central Asian power but a major player in the Persian Gulf, the Middle East, and Southeast Asia.

At the same time, India's search for new vistas in defense acquisition and production relates very much to its rising economic, technological, and military-industrial capabilities as well as to its desire to strengthen existing long-standing partnerships, eg with Russia. For example, beyond the existing $10 billion weapons sales from Russia to India, India is collaborating with Russia on joint production of a fifth-generation fighter that Russia feels vital to its military future. Both are also collaborating on research that is probably tied to missile defense and nuclear systems as well. More broadly, India is the only country with whom Russia is collaborating on joint production of sophisticated and futuristic weapons systems. Likewise India, not China, gets the best weapons currently being produced in Russia, systems that not even Russia's armed forces can obtain. Moscow offers offsets in the form of technology transfer of production skills and know-how to India, one of its largest customers. Although India obviously seeks to diversify its sources of foreign procurement, Russian producers have until now been confident of their ability to obtain the bulk of Indian defense contracts.

Whether or not this confidence is misplaced, time will tell, but diversification and strengthening of India's own capabilities surely would increase India's scientific-technological and manufacturing capabilities for weapons production. This objective also appears to be a major goal of the deals now being made with Russia, Israel, and presumably the United States. We see similar deals with Italian and French firms for joint manufacture of weapons systems.

India's leading defense firm, Hindustan Aeronautics Ltd (HAL), is also pressing an outsourcing program whereby it would help private Indian companies find and choose foreign partners to undertake such high-tech projects as avionics integration, weapons-system integration, and other related efforts to "lay the foundation for a credible domestic aerospace industry base that could meet the majority of India's military aerospace requirements in the next 10 years". And it is no less logical to assume that India would be thrilled to duplicate this particular kind of relationship with Washington, especially as India already has a large space program with military applications and very much wants US conventional-weapons systems and technology transfer.

Indeed, a Pentagon-commissioned study of Indo-American perceptions reported that on the basis of many interviews, a uniform conclusion was reached that "for Indians, technology transfer from the United States is military cooperation's touchstone". Other Indian assessments confirm the great importance that India attaches to transfer of both civil and defense technology as a critical and essential element in any partnership with the US. While India's aspirations in the defense industry are common to other countries that seek the capability for indigenous production of most, if not all of their weapons, it is nevertheless clear that this deal, if it materializes, would utterly transform defense relationships among major players in the defense business: India, the US, Israel, and Russia. The major transformations in Asian security that accelerated after September 11, 2001, have clearly not yet run their course. Nor is it clear when the overall Asian situation will stabilize or when also the rising tide of weapons sales will abate.

But there can be no doubt that major changes are in the offing and that the future holds many more surprises and jolts for all of those who seek to play a key role in the security and defense of Asia.

3

India's Nuclear Weapons Programme

The end of World War II marked a revolution in world affairs - the recasting of nations and relations between nations, and the emergence of a new technology which fundamentally changed the role of warfare. Within the span of two years and two months, from 1945 to 1947, three critical events occurred whose reverberations have brought the threat of nuclear war in South Asia seemingly daily to the front pages of newspapers everywhere. The three events were - in chronological order - the establishment of the United Nations on 26 June 1945; the dramatic demonstration of the destruction of which even crude nuclear weapons are capable in August 1945; and the calamitous partition of British India into the modern states of India and Pakistan at midnight on 14-15 August 1947.

It is clear to everyone that the legacy of partition is a key driving force behind the nuclear standoff that now exists between India and Pakistan. Partition split apart a region that had been united for millenia amid communal massacres on a scale never before seen, leaving in its wake the unresolved issue of contested Kashmir - a Muslim-majority region held by Hindu-majority India. The skirmishing that has continued now for over fifty years, punctuated by outbreaks of full-scale war (in 1947, 1965, and 1971), have given both nations ample motivation to develop potent weapons to gain advantage over — or restore balance with — the other. Another motivation for India's acquisition of nuclear weapons, less often considered in the West, is the potential threat and regional challenge presented by the nuclear-armed state of China, which faces India along much of its northern border. Disputes covering 80,000 square kilometers of this border region exist:

- China currently occupies the Aksai Chin plateau adjacent to Ladakh in Kashmir;
- India occupies the North-East Frontier Agency claimed by China.

These territorial disputes, a legacy of British rule, erupted into the Sino-Indian War on 20 October 1962, when China launched a massive attack on India to which India was powerless to respond. India had relied for years on a warm relationship with the Soviet Union as a counterweight to China, but with the USSR facing down the United States at the same moment in the Cuban Missile Crisis, India was shocked to find the Politburo suddenly switching to support China in an effort to bolster its own position. PM Nehru was forced to appeal to the U.S. for help. U.S. naval air forces arrived off the coast, but before the USAF could deploy to India, China halted its attack on 21 November and partially withdrew. China continues to hold the Aksai Chin region captured in the initial advance. The legacy of this incident was the discovery that the Soviet Union was an unreliable ally, and the deep resolve not to be at a similar disadvantage with respect to China in the future.

Finally, an even less well known factor is a deep-seated drive to achieve international influence commensurate with India's size, and its importance throughout history as one of the world's principle civilizations. At the founding of the United Nations in 1945 the composition of the UN Security Council, the world's most influential and powerful international body, was fixed and has never changed from that time. By an accident of history India was not an independent state at that moment, and its only hope for representation at the conference was the Churchill administration, then in its closing days, which vehemently opposed India's national aspirations. As a result China - with a similar geographic size, population, and state of economic development - was given a seat on Security Council, but India was not. Nuclear weapons did not exist at the time the Security Council composition was debated, but over time the five Council members all acquired nuclear, then thermonuclear, arms. With the signing of the Nuclear Non-Proliferation treaty in 1970, and the replacement on the Council of the non-nuclear Taipei Chinese government with the nuclear armed government in Beijing shortly thereafter, the de facto principle that Security Council permanent members and the "nuclear club" were one and the same was firmly established.

The crucial importance of the desire for recognition of India as a world power in driving forward the nuclear weapons program, even overshadowing considerations of military necessity and deterrence is underscored by remarks by former weapons program leader Raj Ramanna: "There was never a discussion among us over whether we shouldn't make the bomb. How to do it was more important. For us it was a matter of prestige that would justify our ancient past. The question of deterrence came much later. Also, as Indian scientists we were keen to show our Western counterparts, who thought little of us those days, that we too could do it." Thus it should be no surprise that India, now tied for third place among the world's largest economies (with Germany), and soon to become the most populous nation on Earth, has concluded that to be given its due in world affairs, it must become a member of the nuclear club as well.

What is notable however is how the world's largest democracy developed such capabilities. The decisions were made by a handful of people, with virtually no input or oversight by the public or the legislature. India's nuclear weapons program from its outset has answered only to the Prime Minister's office, and only the Prime Minister and a select few of his or her appointees have ever had any say in its development and acquisition.

ORIGIN OF INDIA'S NUCLEAR WEAPON PROGRAM

India's indigenous efforts in nuclear science and technology were established remarkably early. The first step was taken by Dr. Homi Jehangir Bhabha in March 1944 when he submitted a proposal to the Sir Dorab Tata Trust (established in honor of Bhabha's own uncle, Sir Dorab Tata) to found a nuclear research institute, over three years before independence and a year before the first nuclear weapon test. This led to the creation of the Tata Institute of Fundamental Research (TIFR) on 19 December 1945 with Bhabha as its first Director. The new government of India passed the Atomic Energy Act, on 15 April 1948, leading to the establishment of the Indian Atomic Energy Commission (IAEC) not quite one year after independence. At that time Prime Minister Pandit Jawaharlal Nehru declared: We must develop this atomic energy quite apart from war - indeed I think we must develop it for the purpose of using it for peaceful purposes.... Of course, if we are compelled as a nation to use it for other purposes, possibly no pious sentiments of any of us will stop the nation from using it that way."

This note of ambivalence in Nehru's speech foreshadowed his policies on nuclear research for the next decade. Nehru took a prominent role in international politics, founding the Non-Aligned Movement, and advocating nuclear disarmament. However, he refused to foreclose India's nuclear option while other nations maintained nuclear arsenals and supported programs designed to bolster India's weapons potential. In 1954 the Indian nuclear program began to move in a direction that would eventually lead to establishment of nuclear weapons capability. On 3 January 1954 the IAEC decided to set up a new facility - the Atomic Energy Establishment, Trombay (AEET), later to become the "Indian Los Alamos". On 3 August 1954 the Department of Atomic Energy (DAE) was created with Dr. Bhabha as Secretary. This department answered directly to the Prime Minister and has continued to do so down to the present day.

The program grew swiftly. The atomic energy budget increased 12-fold from 1954 to 1956. By 1958 the DAE consumed one third of India's research budget. By 1959 AEET employed over one thousand scientists and engineers. In 1955 construction began on India's first reactor, the 1 MW Apsara research reactor, with British assistance. And in September 1955, after more than a year of negotiation, Canada agreed to supply India with a powerful research reactor - the 40 MW Canada-India Reactor (CIR). Under the Eisenhower Administration's "Atoms for Peace" program the

US agreed to supply 21 tons of heavy water for this reactor in February 1956, and the reactor was dubbed the Canada-India Reactor, U.S. or CIRUS (now commonly written as Cirus).

The acquisition of Cirus was a watershed event in nuclear proliferation. Although the sale was made with the understanding that the reactor would only be used for peaceful purposes (the heavy water contract at least made this explicit), it occurred before any international policies were in place to regulate such technology transfers and no provision for inspections were made. And in fact India was careful to ensure that no effective regulation would accompany the reactor. India refusing to accept fuel from Canada for the reactor and set up a program to manufacture the natural uranium fuel for Cirus indigeneously so as to keep complete control of the plutonium produced there. This program, led by metallurgist Brahm Prakash, succeeded in developing the techniques for producing the precisely manufactured, high purity material demanded by the reactor.

The reactor was a design ideal for producing weapons-grade plutonium, and was also extraordinarily large for research purposes, being capable of manufacturing enough plutonium for one to two bombs a year. The acquisition of Cirus was specifically intended by India to provide herself with a weapons option and this reactor produced the plutonium used in India's first nuclear test in 1974; provided the design prototype for India's more powerful Dhruva plutonium production "research" reactor; and is directly responsible for producing nearly half of the weapons grade plutonium currently believed to be in India's stockpile. The sale further set a precedent for similar technology transfers which greatly assisted Israel in obtaining its own plutonium production reactor from France shortly thereafter. The Atomic Energy Establishment, Trombay was formally inaugurated by PM Nehru on 20 January 1957. It acquired its present name — Bhabha Atomic Research Centre (BARC) — on 12 January 1967 when PM Indira Gandhi renamed it in memory of Dr. Bhabha who died in an airplane crash on 24 January 1966.

Apsara, fueled by enriched uranium from the UK, went critical on 4 August 1957, becoming the first operating reactor in Asia outside of the Soviet Union (though only days ahead of Japan's first reactor). Cirus achieved criticality at BARC on 10 July 1960.

As a nation India has always placed a premium on self-sufficiency. It is, in fact, the most self-sufficient large economy in the world and does not import any nuclear fuel. [The traditionally closed nature of economy though accounts for the import/export based Chinese economy far outstripping its growth from the late seventies to the early nineties.] Due to its vast domestic resources of thorium (a potential fuel for breeder reactors) but limited supplies of uranium, from the start of its nuclear program India has always placed strong emphasis on the development of breeder reactor fuel cycles. Breeder reactors require highly concentrated fissionable material for reactor fuel: either highly enriched uranium or plutonium. This provided a peaceful rationale for developing a plutonium separation capability, but the principal impetus for the India's first fuel reprocessing plant was to obtain a nuclear option.

In July 1958 PM Nehru authorized project Phoenix to build a plant with a capacity of 20 tonnes of fuel a year - sized to match the production capacity of Cirus. The plant was based on the U.S. developed Purex process and an American firm, Vitro International prepared the plans for it. Construction of the plutonium plant began at Trombay on 27 March 1961 and was commissioned in mid-1964.

India's civilian nuclear program was also established during this period. Discussions with American firms to construct India's first nuclear power plants at Tarapur were held in 1960-61. An interesting incident sheds light on Nehru's and Bhabha's thinking at that time. In 1960 Kenneth Nichols, a former U.S. Army engineer who played significant roles in the Manhattan Project, represented Westinghouse in discussions on power plant construction. In a meeting with Nehru and Bhabha, Nichols relates that Nehru turned to Bhabha and asked:

"Can you develop an atomic bomb?" Bhabha assured him that he could and in reply to Nehru's next question about time, he estimated that he would need about a year to do it.... He concluded by saying to Bhabha "Well, don't do it until I tell you to."

DELIVERY SYSTEMS

Agni-I

Thermonuclear warhead (200-300 kt)?, fission/boosted fission warhead (>15 kt)? "Agni" is Hindi for "fire" and is also the name of the Hindu deity of fire. There is some question as to the operational status of the Agni-I. For many years the Agni-I program has been described as a "technology demonstration", which was consistent with the design varaitions that were tried, and the employment of a solid/liquid fuel two stage design that would be undesirable for operational use. However in August 2000 the U.S. defense industry weekly *Defense News* quoted an unnamed senior scientist at DRDO as stating that India had 10 Agni-I missiles in service. He added that the unit cost of the Agni-I is about $5 million.

Agni-I awaiting launch (17 K)

Developed by the Defense Research and Development Laboratory (DRDL) of Hyderabad. The first member of the Agni family was successfully launched on 22 May 1989 from the Chandipur test facility about 250 km southwest of Calcutta at Balasore. The two-stage missile impacted 800 km downrange in the Bay of Bengal. The Agni-I has been tested at a maximum range of 1400 km.

The Agni-I first stage was based on the Indian Satellite Launch Vehicle (SLV-3) used in satellite launches since 1979. The first stage motor was 10 meters long and capable of delivering about 45 tons average thrust with a 50 second burn duration. The second stage was a shortened version of the two chamber liquid fuel motor from the Prithvi. Second stage control was achieved through engine gimballing by its hydraulic actuation system.

Agni-II

The medium range Agni-II system is the first true strategic missile (in the Indian context) deployed by India. The Agni-II is designed to be mobile. It was originally developed in a road-mobile configuration but its deployment is being conducted using a rail-mobile version. The strap-down (limited degree of freedom) inertial guidance system may be replaced in the future with a full inertial system. The RV is reported to have an optical terminal guidance, and speculation has been made about the possible use or future use of a external positioning reference system. The Agni-II is an indigenously developed system, descended from the SLV-3 space launch vehicle via the Agni-I technology demonstrator. A pre-production road mobile Agni-II (Agni-I?) is said to have been made operational during the 1999 Kargil War. The Agni-II costs approximately Rs.400 million per missile and is manufactured by a partnership of the DRDO and Bharat Dynamics Limited (BDL) in Hyderabad. It is expected that BDL will be manufacturing 10-12 missiles every year.

The Agni-II was test fired in April 1999 with a range of 2300 km; on its second test on 17 January 2001 it travelled 2200 km. When the missile system is inducted, India will have the capability to strike at targets at least 2500 km away (up to 3000 km using specific payloads, according to some estimates).

Although the government has on several occasions stated that nuclear weaponization was now complete, the fact remains that the second Agni-II test occurred almost two years after the first and by all accounts more must take place before a true deployable arsenal is available.

In August 2000 Defence Minister George Fernandes stated that the Agni-II had "reached the point of operationalization". A DRDO scientist quoted in *Defense Weekly* reported in August 2000 at that time two pre-production Agni-II missiles were fully operational. He added that the unit cost of the Agni-II about $8 million and that, if required, DRDO's missile research laboratory could produce, in collaboration with Bharat Dynamics Limited, up to 18 Agni-IIs a year. Following the second successful test of Agni-II, on 17 January 2001, Scientific Advisor to the Defence Minister V.K. Aatre said that the Agni-II missile would be inducted into the Indian Air Force by year's end. This test was the first time the Agni-II was test-fired in its final operational configuration.

The Agni-II can be launched in 15 minutes, as opposed to half a day for the Agni-I. It uses far more accurate navigational and guidance systems and is designed to operate on a highly mobile platform which lends flexibility and reduces vulnerability to strikes.

Given its range and India's geopolitical situation, most observers say that the Agni-II was developed as a deterrent against China (it has far more range than is required to cover Pakistan). If that is the case, India has some way to go since with its current range, the Agni-II can at best cover Chinese territory as far as the western cities of Chengdu and Kunming, if based in the central plateau of Bihar. Even if based in Assam, a somewhat improbable scenario, the missile would not be able to reach either Shanghai or Beijing. For this purpose, India is developing the Agni-III, a longer-range missile capable of reaching targets out to 3500 km and beyond. The first test of this vehicle, which will feature entirely new first and second stages, is likely to take place in 2001. Speaking to the Lok Sabha in February 2001 Defence Minister George Fernandes gave the time frame for induction as 2001-2002.

Agni-III

A follow on version to the Agni-II, to be called Agni-III, with a range of 3500 to 5000 km and a 1000 kg payload, is under development. This is expected to be the final variant in the Agni family. According to DRDO sources two approaches are under consideration - an enlarged solid fuel first stage with a 1.8 meter diameter and 36 tonnes of propellant, or an added third stage to the existing Agni-II. The principal objective of the Agni-III would be to develop a missile capable of reaching China's capital of Beijing. The *Deccan Chronicle* reported on 23 September 2000 that Defence Minster George Fernandes had disclosed that the Agni-III had almost completed the development stage and was ready to be test fired soon. *Yahoo India News* reported a senior defence department official as saying India plans to build the third version of the Agni IRBM, but is yet to set a deadline for the project (8 February 2001). "Agni-III will obviously be of a higher range and better capabilities than its predecessor," said the official, who did not want to be identified. "But we have not set a date to test it," the official said on the sidelines of an aerospace conference in Bangalore.

Suriya

A higher performance missile in the ICBM class (the Suriya or Surya) with a range of over 6000 km has been discussed. It would be an entirely new development effort. Dr. APJ Abdul Kalam, Principal Scientific Adviser to the Prime Minister, was quoted in the *Hindustan Times* on 18 September 2000 as saying that "All technologies and industrial complexes are available for an ICBM. It'll not take much time, should India decide on it." He discounted speculation that the ICBM will be the derivative of the GSLV, India's latest space launch vehicle. "Cryogenic engines (used for the GSLV) are good for satellite launch vehicles, not missiles. They require huge fuelling facilities, which can be detected by satellite."

Prithvi

Prithvi (Hindi for "Earth") is a single stage, road-mobile, short-range ballistic missile (SRBM). The missile's corrosive liquid fuel must be loaded immediately prior to launch, which is a serious disadvantage in the field. On the other hand the ability to control the liquid fuel motor, including throttling it or shutting it down (difficult or impossible with solid fuel) gives it great flexibility in range and trajectory, including in-flight maneuvering. The liquid propellant also has higher performance than solid propellants, giving the Prithvi an unusually high payload for its size and range. The inertial navigation system has been reported to have a CEP (Circular Error Probability) equal to.01% of its range, or 15 m for the Army version and 25 m for the Air Force version at maximum range (this is roughly comparable to an ICBM having a 1.5 km accuracy). The missile uses its maneuvering capability to follow up to six different trajectories so as to avoid ABM interception, and confuse launch system counter targeting. Another defense measure the Prithvi has is the use of radar absorbing paint to reduce its radar signature.

The fact that both the Indian Army and the IAF operate versions of the Prithvi is the result of a turf war over control of ballistic missile systems, a scenario that has played out in many other nations. The outcome of this struggle was that the Army controls land based missiles with a range of 150 km or less (a limit that was set by the initial range of the Prithvi) while longer range missiles belong to the Air Force. The DRDO is attempting to increase the payload of the IAF version to 1000 kg, by using higher performance liquid propellants to generate more thrust-to-weight ratio. The missile carries both nuclear warheads and a variety of conventional payloads. A family of warheads have been developed, including high-explosive (HE), pre-fragmented unitary HE, incendiary, cluster munitions (bomblets), sub-munitions, and fuel-air explosives (FAE).

For field operations, Prithvi is transported on an all-terrain, eight wheel Kolos Tatra 4x4 truck. The missile is deployed off this vehicle and fired from a simple launcher. Each battery of four Prithvi carrier vehicles is accompanied by a missile re-supply and loading vehicle, a propellant tanker and a command post vehicle to provide target data to the missile's guidance system before launch. In addition, a variety of other support support vehicles and equipment are used to support the batteries in the field.

Prithvi SS-150 which has been in serial production by Bharat Dynamics Limited in Hyderabad since 1997, following a development program that included 12 test flights.

Due to the limited strategic space of Pakistan (the Indus river valley where most major Pakistani cities are located runs close to the Indian frontier) the Prithvi has significant strategic value despite its short range. If it is deployed in states like Kashmir, Punjab and Gujrat which border Pakistan, it would place the capital of Islamabad, as well as the principal cities of Lahore and Karachi in range, as wells as many of Pakistan's strategic military installations.

In September 2000 *Defense News* reported that India would go ahead with full production of about 300 Prithvis for all three branches of the Indian defense forces. The decision, taken by Defence Minister George Fernandes on 25 August, was prompted by Pakistan's test-firing of its Ghauri-III IRBM 10 days earlier, on Independence Day, a senior Indian ministry official, who was not named, was quoted as saying. The production of 300 Prithvis was estimated to cost $200 million. The state-owned Bharat Dynamics in Hyderabad would invest $100 million to ready itself for production. According to company sources, the Army required 150 Prithvis with a range of 150 km while the Navy needed 100 missiles of equal range. 50 Prithvi missiles with a longer range of 250 km, known as Prithvi-II, have to be produced to meet the requirement of the Air Force, the company said.

The Prithvi is a descendant of an earlier program called "Project Devil", an attempt to reverse engineer the Soviet SA-2 liquid fuel surface-to-air missile by the Defense Research and Development Laboratory (DRDL) at Hyderabad. This latter project, initiated under the leadership of Dr. Basanti Dulal Nag Chaudhuri, was a failure and was cancelled in 1978; nonetheless valuable experience and technical skill was obtained which provided the basis for Prithvi. Development was initiated in 1983 as part of the Integrated Guided Missile Development Programme (IGMDP) under the leadership of Dr. Avil Pakir Jainulabdeen Abdul Kalam, the project manager for the successful SLV-3 program. The Prithvi was intended to be a 150 km tactical missile and was first tested at Sriharikota on 22 February 1988..

In October 1995, 20 pre-production models of the initial Prithvi SS-150 (with a 150 km range) were secretly delivered to the Army to form the 333rd Missile Regiment based in Secunderabad. At this time the Prithvi was not yet equipped with a nuclear warhead. The first deployment of Prithvi missiles (numbering less than a dozen) was at Jalandhar, about 200 km from the Pakistani border in May 1997 prior to its formal operational adoption. Integration and testing of a nuclear warhead was completed in 1997 on the Prithvi SS-150 before these were formally deployed in September 1997. Significantly in December 1998, the Army deployed the Prithvi in a major military exercise code named Shiv-Shakti for the first time since its induction. According to Dr. Sanjay Badri-Maharaj during the 1999 Kargil War four nuclear armed Prithvis were actually deployed for retaliatory strikes. Some units are reported to have been moved to at least two northern locations close to the Pakistani border.

The fourth test flight of the extended range SS-250 was launched on 16 June 2000 at the Interim Test Range (ITR) at Chandipur-on-

Sea on the east coast of India. The liquid-propellant weapon carried multiple warheads over a range of 250 km. At this point the SS-250 had not yet been inducted into service.

There is some question whether the Dhanush is really a Prithvi variant, or simply a new missile design in the same size class.

Jane's Missiles and Rockets reported on 9 August 2000 that John Pike of the Federation of American Scientists (FAS) has detected what it believes is the storage site for Indian's Prithvi missiles. An image of the Research Centre Imarat complex taken earlier this year by the Ikonos imaging satellite revealed an installation which Pike says "is probably the primary Prithvi garrison". The Imarat centre is associated with research and development of technologies for missiles and other advanced weapons. "Although it is reported that the 333rd Missile Group is headquartered in Secunderabad, it is evident that the military cantonment would be an inappropriate location for the actual missiles, given the urban congestion of the area," said Pike. The facility at the Imarat centre consists of three pairs of garages, each of which the FAS estimates to be large enough to house four vehicles, which suggests that each pair is used to house a battery of four launchers plus four support vehicles. The facility is surrounded by a security perimeter which incorporates a series of objects which may be guard houses. A nearby complex of buildings could be an administrative support facility for the Prithvi missiles, but "this complex is devoid of functional signatures that would support this interpretation, and is enclosed within a separate security perimeter that is suggestive of institutional associations unrelated to the Prithvi complex."

Dhanush

The Dhanush (Bow, as in "bow and arrow") is a derivative of the Prithvi program, adapted to naval use and given extended range. The first test firing was conducted on 10 April 2000 from the modified Sukanya class off-shore patrol vessel (OPV), INS *Subhadra* in the Bay of Bengal 20 km off Orissa state. It was a only partially successful with, the missile splashing down 25-30 km from its launch point. The launch platform used was a hydraulically-stabilized, rail-mounted platform built on the helicopter deck of the *Subhadra*. Dhanush is probably intended for deployment on a specialized ballistic missile submarine, either conventionally powered or the nuclear powered Advanced Technology Vessel (ATV). Neither is likely in the near future due to technical and financial constraints.

Sagarika

There have been conflicting reports about this program since Clinton administration officials in the United States reported on 27 April 1998 that India was developing a sea-launched ballistic missile with a 200 mile range intended for submarine deployment. More recent reports describe Sagarika as submarine-launched cruise missile (SLCM) intended for the nuclear-powered submarine known as the Advanced Technology Vessel (ATV). The initial description of Sagarika as a ballistic missile may have been due to confusion with the Dhanush. Sagarika had been expected to enter service by 2002, but the program has been troubled as has the ATV submarine itself. Work on an Indian nuclear powered submarine has proceeded fitfully and unsuccessfully for nearly 25 years.

Nuclear Facilities

The centre piece of India's nuclear weapons program is the Bhabha Atomic Research Centre (BARC) in Trombay near Mumbai (Bombay) which is the centre for nuclear weapons associated work. BARC was founded as the Atomic Energy Establishment, Trombay (AEET) on 3 January 1954 by Dr. Homi Jehangir Bhabha. Bhabha was the also the founder India's entire nuclear industry and infrastructure, and India's first Secretary of the Department of Atomic Energy (DAE) when it was created on 3 August 1954. In its early years BARC was already a very large, but primarily civilian-oriented nuclear research laboratory. When India's first nuclear device was designed and fabricated at there, the work was conducted surreptitiously (often at night) to hide it from the rest of the laboratory. But in May 2000 a watershed was reached in this tension between civilian and military work when the civilian Atomic Energy Regulatory Board (AERB) which had been exercising regulatory oversight was split off from BARC. As S.

Rajagopal oberved, an expert on nuclear affairs and a professor of the Bangalore-based National Institute of Advanced Studies, this decision effectively reclassified BARC as a nuclear weapons laboratory - a laboratory with a primarily military function though also conducting civilian oriented work in a model similar to the U.S. weapons labs. But without much of the civilian oversight and management that the U.S. labs have.

BARC is the site of the two reactors used for weapons-grade plutonium production: the 40 MW CIRUS (Canadian-Indian-U.S.) reactor, and the 100 MW reactor named R-5, but usually called "Dhruva". Both of these are heavy water moderated and cooled natural uranium reactors.

CIRUS was supplied by Canada in 1954, but uses heavy water supplied by the U.S. (hence its name). The reactor is not under IAEA safeguards (which did not exist when the reactor was sold), although Canada stipulated, and the U.S. supply contract for the heavy water explicitly specified, that it only be used for peaceful purposes. Nonetheless CIRUS has produced much of India's weapon plutonium stockpile, as well as the plutonium for India's 1974 Pokhran-I nuclear test. India argued in 1974 that the contract allows its use in producing peaceful nuclear explosives, which is how it characterized this explosion, though in recent years the project director Raja Ramanna has conceded that this was a sham. CIRUS reactor achieved criticality on 10 July 1960. It can produce 6.6-10.5 kg of plutonium a year (at a capacity factor of 50-80%).

In 1977 work began on the larger Dhruva plutonium production reactor, which was developed indigenous but based on the Canadian supplied technology. It was commissioned on 8 August 1985 but startup problems caused by resonance vibrations from the cooling system damaged fuel assemblies soon required shutdown. After modifications were made (spring clips to damp fuel rod vibration) it began operating at one-quarter power in December 1986 and reached full operation in mid-January 1988. It operates at 100 MW and is capable of producing 16-26 kg of plutonium annually (at a capacity factor of 50-80%).

An additional possible source of plutonium are a number of unsafeguarded CANDU power reactors, including Madras Atomic

Power Stations (MAPS, known as Madras I and II, or MAPS-I and MAPS-II); the Narora Atomic Power Stations (NAPS, known as NAPS-I and NAPS-II), and the Kakrapar Atomic Power Station (KAPS). Like CIRUS and Dhruva, the CANDU reactors are heavy-water moderated natural uranium reactors that can be used effectively for weapon-grade plutonium production.

The possible production by MAPS is much larger than CIR and Dhruva combined, although the fuel burnup in power reactors of this type normally produces lower grade plutonium that is less desirable for weapons. Each power station reactor could produce up to 160 kg/yr (at a 60% capacity factor). It is uncertain how practical it is to operate MAPS for weapons grade plutonium production, although even the reactor-grade output has weapons potential. If supergrade plutonium were produced at BARC by short irradiation periods, it could be mixed with MAPS plutonium to extend the plutonium supply. As of November 1998 India had a total of 10 small power reactors operating, with 4 under construction and due to begin operation in 1999, but with 12 more planned or under construction that would boost electrical output by another 5100 MW. Nuclear power supplied 2.65 percent of India's electricity in 1999 and this is expected to reach 10 per cent by 2005. Expectations for nuclear power growth have consistently fallen far short of goals for over 30 years, so this percentage is likely to continue to grow slowly. India's nuclear power program proceeds almost entirely without fuel or technological assistance from other countries.

Partly as a result its power reactors have been among the worst-performing in the world (with regard to capacity factors), reflecting the technical difficulties of the country's isolation, but are apparently now improving significantly. Its industry is largely without IAEA safeguards, though a few plants are under facility-specific safeguards.

In February 2001 India had 14 small nuclear power reactors in commercial operation, two larger ones under construction and ten more planned. The 14 operating ones comprise:

- two 150 MWe BWRs from USA, started up in 1969, now using locally-enriched uranium and are under safeguards,

- two small Canadian PHWRs (1972 & 1980), also under safeguards; and
- ten local PHWRs based on Canadian designs, two of 150 and eight 200 MWe.

The separated plutonium for the 1974 test was produced at the separation plant in Trombay, near to Bombay, capable of processing 50 tonnes of heavy metal fuel/yr. Construction on the first facility there began in the 1950s, and began operating in 1964. In 1974 it was shut down for repair and expansion and reopened in 1983 or 1984. Trombay handles the fuel from both the Cirus and Dhruva reactors. India also can separate plutonium in the Power Reactor Fuel Reprocessing (PREFRE) facility. This plutonium separation plant was built at Tarapur, north of Bombay, and began operating in 1979. The plant has encountered operating problems, but India reports having overcome these by 1990. The nominal annual capacity is given as 100-150 tonnes of CANDU fuel. A much larger plant is now under construction at Kalpakkam sufficient to handle all existing reactors.

Given its immense thorium resources, India is actively interested in developing the thorium/U-233 fuel cycle. India is known to have produced kilogram quantities of U-233 by irradiating thorium in CIR, Dhruva, and MAPS reactors. Substantial production of U-233 is not practical though with natural uranium fueled reactors. The thorium cycle requires more highly enriched fuel to have an acceptable breeding ratio with the non-fissile thorium blanket. Reactor-grade plutonium from MAPS could serve as start-up fuel for U-233 plants in the future. If available U-233 is as effective a weapon material as plutonium.

India has been developing the capability to produce heavy water domestically to provide the moderator load for future reactors. The heavy water for almost all existing reactors was imported however. The 110 tonnes of unsafeguarded moderator for Dhruva and Madras I and II were ironically provided by China.

India has acquired and developed centrifuge technology and built centrifuge enrichment plants in Trombay and Mysore in the 1980s. The larger Rare Metals Plant (RMP), as it is called, at

Mysore has a cascade capable of producing 30% enriched uranium in kilogram quantities, beginning in 1992-93, although reliability has been a problem. These enrichment plants appear to have no role in India's power reactor development plans, so they may be intended to offset the prestige of Pakistan's enrichment capability, or to provide additional standby weapons production capability. India has reported that it plans to build an enriched uranium reactor, and a domestically fueled nuclear submarine.

India's interest in light weight weapon design can be surmised from BARC's acquisition in the 1980s of a vacuum hot pressing machine, suitable for forming large high-quality beryllium forgings, as well as large amounts of high purity beryllium metal. India is known to manufacture tritium, and may have developed designs for fusion-boosted weapons.

India is not a signatory to NPT and has opposed the treaty as discriminatory to non-weapons states. India has previously taken the position that a worldwide ban on nuclear testing, and the production of fissionable material for weapons is called for. Except for China, which continues testing, there is now a de facto halt to testing worldwide, as well as the production of weapons grade plutonium and uranium by the US and Russia. India has shown no interest so far in restricting its own activities despite these changes in the world situation. India has also rejected offers at bilateral negotiation with Pakistan, but in December 1988 the two nations signed an agreement prohibiting attacks on each other's nuclear installations and informing each other of their locations (though not their purposes).

NUCLEAR WEAPONS AND NON-PROLIFERATION TREATY

The Treaty on the Non-Proliferation of Nuclear Weapons, commonly known as the Non-Proliferation Treaty or NPT, is a landmark international treaty whose objective is to prevent the spread of nuclear weapons and weapons technology, to promote cooperation in the peaceful uses of nuclear energy and to further the goal of achieving nuclear disarmament and general and complete disarmament. Opened for signature in 1968, the Treaty entered into force in 1970. On 11 May 1995, the Treaty was extended indefinitely. A total of 190 parties have joined the Treaty, including the five nuclear-weapon States: the United States, Russia, the United Kingdom, France, and China (also the five permanent members of the United Nations Security Council). More countries have ratified the NPT than any other arms limitation and disarmament agreement, a testament to the Treaty's significance. Four non-parties to the treaty are known or believed to possess nuclear weapons: India, Pakistan and North Korea have openly tested and declared that they possess nuclear weapons, while Israel has had a policy of opacity regarding its own nuclear weapons program. North Korea acceded to the treaty in 1985, but never came into compliance, and announced its withdrawal in 2003.

The NPT consists of a preamble and eleven articles. Although the concept of "pillars" is not expressed anywhere in the NPT, the treaty is nevertheless sometimes interpreted as a *three-pillar* system, with an implicit balance among them:

1. *non-proliferation,*
2. *disarmament*, and
3. *the right to peacefully use nuclear technology.*

The NPT is often seen to be based on a central bargain: "the NPT non-nuclear-weapon states agree never to acquire nuclear weapons and the NPT nuclear-weapon states in exchange agree to share the benefits of peaceful nuclear technology and to pursue nuclear disarmament aimed at the ultimate elimination of their nuclear arsenals". The treaty is reviewed every five years in meetings called Review Conferences of the Parties to the Treaty of Non-Proliferation of Nuclear Weapons. Even though the treaty was originally conceived with a limited duration of 25 years, the signing parties decided, by consensus, to extend the treaty indefinitely and without conditions during the Review Conference in New York City on May 11, 1995.

At the time the NPT was proposed, there were predictions of 25-30 nuclear weapon states within 20 years. Instead, over forty years later, only four states are not parties to the NPT, and they are the only additional states believed to possess nuclear weapons. Several additional measures have been adopted to strengthen the

NPT and the broader nuclear nonproliferation regime and make it difficult for states to acquire the capability to produce nuclear weapons, including the export controls of the Nuclear Suppliers Group and the enhanced verification measures of the IAEA Additional Protocol. However, critics argue that the NPT cannot stop the proliferation of nuclear weapons or the motivation to acquire them. They express disappointment with the limited progress on nuclear disarmament, where the five authorized nuclear weapons states still have 22,000 warheads in their combined stockpile and have shown a reluctance to disarm further. Several high-ranking officials within the United Nations have said that they can do little to stop states using nuclear reactors to produce nuclear weapons.

Treaty "pillars"

The NPT is commonly described as having three main "pillars": non-proliferation, disarmament, and peaceful use. This "pillars" concept has been questioned by some who believe that the NPT is, as its name suggests, principally about nonproliferation, and who worry that "three pillars" language misleadingly implies that the three elements have equivalent importance.

First Pillar: Non-proliferation

Five states are recognized by the Non-Proliferation Treaty as nuclear weapon states (NWS): China (signed 1992), France (1992), the Soviet Union (1968; obligations and rights now assumed by the Russian Federation), the United Kingdom (1968), and the United States (1968) (The United States, UK, and the Soviet Union were the only states openly possessing such weapons among the original ratifiers of the treaty, which entered into force in 1970). These five nations are also the five permanent members of the United Nations Security Council. These five NWS agree not to transfer "nuclear weapons or other nuclear explosive devices" and "not in any way to assist, encourage, or induce" a non-nuclear weapon state (NNWS) to acquire nuclear weapons (Article I). NNWS parties to the NPT agree not to "receive," "manufacture" or "acquire" nuclear weapons or to "seek or receive any assistance in the manufacture of nuclear weapons" (Article II). NNWS parties also agree to accept safeguards by the International Atomic Energy Agency (IAEA) to verify that they are not diverting nuclear energy from peaceful uses to nuclear weapons or other nuclear explosive devices (Article III).

The five NWS parties have made undertakings not to use their nuclear weapons against a non-NWS party except in response to a nuclear attack, or a conventional attack in alliance with a Nuclear Weapons State. However, these undertakings have not been incorporated formally into the treaty, and the exact details have varied over time. The U.S. also had nuclear warheads targeted at North Korea, a non-NWS, from 1959 until 1991. The previous United Kingdom Secretary of State for Defence, Geoff Hoon, has also explicitly invoked the possibility of the use of the country's nuclear weapons in response to a non-conventional attack by "rogue states". In January 2006, President Jacques Chirac of France indicated that an incident of state-sponsored terrorism on France could trigger a small-scale nuclear retaliation aimed at destroying the "rogue state's" power centers.

Second Pillar: Disarmament

Article VI of the NPT represents the only binding commitment in a multilateral treaty to the goal of disarmament by the nuclear-weapon States. The NPT's preamble contains language affirming the desire of treaty signatories to ease international tension and strengthen international trust so as to create someday the conditions for a halt to the production of nuclear weapons, and treaty on general and complete disarmament that liquidates, in particular, nuclear weapons and their delivery vehicles from national arsenals.

The wording of the NPT's Article VI arguably imposes only a vague obligation on all NPT signatories to move in the general direction of nuclear and total disarmament, saying, "Each of the Parties to the Treaty undertakes to pursue negotiations in good faith on effective measures relating to cessation of the nuclear arms race at an early date and to nuclear disarmament, and on a treaty on general and complete disarmament." Under this interpretation, Article VI does not strictly require all signatories to actually conclude a disarmament treaty. Rather, it only requires them "to negotiate in good faith." On the other hand, some governments, especially non-nuclear-weapon states belonging to the Non-Aligned Movement, have interpreted Article VI's language as being anything but vague. In their view, Article VI constitutes a formal and specific obligation on the NPT-recognized nuclear-weapon states to disarm themselves of nuclear weapons, and argue that these states have failed to meet their obligation. The International Court of Justice (ICJ), in its advisory opinion on the Legality of the Threat or Use of Nuclear Weapons, issued 8 July 1996, unanimously interprets the text of Article VI as implying that, "There exists an obligation to pursue in good faith and bring to a conclusion negotiations leading to nuclear disarmament in all its aspects under strict and effective international control." The ICJ opinion notes that this obligation involves all NPT parties (not just the nuclear weapon states) and does not suggest a specific time frame for nuclear disarmament.

Critics of the NPT-recognized nuclear-weapon states sometimes argue that what they view as the failure of the NPT-recognized nuclear weapon states to disarm themselves of nuclear weapons, especially in the post–Cold War era, has angered some non-nuclear-weapon NPT signatories of the NPT. Such failure, these critics add, provides justification for the non-nuclear-weapon signatories to quit the NPT and develop their own nuclear arsenals.

Other observers have suggested that the linkage between proliferation and disarmament may also work the other way, i.e., that the failure to resolve proliferation threats in Iran and North Korea, for instance, will cripple the prospects for disarmament. No current nuclear weapons state, the argument goes, would seriously consider eliminating its last nuclear weapons without high confidence that other countries would not acquire them. Some observers have even suggested that the very progress of disarmament by the superpowers—which has led to the elimination of thousands of weapons and delivery systems —could eventually make the possession of nuclear weapons more attractive by increasing the perceived strategic value of a small arsenal. As one U.S. official and NPT expert warned in 2007, "logic suggests that as the number of nuclear weapons decreases, the 'marginal utility' of a nuclear weapon as an instrument of military power increases. At the extreme, which it is precisely disarmament's hope to create, the strategic utility of even one or two nuclear weapons would be huge."

Third Pillar: Peaceful use of Nuclear Energy

The third pillar allows for and agrees upon the transfer of nuclear technology and materials to NPT signatory countries for the development of civilian nuclear energy programs in those countries, as long as they can demonstrate that their nuclear programs are not being used for the development of nuclear weapons.

Since very few of the states with nuclear energy programs are willing to abandon the use of nuclear energy, the third pillar of the NPT under Article IV provides other states with the possibility to do the same, but under conditions intended to make it difficult to develop nuclear weapons.

The treaty recognizes the inalienable right of sovereign states to use nuclear energy for peaceful purposes, but restricts this right for NPT parties to be exercised "in conformity with Articles I and II" (the basic nonproliferation obligations that constitute the "first pillar" of the Treaty). As the commercially popular light water reactor nuclear power station uses enriched uranium fuel, it follows that states must be able either to enrich uranium or purchase it on an international market.

Mohamed ElBaradei, then Director General of the International Atomic Energy Agency, has called the spread of enrichment and reprocessing capabilities the "Achilles' heel" of the nuclear nonproliferation regime. As of 2007 13 states have an enrichment capability.

Because the availability of fissile material has long been considered the principal obstacle to, and "pacing element" for, a country's nuclear weapons development effort, it was declared a major emphasis of U.S. policy in 2004 to prevent the further spread of uranium enrichment and plutonium reprocessing (a.k.a. "ENR") technology. Countries possessing ENR capabilities, it is feared, have what is in effect the option of using this capability to produce fissile material for weapons use on demand, thus giving them what has been termed a "virtual" nuclear weapons program.

Countries that have signed the treaty as Non-Nuclear Weapons States and maintained that status have an unbroken record of not building nuclear weapons.

However, Iraq was cited by the IAEA with punitive sanctions enacted against it by the UN Security Council for violating its NPT safeguards obligations; North Korea never came into compliance with its NPT safeguards agreement and was cited repeatedly for these violations, and later withdrew from the NPT and tested multiple nuclear devices; Iran was found in non-compliance with its NPT safeguards obligations in an unusual non-consensus decision because it "failed in a number of instances over an extended period of time" to report aspects of its enrichment program; and Libya pursued a clandestine nuclear weapons program before abandoning it in December 2003. In 1991 Romania reported previously undeclared nuclear activities by the former regime and the IAEA reported this non-compliance to the Security Council for information only. In some regions, the fact that all neighbors are verifiably free of nuclear weapons reduces any pressure individual states might feel to build those weapons themselves, even if neighbors are known to have peaceful nuclear energy programs that might otherwise be suspicious. In this, the treaty works as designed.

INDIA'S THREE STAGE NUCLEAR POWER PROGRAMME

India's three stage nuclear power programme was formulated by Dr. Homi Bhabha in the 1950s to secure the country's long term energy independence, through the use of uranium and thorium reserves found in the monazite sands of coastal regions of South India. The ultimate focus of the programme is on enabling the thorium reserves of India to be utilized in meeting the country's energy requirements. Thorium is particularly attractive for India, as it has only around 1-2% of the global uranium reserves, but one of the largest shares of global thorium reserves at about 30% of the total world thorium reserves.

Since the inception of the programme in the 1950s, India has built up its capacity in the area of nuclear research to the extent that it is now generally considered as the leader of thorium based research in the world. The country published about twice the number of papers on thorium as its nearest competitors, during each of the years from 2002 to 2006. The Indian nuclear establishment estimates that the country could produce 500 GWe for at least four centuries using just the country's economically extractable thorium reserves.

As of 2012, the first stage consisting of the PHWRs is near completion of its planned goals, the second stage consisting of fast breeder reactors is poised to go into operation within one year, and the third stage consisting of AHWRs (one among several technology options) is slated to begin construction so that its commissioning can be done by 2020. The recent Indo-US Nuclear Deal and the NSG waiver, which ended more than three decades of international isolation of the Indian civil nuclear programme, have created many hitherto unexplored alternatives for the success of the three stage nuclear power programme.

Origin and rationale

Dr. Homi Bhabha conceived of the three-stage nuclear programme as a way to develop nuclear energy by working around India's limited uranium resources. Thorium itself is not a fissile material, and thus cannot undergo fission to produce energy. Instead, it must first be converted into the fissile isotope uranium-233 by transmutation in a reactor fueled by other fissile materials. The first two stages, natural uranium-fueled heavy water reactors and plutonium-fueled fast breeder reactors, are intended to generate sufficient fissile material from India's limited uranium resources, so that all its vast thorium reserves can be fully utilised in the third stage of thermal breeder reactors.

Bhabha summarized the rationale for the three stage approach as follows:

"The total reserves of thorium in India amount to over 500,000 tons in the readily extractable form, while the known reserves of uranium are less than a tenth of this. The aim of long range atomic power programme in India must therefore be to base the nuclear power generation as soon as possible on thorium rather than uranium... The first generation of atomic power stations based on natural uranium can only be used to start off an atomic power programme... The plutonium produced by the first generation power stations can be used in a second generation of power stations designed to produce electric power and convert thorium into U-233, or depleted uranium into more plutonium with breeding gain... The second generation of power stations may be regarded as an intermediate step for the breeder power stations of the third generation all of which would produce more U-233 than they burn in the course of producing power."

In November 1954, Bhabha presented the three stage plan for national development, at the conference on "Development of Atomic Energy for Peaceful Purposes" which was also attended by India's first Prime Minister Jawaharlal Nehru. Four years later in 1958, the Indian government formally adopted the three stage plan. Indian energy resource base was estimated to be capable of yielding a total electric power output. Indian government recognized that thorium was a source that could provide power to the Indian people for the long term.

Energy Resource Type	*Amount (tonnes)*	*Power Potential (TWe-year)*
Coal	54 billion	11
Hydrocarbons	12 billion	6
Uranium (in PHWR)	61,000	0.3 - 0.42
Uranium (in FBR)	61,000	16 - 54
Thorium	~300,000	155 – 168 or 358
		Fuel reserves and research capability

According to a report issued by the IAEA, India has limited uranium reserves, consisting of approximately 54,636 tonnes of "reasonably assured resources", 25,245 tonnes of "estimated additional resources", 15,488 tonnes of "undiscovered conventional resources, and 17,000 tonnes of "speculative resources". According to NPCIL, these reserves are only sufficient to generate about 10 GWe for about 40 years. In July 2011, it was reported that a four year long mining survey done at Tumalapalli mine in Kadapa district near Hyderabad had yielded confirmed reserve figure of 49,000 tonnes with a potential that it could rise to 150,000 tonnes. This was a rise from an earlier estimate of 15,000 tonnes for that area. Thorium reserves

India has only around 1-2% of the global uranium reserves, but one of the largest shares of global thorium reserves at 12-33%, according to IAEA and US Geological Survey. Several brief third party news reports quote Indian share of global thorium reserves as being at 25% or 30%. Several in-depth independent studies put Indian thorium reserves at 30% of the total world thorium reserves.

As per official estimates shared in the country's Parliament in August 2011, the country can obtain 846,477 tonnes of thorium from 963,000 tonnes of ThO2, which in turn can be obtained from 10.7 million tones of monazite occurring in beaches and river sands in association with other heavy metals. Indian monazite contains about 9-10% ThO2. The 846,477 tonne figure compares with the earlier estimates for India, made by IAEA and US Geological Survey of 319,000 tonnes and 290,000 to 650,000 tonnes respectively. The 800,000 tonne figure is given by other sources as well.

It was further clarified in the country's Parliament on 21st March 2012 that, "Out of nearly 100 deposits of the heavy minerals, at present only 17 deposits containing about ~4 million tonnes of monazite have been identified as exploitable. Mineable reserves are ~70% of identified exploitable resources. Therefore, about 225,000 tonnes of thorium metal is available for nuclear power programme."

Research capability

India is generally considered as the leader of thorium based research in the world. It is also, by far the most committed nation as far as the use of thorium fuel is concerned, and no other country has done as much neutron physics work on thorium. The country published about twice the number of papers on thorium as its nearest competitors, during each of the years from 2002 to 2006. Bhabha Atomic Research Centre (BARC) had the highest number of publications in the thorium area, across all research institutions in the world during the period 1982-2004. During this same period, India ranks an overall second behind the United States in the research output on Thorium. Analysis shows that majority of the authors involved in thorium research publications appear to be from India. According to Siegfried Hecker, a former director (1986-1997) of the Los Alamos National Laboratory in the U.S., "India has the most technically ambitious and innovative nuclear energy program in the world. The extent and functionality of its nuclear experimental facilities are matched only by those in Russia and are far ahead of what is left in the US."

Stage I - pressurised heavy water reactor

In the first stage of the programme, natural uranium fuelled pressurised heavy water reactors (PHWR) produce electricity while generating plutonium-239 as by-product. PHWRs was a natural choice for implementing the first stage because it had the most efficient reactor design in terms of uranium utilization, and the existing Indian infrastructure in the 1960s allowed for quick adoption of the PHWR technology. India correctly calculated that it would be easier to create heavy water production facilities (required for PHWRs) than uranium enrichment facilities (required for LWRs). Natural uranium contains only 0.7% of the fissile isotope uranium-235. Most of the remaining 99.3% is uranium-238 which is not fissile but can be converted in a reactor to the fissile isotope plutonium-239. Heavy water (deuterium oxide, D_2O) is used as moderator and coolant.

Indian uranium reserves are capable of generating a total power capacity of 420 GWe-years, but in order to ensure that existing plants get a lifetime supply of uranium, it becomes necessary to limit the number of PHWRs fueled exclusively by indigenous uranium reserves. US analysts calculate this limit as being slightly over 13 GW in capacity. Several other sources estimate that the known reserves of natural uranium in the country permit only about 10 GW of capacity to be built through indigenously fueled PHWRs. The three stage programme explicitly incorporates this limit as the upper cut off of the first stage, beyond which PHWRs are not planned to be built.

Almost the entire existing base of Indian nuclear power (4780 MW) is composed of first stage PHWRs, with the exception of the two Boiling Water Reactor (BWR) units at Tarapur. The installed capacity of Kaiga station is now 880 MW, making it the third largest after Tarapur (1400 MW) and Rawatbhata (1180 MW). The remaining three power stations at Kakrapar, Kalpakkam and Narora all have 2 units of 220 MW, thus contributing 440 MW each to the grid. The 2 units of 700 MWe each (PHWRs) that are under construction at both Kakrapar and Rawatbhata, and the one planned for Banswara would also come under the first stage of the programme, totalling a further addition of 4200 MW. These additions will bring the total power capacity from the first stage PHWRs to near the total planned capacity of 10 GW called for by the three stage power programme.

Capital costs of PHWRs is in the range of Rs. 6 to 7 crore per MW, coupled with a designed plant life of 40 years. Time required for construction has improved over time and is now at about 5 years. Tariffs of the operating plants are in the range of Rs. 1.75 to 2.80 per unit, depending on the life of the reactor. In the year 2007-08 the average tariff was Rs.2.28. The tariffs of new plants to be set up, both indigenous and imported, are expected to be about Rs. 2.50 in the year 2015 (at 2007 prices).

Stage II - fast breeder reactor

In the second stage, Fast breeder reactors (FBRs) would use a mixed oxide (MOX) fuel made from plutonium-239, recovered by reprocessing spent fuel from the first stage, and natural uranium. In FBRs, plutonium-239 undergoes fission to produce energy, while the uranium-238 present in the mixed oxide fuel transmutes to additional plutonium-239. Thus, the Stage II FBRs are designed to "breed" more fuel than they consume. Once the inventory of plutonium-239 is built up thorium can be introduced as a blanket material in the reactor and transmuted to uranium-233 for use in the third stage.

The surplus plutonium bred in each fast reactor can be used to set up more such reactors, and thus grow the Indian civil nuclear power capacity till the point where the third stage reactors using thorium as fuel can be brought online, which is forecasted as being possible once 50 GW of nuclear power capacity has been achieved. The uranium in the first stage PHWRs that yield 29 EJ of energy in the once-through fuel cycle, can be made to yield between 65 and 128 times more energy through multiple cycles in fast breeder reactors.

The design of the country's first fast breeder, called Prototype Fast Breeder Reactor (PFBR), was done by Indira Gandhi Centre for Atomic Research (IGCAR). Bharatiya Nabhikiya Vidyut Nigam Ltd (Bhavini), a public sector company under the Department of Atomic Energy (DAE), has been given the responsibility to build the fast breeder reactors in India. The construction of this PFBR at Kalpakkam is due to be completed in 2012. The commissioning date of the reactor should be known by mid 2012. Loading of the fuel is expected in the early part of 2013, followed by one year of system testing after the reactor achieves criticality. Commercial generation of electricity can be expected by 2015.

In addition, the country proposes to undertake the construction of four FBRs as part of the 12th Five Year Plan spanning 2012-17, thus targeting 2500 MW from the five reactors. One of these five reactors is planned to be operated with metallic fuel instead of oxide fuel, since the design will have the flexibility to accept metallic fuel, although the reference design is for oxide fuel. Indian government has already allotted Rs.250 crore for pre-project activities for two more 500 MW units, although the location is yet to be finalised. India's fast breeder reactor is based upon the liquid metal fast breeder reactor. To sustain a chain reaction using fast neutrons, the reactor fuel must be relatively rich in fissile material. The superior neutron economy of a fast neutron reactor makes it possible to build a reactor that, after a relatively large initial fuel charge of plutonium, requires only natural (or even depleted) uranium feedstock as input to its fuel cycle.

Doubling time

Doubling time refers to the time required to extract as output, double the amount of fissile fuel, which was fed as input into the breeder reactors. This metric is critical for understanding the time durations that are unavoidable while transitioning from the second stage to the third stage of Bhabha's plan, because building up a sufficiently large fissile stock is essential to the large deployment of the third stage. In Bhabha's 1958 papers on role of thorium, he pictured a doubling time of 5-6 years for breeding U-233 in the Th-U233 cycle. This estimate has now been revised to 70 years due to technical difficulties that were unforeseen at the time. Despite such setbacks, according to publications done by DAE scientists, the doubling time of fissile material in the fast breeder reactors can be brought down to about 10 years by choosing appropriate technologies with short doubling time.

Type	*U238- Pu Cycle*	*Th-U233 Cycle*
oxide	17.8	108
carbide-Lee	10	50
metal	8.5	75.1
carbide	10.2	70

Another report prepared for U.S. Department of Energy suggests a doubling time of 22 years for oxide fuel, 13 years for carbide fuel and 10 years for metal fuel.

Stage III - thorium based reactors

A Stage III reactor or an Advanced nuclear power system involves a self-sustaining series of thorium-232-uranium-233 fuelled reactors. This would be a thermal breeder reactor, which in principle can be refueled - after its initial fuel charge - using only naturally occurring thorium. According to the three stage programme, Indian nuclear energy could grow to about 10 GW through PHWRs fueled by domestic uranium, and the growth above that would have to come from FBRs till about 50GW. The third stage is to be deployed only after this capacity has been achieved. According to replies given in Q&A in the Indian Parliament on two separate occasions, 19 August 2010 and 21 March 2012, large scale thorium deployment is only to be expected "3 - 4 decades after the commercial operation of fast breeder reactors with short doubling time". Full exploitation of India's domestic thorium reserves will likely not occur until after the year 2050.

Parallel approaches

As there is a long delay before direct thorium utilization in the three stage programme, the country is now looking at reactor designs that allow more direct use of thorium in parallel with the sequential three stage programme. Three options under consideration are the Accelerator Driven Systems (ADS), Advanced Heavy Water Reactor (AHWR) and Compact High Temperature Reactor. Molten Salt Reactor may also be under consideration based on some recent reports.

Advanced Heavy Water Reactor (AHWR)

Of the options, the design for AHWR is ready for deployment. AHWR is a 300 MWe vertical pressure tube type, boiling light water cooled and heavy water moderated reactor, using uranium233-thorium MOX and plutonium-thorium MOX. It is expected to generate 65% of its power from thorium and can also be configured to accept other fuel types in full core including enriched uranium and uranium-plutonium MOX. There was a plan for constructing such an AHWR with a plutonium-thorium core combination in 2007. This AHWR design was sent for an independent pre-licensing design safety review by the Atomic Energy Regulatory Board (AERB), the results of which were deemed satisfactory. AHWR would offer very little growth for the fuel build up that is essential for wide deployment of the third stage, and perhaps the impact on the accumulated fissile material could even be negative.

The AHWR design that will be taken up for construction is to be fueled with 20% low enriched uranium (LEU) and 80% thorium. The low enriched uranium (LEU) for this AHWR design is readily available on the world market. As of November 2011, construction will start after the site is identified in 6 months time. It will take another 18 months to get clearances on regulatory and environmental grounds. Construction is estimated to take six years. If everything goes according to plan, AHWR could be operational in India by the end of this decade.

4

Atomic Diplomacy of India

HISTORICAL SUMMARY OF ARSENAL DEVELOPMENT

Although India first tested a nuclear explosive in 1974 (euphemistically called the PNE, for "peaceful nuclear explosive") it did not become a nuclear weapons state - in the sense of having the ability to deliver nuclear weapons until 1986-88 when, according to Dr. Sanjay Badri-Maharaj author of *The Armageddon Factor*, a rudimentary delivery system was in place [Indian Express, 18 June 2000]. This presumably refers to a developmental delivery system based on the Mirage 2000 that began development in 1986, after an attempt to integrate a DRDO developed nuclear bomb with the Jaguar fighter-bomber failed. This system provided India with a usable but limited nuclear weapons capability, but the weapon system did not actually enter service until it passed a full field drop test in May 1994 at Balasore, though most observers thought that this milestone had been passed years before.

The US CIA testified before congress in 1993 that it did not believe that India maintains assembled or deployed nuclear weapons, although it believed India was producing weapon components. The CIA's HUMINT (human intelligence, as opposed to electronic intelligence) reggarding India's nuclear program is famously poor however (witness the U.S. intelligence communities surprise about the 1998 tests) so it cannot be accorded great weight; nonetheless it could be true that in 1993 India still had not taken the step of maintaining weapons in a ready-to-use state. There is a vague report though of "a few" weapons existing as early as the early 1980s.

Chengappa relates that hardened concrete bunkers were built in the early 1980s at Mumbai to house India's weapons plutonium stocks, a few weapons. Gen Sundarji was shown these weapons in the mid-80s, an unusual step since the military chiefs of staff had not been briefed on India's nuclear capability even as late as 1990. These weapons may not have been kept fully assembled, but there is little doubt that India could have made them ready in a matter of hours (or days at the most).

India has several aircraft that are nominally considered "nuclear capable", the Mirage 2000, Mig-27, and the Jaguar. Due to the cost of integrating and qualifying an aircraft for nuclear delivery, and maintaining a cadre of specially trained pilots, it is unlikely that India would choose to deploy nuclear weapons on more than one or two aircraft types.

Only the Mirage 2000 is known to have been qualified as a nuclear delivery platform, and the Jaguar is known to have been abandoned for nuclear weapons delivery due to technical problems. Thus it may be that the Mirage 2000 remains the sole air breathing nuclear weapon delivery system.

India has developed short and medium-range nuclear-capable missiles. These are the Prithvi (range 250 km, payload 500 kg), and the Agni-II (range 2500 km, payload 1000 kg). The first operational capability of a missile deliverable nuclear warhead was probably soon after the official deployment of the Prithvi SS-250 missiles in September 1997, which occurred after the successful completion of integration and testing of the warhead and missile during 1996-97. Reportedly four nuclear armed Prithvis were deployed during the Kargil War in June 1999. Also during this war was the first deployment of the medium range Agni-II, apparently consisting of a single preproduction model. The Agni-II was not qualified for full production and deployment until after the second Agni-II test occurred on 17 January 2001 at 10:01 a.m. IST (Indian Standard Time) when it was tested in its final deployment configuration. India reportedly is investigating development of an ICBM-class missile called Suriya.

DEVELOPMENT OF CURRENT ARSENAL IN INDIA

There are no official figures for weapon stockpiles at any stage of development of India's arsenal. The only figures that can be offered are either explicit estimates made from considerations of India's probable ability to produce critical raw materials and considerations of likely production plans; or are unofficial statements of uncertain provenance and authenticity. To show the problems with figures of the latter sort we have only to look at the statement by K. Subrahmanyam, a leading strategic theorist, that by 1990 India had stockpiled at least two dozen unassembled weapons, versus the May 1998 estimate by G. Balachandran, an Indian nuclear researcher, that India had fewer than 10 weapons ready to be assembled and mounted on warplanes or missiles.

The types of weapons India is believed to have available for its arsenal include:

- a pure fission plutonium bomb with a yield of 12 kt;
- a fusion boosted fission bomb with a yield of 15-20 kt, made with weapon-grade ploutonium;
- a fusion boosted fission bomb design, made with reactor-grade plutonium;
- low yield pure fission plutonium bomb designs with yields from 0.1 kt to 1 kt;
- a thermonuclear bomb design with a yield of 200-300 kt.

All of these types should be available based on the tests conducted during Operation Shakti (Pokhran-II). It may be possible to extrapolate significantly from these device classes however without further testing. There is reasonable doubt about whether the thermonuclear device actually performed as designed. Even if this so, it does not rule out the possiblity that sufficent test data was collected to field a successful design with reasonable confidence of good performance. Interest has been expressed in the development of a neutron bomb (a very low yield tactical thermonuclear device), but this would probably require additional testing to perfect.

The most widely accepted estimates of India's plutonium production have been made by David Albright ([Albright et al

1997], [Albright 2000]). His most recent estimate (October 2000) was that by the end of 1999 India had available between 240 and 395 kg of weapon grade plutonium for weapons production, with a median value of 310 kg. He suggests that this is sufficient for 45 - 95 weapons (median estimate 65). The production of weapon grade plutonium has actually been greater, but about 130 kg of plutonium has been consumed - principally in fueling two plutonium reactors, but also in weapons tests. His estimate for India's holdings of less-than-weapons-grade plutonium (reactor or fuel grade plutonium) are 4200 kg of unsafeguarded plutonium (800 kg of this already separated) and 4100 kg of IAEA safeguarded plutonium (25 kg of this separated). This unsafeguarded quantity could be used to manufacture roughly 1000 nuclear weapons, if India so chose (which would give it the third largest arsenal in the world, behind only the U.S. and Russia).

Indian Nuclear Force Planning

Nothing is publicly known about official Indian nuclear force planning, but assessments made by opinion leaders provide a context for judging the prevailing attitude in Indian government circles

India's first effort to formulate a nuclear policy and the determine the means needed to implement it was an informal but authoritative study group that was set up in November 1985 to answer queries by Rajiv Gandhi regarding defense planning. It encompassed the three services (Navy Chief of Staff Adm. Tahliani, Army Vice Chief of Staff Gen. K. Sundarji, Deputy Cheif of Air Staff John Greene), leaders of BARC (Ramanna), the DRDO (Abdul Kalam), and the AEC (Chidambaram), and India's most prominent strategic analyst K. Subrahmanyam. The outcome of the group's deliberations was to recommend building a minimum deterrent force with a strict no first use policy. The arsenal envisioned was 70 to 100 warheads at a cost of about $5.6 billion.

In 1994 K. Subrahmanyam suggested that a force of 60 warheads carried on 20 Agnis, 20 Prithvis and the rest on aircraft would cost about Rs 10 billion over 10 years. In 1996 Sundarji suggested a cost of some Rs 27.5 billion — Rs 6 billion for 150 warheads, Rs 3.6 billion for 45 Prithvis and Rs 18 billion for 90 Agni missiles.

INDIA'S FIRST BOMB: 1967-1974

India's nuclear weapons program moved in to full swing with Raja Ramanna at the helm. As Ramanna admitted in an interview on 10 October 1997, the "Peaceful Nuclear Explosive" (PNE) program - implying an intention to develop the nuclear explosives for civilian engineering work - was simply a cover for a program aimed from the beginning to develop a weapons capability, in truth there was little if any interest in Plowshare type peaceful applications. On the other hand, there was also no involvement of the military in the development program. There was no attempt to devise a military role for the nuclear explosive, or to seek the military's input for requirements. The military's public statements on nuclear weapons at this time were far from enthusiastic - essentially mirroring Sarabhai's views - so the advocates of nuclear weapons development had little incentive to seek their collaboration.

Even with the peaceful cover story, India found it necessary to keep as a low a profile on the project as possible to avoid inevitable attempts by other nations to obstruct it by denying access to nuclear technology and knowledge.

During December 1968 - January 1969 P.K. Iyengar visited the Soviet Union with three colleagues and toured the nuclear research facilities at Dubna. He was very impressed by the plutonium fueled pulsed fast reactor he saw there. This type of reactor is an unmoderated fast neutron reactor, that is allowed to go prompt supercritical to produce an intense very short pulse of neutrons. These are all characteristics of the cores of fission bombs, the principal difference between them being that in pulsed reactors the degree of supercriticality is very slight and ordinary thermal expansion of the reactor core is sufficient to shut down the reaction, while in fission bombs the degree is very large and the core cannot expand fast enough to shut down the reaction until vast amounts of energy are released. Pulsed fast reactors provide an excellent laboratory model of fission bomb behaviour, having been used for that purpose during the Manhattan Project (the famous Dragon experiments) and afterward (the Godiva, Popsy and Topsy reactors).

Recognizing this, Iyengar set about developing just such a reactor for India. The scientific leadership approved the plan in January 1969, the kick-off meeting for this reactor, called Purnima (an approximate acronym for Plutonium Reactor for Neutron Investigation in Multiplying Assemblies), took place in March 1969. Attending this meeting was Iyengar, Ramanna, Homi Sethna, and Sarabhai. Sarabhai's presence clearly indicates that with or without formal approval, the work at BARC toward weapon design now had Sarabhai's support. Chengappa indicates in fact that Sarabhai approved a one million rupee budget for Purnima (about $125,000, a figure could have covered only incidental costs - not the value of the plutonium).

Purnima was designed to use a hexagonal core of 177 stainless steel pencil shaped rods containing 18 kg of plutonium as 21.6 kg of plutonium oxide pellets (enough for three Fat Man type bombs) with a nominal average power of 1 watt. Mahadeva Srinivasan developed a sophisticated physics model for criticality calculations in 1970, and later became the reactor's chief physicist.

Construction began that year when sufficient separated plutonium finally became available. Purnima went critical on 18 May 1972. With Purnima as a test bed the Indian physicists were able to refine their understanding of the physics of fast fission and fast neutrons. While not formally part of the later bomb development team Srinivasan's expertise in fast critical systems underlay the nuclear design of the device.

1970 saw expansion of the nuclear weapons program in many ways. Due to the requirements of Purnima the program needed to develop facilities and experience in handling large amounts of plutonium (developed under the supervision of P.R. Roy), and work also began on fabricating plutonium metal alloys for the eventual construction of the bomb core. To advance the development of the essential implosion system V.S. Ramamurthy also began performing numerical implosion simulations on an antiquated Soviet Besm 6 computer

Development of the technology for implosion got underway in April 1970 when Ramanna sent Pranab Rebatiranjan Dastidar, the electronics expert at BARC, to Waman Dattatreya Patwardhan at the Explosive Research and Development laboratory (ERDL) at Pune to begin work on the detonation system for the bomb. Patwardhan was well known to the BARC scientists, since he helped them with the explosives tests years before as part of SNEPP. In July nuclear physicist Dr. Basanti Dulal Nag Chaudhuri took over as science adviser to the Defense Minister, and as Director of the Defense Research and Development Organization (DRDO). The following month, he and Ramanna began working together to recruit the Terminal Ballistics Research Laboratory (TBRL), located in Chandigarh, to develop the explosive lenses for the implosion system.

During 1971 work on weapon design continued. Srinivasan working with K. Subba Rao developed models of the fission process on a nuclear bomb, and equations to predict its efficiency. Chidamabaram completed his work on the plutonium equation of state, and Ramamurthy developed computational models of the implosion, nuclear reaction, and disassembly process to predict the devices behaviour. Throughout this period Ramanna and his lieutenant, P.K. Iyengar, held frequest reviews of the projects progress.

In April 1971 Nag Chaudhuri appointed Nagapattinam Sambasiva Venkatesan to Director of TBRL with specific instructions to assist in developing the nuclear device.

The 1971 Indo-Pakistani War influenced India's resolve to test a nuclear device, but in a curious and indirect way. This war developed when the bi-regional state of Pakistan, split into East and West Pakistan on either side of India, held its first national election in December 1970. The dominant party of the more populous East Pakistan won a majority of the seats in parliament, but West Pakistan, accustomed to monopolizing political and military power, responded by ignoring the election result. And on 25 March 1971 West Pakistan forces arrested the winner Mujibur Rahman, and launched a campaign brutal military repression on the Bengalis of East Pakistan. This resulted in tens of millions of refugees spilling into India, some of whom took up arms against the Pakistani government. By autumn the Indian-East Pakistani border had become something close to a combat zone, with India and Pakistan trading intense firing across the border, while armed rebels operated from safe havens in India. In late November PM Gandhi authorized Indian forces to cross the border to "pursue" Pakistani forces. Pakistan responded by a massive strike against Indian airbases in western India on 3 December, and declaring war on 4 December. India had spent months preparing for this escalation, indeed had deliberately provoked it, and launched an overwhelming 3-pronged attack into East Pakistan. Unable to hold back the Indian invasion, Pakistan attempted to counter with an attack in Kashmir, gaining several miles of territory before being halted by Indian forces. The Indian army on the other hand had surrounded Dacca, the capital of East Pakistan by 15 December, and its garrison surrendered the next day. On 17 December a cease-fire was accepted by both sides, effectively ending the war.

The war had been a crushing defeat for Pakistan, which had lost more than half its population. As the crisis developed throughout 1971 China and Pakistan had grown closer to the U.S. while India had grown closer to the Soviet Union.

The keystone of the Nixon administration's foreign policy had been its reapproachment with China (announced 15 July), to place the Soviet Union between the pincers of two major opposing powers. Pakistan had played a critical role in facilitating secret negotiations with China.

India had at the same time strengthened its ties to the U.S.S.R. culminating in a formal treaty of friendship on 9 August. Chinese support for Pakistan during the most extreme crisis of Pakistan's existence came to nought however. China failed to provide any significant assistance for Pakistan, such as applying pressure on India's border. The net result was that Pakistan suffered both a serious military defeat, demonstrating its inferiority to India in military terms, and a permanent irreparable loss in its strategic position by the new found independence of East Pakistan. And the much feared Pakistan-China axis had turned out to be a "paper tiger".

Unsurprisingly this did bolster India's sense of security, but it did not stem the momentum toward the testing of a nuclear device as one might have supposed.

On 30 December 1971 Sarabhai died, and Homi Sethna - already head of BARC - took his place as chairman of the IAEC. Thus the only prominent voice in Indian government counciling restraint in pursuing the nuclear option was replaced by one of its most ardent advocates.

And the hostile attitude taken toward India by the U.S. during the crisis had along lasting effect on Indian attitudes. Pres. Nixon and Sec. of State Kissinger chose to view India's actions as hostilities aimed at a U.S. ally and thus as an act hostile to the United States, rather than a case of a western-style democracy coming to the defense of a people being brutally persecuted by a military dictatorship for attempting to exercise its democratic rights. The U.S. even went so far as to dispatch an aircraft carrier battle group to the Indian Ocean in an ill-conceived, obscurely reasoned, and ineffectual attempt to pressure India. The feeling that a superpower had attempted to coerce India in affairs affecting India's vital interests became a cause celebre for advocates of the nuclear option (although they never clearly explained how a limited nuclear capability would counter U.S. pressure).

Bhabhani Sen Gupta ably described the shift in India's views toward the nuclear option in the wake of the 1971 war:

> The Chinese bomb ceased to be the main argument for the Indian bomb, perhaps becasue of the Chinese inability to help Pakistan in the 1971 war and also becasue of the initiatives taken by India to normalize relations with China. The arguments for the bomb now were that without it India could not expect to be admitted to the corridors of global power, nor enjoy the status of the dominant regional power; that the bomb might quicken the process of normalizing relations with China; that it would proclaim India's independence of the Soviet Union and compel the United States to change its attitude of hostility or benign neglect.

By the beginning of 1972 the basic design for India's first nuclear device was complete, and other parts of the program for developing the necessary expertise to implement the design were coming along. During that year the data from operating Purnima (starting in May) began flowing in allowing confirmation and refinement of the device's nuclear design; and the work in plutonium metallurgy reached the point where the device could be successfully fabricated.

The decision to go ahead and manufacture the device and prepare for a test was made later in the year, while Indira Gandhi was still near the peak of her post-war popularity. Early in the year PM Gandhi had seemed ambivalent about the wisdom of conducting an actual test. But by this time the internal momentum of the nuclear development program, the now well established popularity of the nuclear option among India's literate urban elite, the lack of any significant restraining counsel, and Gandhi's sense of strength all seem to have combined to make the decision one of when, not if, the test would come. The decision to move forward was made by PM Gandhi on 7 September 1972, a day in which she toured BARC on the occasion of the tenth convocation of the Indian Institute of Technology at Bombay. During this tour she was shown a wooden model of the device. Upon seeing the model she gave the scientists present verbal authorization to construct it and prepare for testing, but not to test it without explicit approval from herself.

One change made by Sethna soon after assuming the chairmanship was to split the Indian space program, then part of the Department of Atomic Energy, into a separate agency - observing quite reasonably that to have the DAE developing *both* nuclear explosives and missile technology would wave a red flag for observers concerned about proliferation, no matter what claims were made about the peaceful intent of both programs.

THE "PEACEFUL NUCLEAR EXPLOSION" AND AFTER

On May 24, 1974, at the height of a nationwide railway strike (led by the current Defense Minister, George Fernandes), India conducted its first nuclear test at Pokharan in the desert in Rajasthan. The telegram sent to the Prime Minister Indira Gandhi by Raja Ramanna, the leader of the team that carried out the explosion, read "The Buddha is Smiling" – a phrase that has become the source of several article titles. The device tested is believed to have been large and heavy with a yield of about 8-12 kilotons, a little less than the weapon that was dropped on Hiroshima. India termed the test a "Peaceful Nuclear Explosion" and launched a diplomatic offensive trying to prove that it was indeed peaceful. Part of the motivation to call the tests "peaceful," was to maintain technological ties with the U.S. and Canada. When Canada and the US agreed to provide assistance in building and operating India's CIRUS research reactor, India pledged to use the facility and the fissile material coming out of it for purely peaceful purposes. By terming its test a peaceful nuclear explosion - which was well within the terms of nuclear discourse at that time - India maintained that it had not violated its pledge. Despite this, the test led to the withdrawal of practically all cooperation in nuclear technology with the US and Canada.

To avoid such problems in the future, India subsequently built a similar, but larger, research reactor called Dhruva. Dhruva started functioning in 1985. It has been estimated that India could have accumulated about 300-500 kgs of Plutonium from these two reactors. Judging from the sophistication of the recent tests, Indian designs probably use less than 5 kg of Plutonium for each nuclear bomb. Hence, India has sufficient stocks of fissile material for over 60 to 100 bombs.

It is striking that all the leaders of the group that conducted the 1974 test went on to head the Department of Atomic Energy. The first, Raja Ramanna, is known for his hawkish views. He went on to become the science advisor to the Minister of Defense in 1977-1979 and the minister of state for Defense in 1989-91. According to recent revelations, it was during his tenure as science advisor that the manufacture of nuclear weapon components, which had been temporarily stopped after the 1974 test, was restarted.

The next of the Pokharan leaders who went on to head the Department of Atomic Energy, P. K. Iyengar, also continued to expand the infrastructure to make nuclear weapons. The third leader of the group to also become head the DAE was R. Chidambaram. In a 1994 interview, while denying reports of radioactivity releases from the 1974 test explosion, he went on to triumphantly assert, "that's how good our bomb was." This was the first time a high official within the Department of Atomic Energy had publicly called the "peaceful nuclear explosion" what it was - a bomb.

The Missile Program

The quest for nuclear capability also extended to developing vehicles for delivering nuclear weapons. In 1983, the Integrated Guided Missile Development Program (IGMDP) was set up. The guiding force behind the program, Abdul Kalam, was born in a poor family in Southern India.

Inspired by an article on the British Spitfire, he took up Aeronautical Engineering at the Madras Institute of Technology (known locally as MIT!). After working as a leading scientist in India's defense related research agencies, he headed the Satellite Launch Vehicle Program in India's civilian space program, before finally leading the missile program.

Abdul Kalam brought a more open management style practiced in the Indian civilian space program to the relatively closed defense research program. This included involving academic institutions in defense research as well as subcontracting projects and the manufacture of components to private firms. He also acquired technology from the civilian space program for the military missile program. This form of integration of civilian scientific programs with national security goals was clearly a result of the 1974 test. Kalam won great acclaim for his role in successfully developing guided missiles. He was appointed to head India's main defense research agency, and was subsequently awarded India's highest civilian honor - the Bharat Ratna.

The Indian guided missile program started with the development of five missile systems - the short range Prithvi (Earth), the intermediate range Agni (Fire), the surface to air missiles Akash (Sky) and Trishul (Trident), and the guided anti-tank Nag (Snake). By 1988, the results of the new program were visible - the first test of Prithvi was conducted on 25 February 1988. This was followed the next year with a test of Agni. More recently, other missile systems are under development – the Pinaka, the Sagarika and the Astra.

Round Two of the Non-Proliferation Treaty (NPT)

The indefinite extension of the NPT in 1995 was another blow to the Indian position on nuclear disarmament. Under the NPT, Non-Nuclear Weapon-States abjure nuclear weapons and in exchange Nuclear-Weapon States agreed to "pursue negotiations in good faith on effective measures relating to cessation of the nuclear arms race at an early date and to nuclear disarmament, and on a Treaty on general and complete disarmament under strict and effective international control." While the Non-Nuclear Weapon-States have almost without exception kept their end of the bargain, the Nuclear Weapon-States have failed to keep theirs. Since the NPT was signed, the Nuclear Weapon-States have conducted innumerable nuclear weapons tests and increased the size and destructive power of their arsenals.

In 1995, the NPT came up for review and a decision about extending it had to be made. Despite opposition by the Non Nuclear Weapon-States, the Nuclear Weapon-States, led by the US, forced through an indefinite extension of the NPT. This was widely interpreted in India as the permanent entrenchment of an unequal system. The indefinite extension of the NPT strengthened the position of the bomb lobby in debates over Indian nuclear policy and provided grounds for a renewed campaign for nuclear weapons.

Debating the Comprehensive Test Ban Treaty

The first effect of this campaign was that India voted against the CTBT in 1996, a treaty it had championed for forty years. This came as a big surprise since India had consistently supported non-discriminatory global arms control measures such as the CTBT and a cutoff on the production of fissile material (fissban). Even as late as 1994, it co-sponsored the CTBT at the United Nations, along with the USA. However, after the indefinite extension of the NPT, things had changed.

In the domestic debate, the Indian bomb lobby argued that the indefinite extension implied nuclear weapons were going to be around forever. Hence India should either develop nuclear weapons or settle for permanent second-class status. To develop militarily useable nuclear weapons India had to test. Therefore it had to reject the CTBT.

In international forums, as well as official circles, two main arguments were used against the CTBT. First, the CTBT did not really constrain the weapons development programs of the Nuclear Weapon-States, especially the U.S. The U. S. had started a multi-billion dollar Science Based Stockpile Stewardship Program involving the construction of several facilities that could develop new weapons designs. This was not the case when the CTBT was first proposed in the 1950s. It was the hundreds of tests conducted in the intervening period that allows the U.S. to design new weapons without nuclear testing.

Second, the CTBT was no longer a step towards disarmament as had always been envisioned. Instead, the Nuclear Weapon-States viewed it as merely a measure that would, in the words of the head of the erstwhile Arms Control and Disarmament Agency of the USA, "freeze countries on the nuclear learning curve."

The rationale for the Stockpile Stewardship Program was to ensure the US nuclear arsenal would remain functional for the foreseeable future. India demanded that the CTBT be coupled to a time-bound program for nuclear disarmament. The Nuclear Weapon-State were completely opposed to this.

A less noticed, but important, shift in India's stance was the perceived role of its nuclear weapons. While refusing to sign discriminatory agreements and continuing to build its nuclear infrastructure in the past, India had always maintained that nuclear weapons were immoral and deterrence, an abhorrent doctrine. As late as March 1996, the Indian Foreign Secretary, Salman Hyder said "We do not believe that the acquisition of nuclear weapons is essential for our national security and we have followed a conscious decision in this regard." This was in line with the traditional Indian view.

However, when the Indian Ambassador to the Conference on Disarmament, Arundhati Ghose, rejected the CTBT in the present form on 20 June 1996, she said the CTBT was not "in India's national security interest" and "our national security considerations (have) become a key factor in our decision-making." This shift points to the dangerous impact on Indian nuclear policy of arguments advanced by the bomb lobby.

THE LONG PAUSE: 1974-1989

A long hiatus in overt nuclear weapons development followed the 1974 test. The driving force behind the development of the Peaceful Nuclear Explosive (or PNE), as it was officially called, had always been the scientists at BARC rather than any initiative from the military, the Prime Minister, of any other part of the Indian government. They had required no encouragement and had worked toward such a test whenever they had not been actually prevented from doing so. This shared mission, of proving that India as a country and they as scientists were equal to such a task, had given the BARC leadership a unity of purpose that overcame any tensions among them. After the test, this unity was lost and the teamwork that had developed the PNE collapsed. The disintegration unfolded during the remainder of 1974. Initially the test was well received by the Indian public and the Lok Sabha. PM Gandhi's poll rating jumped - from very low to above average; the opposition Jana Sangh party was enthusiastic. But by September, Gandhi's popularity had fallen to the lowest level ever.

International reaction was negative, but varied. Henry Kissinger (operating in a leadership vacuum in the wake of Pres. Nixon's resignation) atoned for his policy blunders toward India in 1971 by declining to take a critical stance, and actively working to improve U.S.-Indian ties. On the other hand the U.S. also boosted aid to the increasingly beleaguered Pakistan, including restarting military aid. The test sharply escalated international attention to proliferation, and support for India's nuclear program from abroad disappeared. Canada cut off virtually all nuclear assistance four days after the test, bringing two nuclear power projects - Rajasthan II reactor and the Kota heavy water plant - to a halt. Indeed the nuclear non-proliferation regime that exists today came about as a direct result of this test.

Pakistani PM Ali Bhutto increased funding for his own nuclear program, which had been started in January 1972, but found itself hamstrung by the nuclear technology restrictions imposed abroad after the Indian test. The impact of the test on India's civilian nuclear program was severe. The civilian nuclear power program had struggled for years to gain credibility, its progress crippled by the lack of indigenous resources and almost wholly dependent on imported technology and technical assistance. No effort had gone into analyzing the likely international reaction to the PNE, or in preparing the nuclear power program for the effects of an embargo. The cut-off of supplies of heavy water, and of technical assistance in building its own heavy water plants hit India particularly hard as its reactor designs were all dependent upon it. Even worse, the group that had triggered these handicaps was treated with accolades while the engineers that bore their consequence struggled on in anonymity.

The adverse international reaction, and its effect on aid and access to technology came as a surprise since foreign policy experts had not been consulted for an assessment prior to the test. The luster of the test wore off in other ways - it soon became clear that the test had produced *no* information of scientific value for peaceful uses or otherwise, beyond the simple demonstration that the device actually worked. Once the popularity boost of the 1974 test had swiftly faded Gandhi came to feel that her decision to break with Nehru's policies had been for no gain, and she lost interest in the program. Her visit to Pokhran on 22 December was perfunctory.

Although Gandhi declared that India was not pursuing the nuclear option, she did authorize preliminary work on developing a fusion boosted fission design. At BARC efforts were begun to organize projects in fusion boosting, levitated pit design for greater implosion compression, and improved neutron initiators. Sethna and Ramanna had begun feuding however, as differences in style and approach came to the surface, aided by bad blood that had built up over various disagreements through the years, and the pressures and temptations of sudden fame. The visit by Indira Gandhi to Pokhran in December was the breaking point, Sethna and Ramanna rarely spoke after that. The Indian nuclear program was left with a vacuum of leadership and even basic management. The effects of the feud trickled down through the organization, with those closely associated with Ramanna (like PK Iyengar) feeling persecuted. Early in 1975 a group had been set up to work on the fusion boosted design headed by M. Srinivasan, but progress was slow.

In June 1975 Indira Gandhi was convicted of election law violations; her response was to declare martial law on 25 June - suspending democracy for the only time in the history of Indian independence. Twenty six political organizations were banned and over 100,000 Indian citizens were arrested. During her next two years as dictator the nuclear programs languished, and then she was defeated in the general election in early 1977

Morarji Desai had been an opponent of pursuing the nuclear option for years before becoming Prime Minister in March 1977, and vocally opposed nuclear tests peaceful or otherwise, and the nuclear option, throughout his term in office. The feud between Sethna and Ramanna continued to fester, paralyzing BARC. Finally in June 1978, in an effort to defuse the situation Desai had Ramanna removed from his position as director of BARC. In compensation the famed Ramanna was made secretary of defense research, scientific advisor to the Ministry of Defense, and later also Director General of DRDO (Defense Research and Development Organization), positioning that would later give Ramanna considerably increased influence. This didn't improve the situation at BARC though since Sethna continued to harass Ramanna's allies, keeping the nuclear program demoralized. Worse still, Ramanna's supporters successfully thwarted Sethna's efforts to replace Ramanna - leaving BARC without a director.

Despite Desai's opposition to nuclear explosives, and the chaotic state of BARC, the Desai era was not entirely without progress in nuclear weapon development. Shortly after taking office PM Desai gave verbal authorization for efforts to improve the 1974 device design, to make it more compact so that it could actually be delivered [Chengappa 2000; p. 219]. In 1978 he approved the purchase of four squadrons of Jaguar aircraft, the first aircraft acquired by India that were suitable for nuclear weapons delivery. Also in 1977 work began on a new larger 100 MW plutonium production reactor at Trombay named R-5, but usually called

"Dhruva" (other accounts place the start of the Dhruva project in 1973 - possibly indicating a preliminary phase of planning). Efforts to rectify the severe shortage of heavy water had mixed success. In 1976 and 1977 assurances of 200 tonnes were obtained from the Soviets, the first 50 tonnes without safeguards, but for the rest India was forced to accept safeguard monitoring. In late 1977 the Baroda heavy water plant went on-line but in December it suffered an explosion and had to be shut down. India's civilian nuclear power program, already more than a decade behind schedule, fell even further behind.

Disturbing developments occurred in Pakistan during 1977 and 1978. As had happened in 1971, an attempt to conduct national elections led to chaos and military action. PM Zulfikar Bhutto held elections in March, which his party (the Pakistan Peoples Party) won, leading to charges of fraud; in April Bhutto declared martial law in three major cities; in June this order was declared illegal by the supreme court and was rescinded, new elections were scheduled for October; on 5 July Army General Zia-ul-Haq launched a coup that took over the government.

The military quickly took control of the nuclear weapons program, control it is maintained to this day - placing Pakistan's nuclear arms outside of the authority of the civilian government (when it has had one). It was during 1977-78 that India, and other nations, became aware of the scope of Pakistan's nuclear program. It soon became apparent that unlike many abortive nuclear projects initiated in other nations, Pakistan's program was huge, lavishly funded, well organized, and likely to succeed. The creation of a vast militarized nuclear weapons program in a neighbouring enemy state seems to have provided little immediate impetus to India's own program however.

The Desai government was fairly short lived. Internal dissension led to the collapse of the governing coalition in early-mid 1979. First Desai was replaced as head of the Janata government by Charan Singh, and then when elections were held in August Indira Gandhi was re-elected with 65% of the seats in the Lok Sabha. 1979 witnessed additional events that adversely shifted the Pakistani situation in the eyes of India. In March U.S. intelligence announced that the Kahuta uranium enrichment plant in Pakistan had been commissioned. On 4 April the hard line nature of Zia-ul-Haq's regime was emphasized when former prime minister Bhutto was hanged. Finally on 25 December the Soviet Union invaded Afghanistan, ensuring that despite its nuclear weapons program Pakistan would be the beneficiary of a massive infusion of U.S. weaponry, as well as U.S. economic and diplomatic support. The possibility that the U.S. would impose sanctions of any kind on Pakistan to undermine its nuclear program became slim, then nil when the aggressively anti-Soviet Reagan administration came to power. By this time concern over China had faded from view, and relations between India and China were becoming warmer.

Gandhi returned to power with a renewed interest in the nuclear weapons program. Now stationed in New Delhi, Raja Ramanna had much greater opportunity to influence the Prime Minister. In January 1981 she reappointed Ramanna as Director of BARC, in addition to his other positions. That month he proposed to her that India begin work on constructing and testing the two weapon designs that had been developed in the intervening 6 years - the fusion boosted device, and the compact pure fission device. The weight of the fission device had been shrunk from 1400 kg to 170-200 kg, along with many other improvements in its components. Gandhi agreed, and in February two new test shafts work began on sinking two new shafts at Pokhran. Construction work continued on the test shafts into May 1982; these shafts would remain idle for 17 years, until the 1998 Pokhran II (Operation Shakti) test series when these shafts would be code named "White House" and "Taj Mahal".

This work was quickly detected by U.S. satellites, and this activity was made public by Sen Alan Cranston in April (he also revealed that Pakistan was constructing a test shaft in Baluchistan). In August 1981 Mumbai journalist Yogi Aggarwal reported that since the end of 1980 work had accelerated at BARC in manufacturing bomb components, including the preparation of 12 kilograms of plutonium metal. He also revealed that plutonium from the CIRUS reactor was now being separated at the Tarapur processing plant which began operation in 1977. He specifically claimed that plutonium had been diverted from Tarapur for weapons use in March and April of 1981 [Perkovich 1999; p. 228-229]

In May 1982 (according to Chengappa), the time had arrived to decide whether to conduct the new nuclear tests. For the first time a leader of the Indian armed forces, Army Gen. K.V. Krishna Rao, was pushing for the nuclear option. On the other hand both Gandhi and the Reagan administration were working on a rapprochement to improve Indian-U.S. relations, and this time PM Gandhi was very much aware of India's vulnerability to likely international repercussions. Gandhi had also introduced a new element into the nuclear decision making process. Up until them Gandhi had held the portfolio of Defense Minister herself, now she transferred it to Ramaswami Venkataraman, a highly experienced, highly respected, and politically savvy senior official. Now a powerful and independent source of counsel, well aware of political and foreign policy implications, had been added to the nuclear decision making process. Unfortunately this was not the shape of things to come, while nuclear decisions in the future tended to have a broader institutional base than they had up through Smiling Buddha and afterward, up at least until the 1998 Shakti tests a formal policy making apparatus never became established and decisions (including the 1998 decision to test) remained ad hoc.

Gandhi held a meeting with Ramanna and Venkataraman as well as her new science adviser V.S. Arunachalam, and her top advisers Principal Secretary P.C. Alexander and Cabinet Secretary K. Rao Sahib, to decide on whether the test would be conducted. Chengappa and Perkovich offer somewhat different accounts of this meeting. Chengappa places it in May, and asserts that no decision was made at the meeting; but that Gandhi approved the test (or tests) after the meeting ended. Perkovich says that it was late in the year, even in early 1983, and that Gandhi did approve the test at the meeting. Both agree that within hours of her decision to test, she reversed herself and decided against it.

The Kargil Review Committee Report [Kargil 2000] states that "Former President Venkataraman and the then Scientific Adviser,

Dr. V.S. Arunachalam, both said that Indira Gandhi agreed to a nuclear weapons test in 1983 but called if off under US pressure." Chengappa offers a interesting (and somewhat dubious) account.

In advance of a planned visit to Washingon by PM Gandhi, India's Foreign Secretary Maharaja Krishna Rasgotra made a trip to resolve outstanding disagreements over the deliver of nuclear fuel for the Tarapur reactor. A compromise was reached (with the U.S. agreeing not to object if France supplied the fuel). Chengappa relates that afterward Rasgotra was confronted by US Undersecretary of Foreign Affairs, Lawrence Eagleburger. Rasgotra was shown classified satellite photographs of Pokhran, and Eagleburger demanded an explanation for the shaft construction that US intelligence had detected. Rasgotra was surprised, knowing nothing of the test preparations. Furious at being blind sided, upon returning to India Rasgotra briefed the Prime Minister about his experience and warned her of a severe reaction if a test were held. This meeting with Gandhi occurred only hours after she had approved a new nuclear test series, and minutes later she rescinded her approval. Chengappa add that later on Gandhi indicated in conversations to Gen. Rao and others that concern about economic reprisals certain to follow such a test was the key reason for postponement.

A problem with Chengappa's account is that the site preparation work at Pokhran was scarcely a secret by May 1982, having been discussed in the Indian (and international) press for over a year at that point. While Rasgotra may well have counseled her not to test, and concern regarding international reprisal very likely was the reason that the tests were suspended, the dramatic account Chengappa provides of Rasgotra being surprised, shocked, and outraged by U.S. revelations is difficult to credit. Nonetheless it would appear that Rasgotra was the conduit of pressure from the U.S. leading Indira Gandhi to cancel the test.

The key role of the threat of international sanctions is borne out by the fact that Indira Gandhi never revisited her decision after her rejection, refusing to permit even a rehearing of the matter even as the security situation with Pakistan grew more serious over the next three years and the growing interest within the military for exercising the nuclear option. This last trend found its greatest expression in a 30 page letter to the Defense Minister drafted by the joint chiefs of staff in June 1983, the first time the Indian military went on record supporting the acquisition of nuclear weapons [Chengappa 2000, pp. 286-287].

Despite Gandhi's rejection of testing, India's nuclear infrastructure continued to advance. One of the most notable achievements of the new leadership provided by Venkataraman and Arunachalam was the establishment of an ambitious ballistic missile program in 1983 that would lead to the successful development of the short range Prithvi missile, and the long range Agni missile series that are a key element of India's nuclear arsenal today. India had developed a significant level of missile related technology as a result of the Department of Space's solid fuel SLV-3 (Satellite Launch Vehicle), begun in 1973 and first successful test launched in July 1980; and as a result of "Project Devil", an attempt to reverse engineer the Soviet SA-2 liquid fuel surface-to-air missile by the Defense Research and Development Laboratory (DRDL) at Hyderabad. This latter project, initiated under the leadership of Dr. Dr. Basanti Dulal Nag Chaudhuri (who had supported the development of the device for "Smiling Buddha", the 1974 nuclear test at Pokhran), was failure and was cancelled in 1978; nonetheless significant experience and technical skill was obtained which provided the basis for additional work on liquid fueled missiles.

The new missile effort was based at DRDL and was led by Dr. Avil Pakir Jainulabdeen Abdul Kalam, and extremely talented engineer and project manager who had been instrumental in the success of the SLV-3 program. Kalam had been transferred to DRDL in 1982 at the instigation of Raja Ramanna, and in 1983 had put together an ambitious development program for five missiles based on a family of related technologies. Venkatarman not only endorsed the program, he encouraged Kalam to be even more aggressive and develop all of the missiles in parallel rather than one at a time. In August 1983 the Integrated Guided Missile Development Programme (IGMDP) was born with a budget of 38.8 billion rupees ($370 million). One of the reasons for the ambitious nature of the program was that the Indians correctly anticipated the tightening of international restrictions on the export of missile technology, which was realized as the Missile Technology Control Regime that was signed in 1987.

Both the Prithvi and the Agni were intended to carry nuclear warheads. The Prithvi was a 150 km liquid fueled missile derived from "Project Devil", and the Agni was a long range (1500+ km) two stage solid fuel (first stage)/liquid fuel (upper stage) design derived both from the SLV-3 and "Project Devil".

Even without approving the testing the new lightweight fission bomb, Gandhi authorized India's first attempt to weaponize a nuclear weapon - that is, package it so that it could be delivered by the military in wartime, and develop the necessary support systems so that it would be integrated into military operations. It is not enough to have a nuclear explosive device, or even to install it in a bomb casing with suitable fuzing and safety systems. Aircraft have to modified to carry it, and techniques for everything from delivery, to routine maintenance, to security must be developed. In late 1982 Arunachalam began a project to develop these capabilities. Dr. Nagapattinam Sambasiva Venkatesan, who had previously directed the laboratory which developed the bomb's high explosive implosion system, had now moved to the Armament Research and Development Establishment (ARDE) in Pune and was given the task of developing the ballistic case for the bomb. Arunachalam also contacted Air Marshal Chandrakant Gole, the deputy chief of air staff, to arrange for the adaptation and testing of a Jaguar combat aircraft for the role of nuclear bomb delivery. Unfortunately the Indian Air Force was not informed about the project (the purpose for which the test Jaguar had been allocated was not disclosed) although they had little trouble in guessing. The modified aircraft thus remained entirely outside the regular military system [Chengappa 2000, pp. 284-285].

This initial attempt to develop a usable nuclear weapon capability was stillborn. A more professional weaponization effort made several years later that eventually incorporated the full participation of the Air Force showed the importance of consulting with the Air Force from the outset to develop a viable weapon system. This later effort had several false starts, took over four years to complete, and found the Jaguar to be an unsuitable delivery aircraft. This smaller armament lab run project clearly produced nothing usable.

After returning to BARC Ramanna pushed forward efforts in other areas. The work on Dhruva had been languishing but Ramanna made its completion a top priority in 1981, making Anil Kakodkar a principal engineer on the project (later to play an important role an the 1998 test series). Perhaps stimulated by Pakistan's evident success with uranium enrichment, Ramanna initiated an Indian uranium enrichment program in the early 1980s. Approved by Indira Gandh and run by BARC, this highly classified project was located at Mysore, Karnataka. Reminiscent of the "tube alloy" code name used by the Manhattan Project's uranium enrichment program, this project was deemed the "Rare Minerals Plant".

The cut-off of legal external supplies of heavy water, and the failure of Indian domestic production efforts, created a serious problem for India's reactor projects in the 1980s. This affected not only Dhruva, but a number of civilian reactors such as Madras I (also called MAPS I). India resolved the problem through covert means, importing over 180 tonnes of heavy water from China (60 tonnes), Norway (15 tonnes), and the Soviet Union (at least 4.7 tonnes) through a German middleman, Alfred Hempel by the end of 1983. None of the supplier nations knew of the destination of these shipments, and the revelation that India was receiving Hempel's shipments probably caused the cessation of supply from China and Norway.

In the early 1980s it was clear that none of India's principal problems - economic development and internal stability - could be aided with nuclear weapons, a fact that diverted interest in testing or deployment. The internal stability problem arose from separatist movements in north eastern and north western India. By far the most serious was the Sikh movement in Punjab to create a new state of Khalistan.

Inevitably any part of the Indian national territory would be deemed essential by the Indian state, but Punjab was more essential than most. The most productive agricultural region in an agricultural economy struggling to feed itself, it was also adjacent to Kashmir - the fortified, restive, and contested region bordering Pakistan. In the early 1980s an armed insurrection took hold in Punjab led by Sant Bhindranwale, who made the Sikh's sacred Golden Temple of Amritsar his headquarters and fortress in 1982. Efforts to stabilize the situation failed, and on 5 June 1984 "Operation Blue Star" was carried out by the Indian Army under the command of Gen K. Sundarji - the assault on the Golden Temple. At least 493 Sikhs were killed in the attack (the Indian government official count, though outside observers estimate hundreds more died) including Bhindranwale, as well as 83 soldiers. Although it inflamed Sikh anger, and thus did nothing to reconcile Punjab, the attack accomplished its objective in breaking the back of organized armed opposition to Indian rule. In a sense though the Sikhs had the last word. India arranged a formal settlement with the principal political party in Punjab - the Akali Dal - in 1985, giving Punjab sovereignty over the Sikh-majority city of Chandigarh, which became the capital of Punjab. But it was not Indira Gandhi who made this settlement, it was her son Rajiv. Indira Gandhi was assassinated by her Sikh bodyguards on 31 October 1984.

Rajiv Gandhi, an airline pilot by profession, became Prime Minister less than 9 hours after Indira Gandhi's death, but ratified his position with the largest landslide in India's history, taking 415 out of 542 seats in the Lok Sabha in late December. Rajiv Gandhi's general orientation was toward technology and modern technological culture, thus he took great interest in the technical aspects of issues and actively promoted technological advance. He had a strong antipathy to nuclear weapons and did not support testing or deploy, and the refinement of weapon designs, and laboratory research required to support further advances in nuclear arms. His policies toward nuclear weapons thus were basically a continuation of the approach of his mother during her second term in office. Also like Indira Gandhi in her later years he had an ambivalent relationship with the scientific leadership at BARC - supporting their work but treating their advice skeptically, leaning perhaps even farther toward skepticism than Indira. In large part his opposition to proceeding with testing or deployment was *because* of his technology orientation. Rajiv recognized that India needed access to the advanced technology of the United States and that detectable progress toward acquiring nuclear weapons would slam many of those doors shut. In addition there seems to have been significant antipathy by Gandhi toward Ramanna, the leading figure in the nuclear establishment.

The mid-eighties saw indications of the growing nuclear capability of Pakistan pile up. Drawn to the limelight, the leader of Pakistan's uranium enrichment program Dr. Abdul Qader Khan held periodic interviews boasting about Pakistans nuclear prowess. It was in such an interview in February 1984 that he first made the claim that Pakistan had achieved nuclear weapons capability. Periodic revelations confirming the successful advance of the Pakistani program turned up with some regularity. In July 1984 the *New York Times* reported that US intelligence had learned that the previous year that China had supplied Pakistan with the design of an actual tested nuclear device. In March 1985 a West German court convicted a German businessman of smuggling a complete uranium hexafluoride manufacturing plant to Pakistan. Also in March the US concluded that Pakistan had made such progress in uranium enrichment capability that the Reagan administration sought an assurance from President Zia that Pakistan would refrain from enriching uranium above the level of 5%. In July 1985 it was reported by ABC that Pakistan had successfully conducted a "cold" implosion test - firing a complete implosion system with an inert natural uranium core. Taken together these indicators pointed to Pakistan acquiring the ability of conducting a nuclear test if it chose to do so within the next year. One factor helping to dampen Indian reaction to these developments is a distinct Indian tendency to discount Pakistani capabilities and accomplishments, even in the face of evidence.

Dhruva went critical on 8 August 1985, but soon after start-up serious problems arose requiring a shut-down. Radioactive contamination developed in the coolant system, indicating a severe fuel leak. The problem was traced to vibrations induced by the cooling system which coincided with the natural resonance frequency of the core. The strong vibrations caused stress on the fuel elements, leading to failure of the aluminum cladding. The problem was solved by attaching spring clips to each of the 192 fuel elements thereby damping the oscillations. It was restarted in December 1986 and operated at one-quarter power from then until spring of 1987. Dhruva finally achieved full power on 17 January 1988, becoming the workhorse of the Indian nuclear weapons production program.

During Rajiv Gandhi's term in office infrastructure was developed to support the manufacture of more sophisticated lightweight fission weapons. In 1984 India had imported 100 kg of high purity beryllium from West Germany, enough to provide the neutron reflecting tampers for a dozen or more weapons, but now India commissioned its own beryllium production plant in Mumbai, drawing on indigenous ores from Kerala. Around this time India also acquired a vacuum hot pressing machine, suitable for forming large high-quality beryllium forgings. Work also began at BARC to lay the foundation from thermonuclear weapon development and the manufacture of boosted fission weapons. The Department of Atomic Energy (DAE) announced that it would develop an inertial confinement fusion facility, a research tool that produces on a small scale physical conditions similar to those found in thermonuclear weapons. BARC also began manufacturing tritium by irradiating lithium in nuclear reactors, useful for neutron initiators and boosting fuel for fission weapons; and developing the capability of isotope enrichment of lithium - useful for tritium production and as fusion fuel for thermonuclear weapons. Throughout Rajiv Gandhi's term in office the BARC and DRDO establishments continued to develop and refine weapon designs and related technologies in the laboratory and the testing ground, much as they had since the early 60s. This was standard operating procedure within the nuclear establishment, they felt within their authority to proceed with weapon development without specific direction from the administration as long as they didn't proceed with the final assembly of a device.

India's first effort to formulate a nuclear policy and the determine the means needed to implement it was an informal but authoritative study group that was set up in November 1985 to answer queries by Rajiv Gandhi regarding defense planning. It encompassed the three services (Navy Chief of Staff Adm. Tahliani, Army Vice Chief of Staff Gen. K. Sundarji, Deputy Cheif of Air Staff John Greene), leaders of BARC (Ramanna), the DRDO (Abdul Kalam), and the AEC (Chidambaram), and India's most prominent strategic analyst K. Subrahmanyam. The outcome of the group's deliberations was to recommend building a minimum deterrent force with a strict no first use policy. The arsenal envisioned was 70 to 100 warheads, and would require a 9% boost to the defense budget for 10 years to finance (about $5.6 billion).

No formal action was taken on this report, but it appears to have inspired Rajiv Gandhi to take additional preparedness measures. In 1986 Gandhi instructed Arunachalam to develop a properly engineered aircraft delivery system, with suitable control and security measures and improved reliability to replace the stopgap system developed two years earlier.

Arunachalam recruited K. Santhanam as technology adviser on the project. The development effort of the improved bomb system was code named "New Armament Breaking Ammunition and Projectile", or NABAP, and was headed by Muthuswamy Balakrishnan at the Terminal Ballistics Research Laboratory (TBRL) in Chadigarh.

Venkatesan, Director of ARDE, was given the task of developing a superior aerodynamic case for the weapon and associated carriage and release mechanisms and to manufacture a certain number of units. This time the Air Force was involved in the development activities from the beginning, with Deputy Chief of Air Staff Surinder Kumar Mehra heading the Air Force team participating in the project. Problems with the existing bomb design and integration plan quickly surfaced.

The bombs developed by the DRDO and ARDE turned out to weigh to much for the Jaguar and had ground clearance of only two inches. By late 1986 the Air Force rejected the Jaguar as unsuitable, and efforts switched to integrating the bomb with the recently acquired Mirage 2000[Chengappa 2000, p. 327]. Considerable integration difficulties continued to be encountered and final qualification of deployed delivery system was not complete until May 1994 [Chengappa 2000; p. 382]. Dr. Badri-Maharaj, author of *The Armageddon Factor*, has stated that a rudimentary delivery system was in place from 1986-88, presumably referring to the developmental Mirage 2000 delivery system [Indian Express, 18 June 2000]. This effort provided India with it first genuinely usable nuclear weapons capability. By the end of the 80s the Indian Air Force, now equipped with nuclear capable Mig-27 as well, began routinely practicing loft bombing techniques for nuclear bomb delivery.

There some significant ups and downs in the Indo-Pakistani relationship from late 1985 through early 1987. The rapidly developing Pakistani nuclear capability provided motivation to establish a modus vivendi between the two nations.

In December 1985 Zia and Gandhi met in New Delhi and agreed to a pact not to engage in attacks on each others nuclear facilities (a situation that would left India rather the worse off due to the proximity of its production reactors to urbanized areas). It would not be signed until 31 December 1988, or fully implemented (through an exchange of data about their facilities) until 1993. In the year following this promising development, an ambitious but poorly managed military exercise by India lead to an unexpected crisis.

This crisis was precipitated by Exercise Brasstacks, the largest military exercise in Indian history conducted to test and demonstrate India's ability to deal with a major war with Pakistan. This exercise was planned by Gen. K. Sundarji, now Army Chief of Staff and began in July 1986.

It reached its crisis stage in December when India had a total of nine divisions deployed in Rajasthan adjacent to the Pakistani province of Sindh. India had not undertaken any measures to alleviate Pakistan's concerns about having such a massive armed force so close to its border, such as inviting observers, or sending advance notice of maneuvers. Pakistan accordingly mobilized its own forces - sending Army Reserve North and Army Reserve South to locations close to India's border where they could strike at Punjab or Kashmir. Pakistan's concern was not unwarranted, military maneuvers have been used to mask planned attacks before

- notably Operation Badr, the stunningly successful Egyptian and Syrian surprise attack that opened the 1973 Yom Kippur War. Poor intelligence and communications, and a disengaged and voltaile Rajiv Gandhi made a bad situation worse in January, leading to an atmosphere of real crisis on 18 January 1987.

Gandhi's decision to begin airlifting troops to Punjab on 20 January threatened to escalate the crisis out of control. But both governments soon after tried to bring the situation under control. A hotline was activated between India and Pakistan on 23 January, and a systematic plan for standing down agreed to on 4 February. A curious footnote to the exercise were threatening remarks by A.Q. Khan to Indian journalist Kuldip Nayar on 28 January, near the height of the crisis.

Nayar however shopped the story around for a few weeks, and it was not published until 1 March, after the matter had been resolved. Nonetheless it left a lingering sense of nuclear threat associated with the Brasstacks affair. The potential for even non-hostile actions to create dangerous situations has unfortunately not been a lesson well learned, judging from crises that have followed in 1990, 1998 and 1999.

Crippled by international sanctions imposed after the 1974 nuclear test, India's civilian nuclear power program fell further behind objectives throughout the 80s. One possible avenue for bolstering the program was to import nuclear reactors from supplier countries (like Russia) which were available on the condition that India operate them under IAEA safeguards.

The weapons establishment, maintaining their obsession with nuclear technology as a symbol of national pride, vigorously opposed taking this step. This obstructionist attitude displeased Rajiv Gandhi, and upon the expiration of Ramanna's term as AEC chairman in 1987 resulted in an occasion of considerable controversy (and horse trading) within the government. Ramanna and his allies insisted that P.K. Iyengar then head of BARC be appointed to the position, and Iyengar threatened to resign from BARC if he was passed over. Iyengar was, like Ramanna, a physicist that had had a leading role in the 1974 nuclear test. Rajiv Gandhi preferred M.R. Srinivasan, a nuclear engineer who was in charge of the nuclear power program and thus disposed to place the priorities of that program first. In the end a deal was struck in which Srinivasan was appointed to the position, but Iyengar was promised that he would be Srinivasan's successor.

Ever since China's first nuclear test, the position it held as a threat in the Indian psyche had been on the decline as Pakistan's position had risen. A brief resurgence in the border dispute with China coincided with the Brasstacks debacle, but with a more favorable outcome for India.

In late 1986 India's Parliament amended the Indian constitution to make the Northeast Frontier Agency (Arunachal Pradesh) a full state of the Indian union. Since a large parcel of territory claimed by China lies in Arunachal Pradesh, China protested and on 17 December demanded territorial concessions.

This led to large deployments of armed forces on both sides of the border over the next several months, reaching 200,000 on each side by May 1987. At the same time Gen. Sundarji began another exercise, "Chequerboard", this time on the Chinese border in the northeast Himalayan region.

Sundarji appears to have learned lessons from the just concluded Brasstacks and went to some pains to reassure the Chinese that the operation would not infringe on disputed territory. The vigorous and well executed movements of forces by India appears to have impressed China sufficiently once the deployments wound down, it was willing to resume talks on the border that had been suspended. The contrast of this denouement with that of Khan's bellicose talk at the close of Brasstacks served to further elevate India's apprehension of threat from Pakistan over China.

Two dramatic changes altered the strategic environment for India in 1988. The first was the Soviet decision in February 1988 to withdraw its forces from Afghanistan, a move that removed the geopolitical rationale for the U.S. support for the military regime, and the reluctance to pressure Pakistan on account of its nuclear weapons program. The second change was on 17 August 1988, when President Zia Ul-Haq, the architect of the militarization of the nuclear program, was killed along with thirty other people, when the aircraft in which he was travelling crashed in what is suspected to be an assassination.

In the aftermath of Zia's death, the military stepped aside and permitted the return of Pakistan to democracy three months later. In November 1988 Benazir Bhutto, the daughter of Prime Minister Zulfikar Ali Bhutto who had been overthrown and executed by Zia, became Prime Minister herself. The nuclear weapons complex remained in the hands of the military, who formed an independent center of power not under the control of the civilian government. PM Bhutto was in fact unaware of the status of the nuclear program, and when Pakistan passed the milestone of manufacturing fissile cores for weapons she first learned of it from the U.S. Ambassador to Pakistan.

5

Nuclear Power of India

INDIA AS A NUCLEAR POWER: 1998-2001

The immediate aftermath of the nuclear tests conducted by India, and then by Pakistan was not an encouraging one. In the two weeks since the conclusion of testing the Indian government has been a source of both conciliatory and potentially threatening remarks. While repeated statements have been made, most notably by Principal Secretary to the Prime Minister Mr. Brajesh Mishra on 22 May, and PM Vajpayee himself on 26 May, that India has declared a unilateral moratorium on testing, and that the weapons are not intended for aggressive purposes. India has also offered to open talks with Pakistan to discuss issues of contention and a possible nuclear weapon "no first use" agreement.

On Monday 18 May, just one week after the first test, Home Minister L.K. Advani issued sharp warnings to Pakistan about interfering in Indian-controlled Kashmir. PM Sharif responded the next day with an accusation that India had threatened to attack the territory under Pakistan's control. Although sporadic exchanges of gunfire have occurred over the years along the Line-Of-Control (LoC) that intersects Kashmir and separates the Indian and Pakistani armies, in the days following Advani's warnings there was a pronounced escalation of small arms and artillery fire on a daily basis. On 22 May B. Mishra stated "Let it not be forgotten that PoK (Pakistan occupied Kashmir), including the so-called northern areas, is an integral part of India. After all the unanimous resolution of the Indian Parliament in February 1994 to this effect is absolutely clear." Pakistan just as firmly believes that Indian controlled Kashmir is an integral part of Pakistan. Two of the three Indo-Pakistani wars have been fought over this same territory. The increasingly aggressive Indian posture, coupled with the current outbreak of armed conflict on the LoC, raised a very real possibility of war returning to the region after a 17 year absence.

Over the next year however this threat seemingly receded. On 20 February 1999 Indian PM Atal Behari Vajpayee made history when he crossed over the Pakistani border by bus to meet Pakistani President Nawaz Sharif at Lahore, raising hopes that with the nuclear arsenals now out of their closets the two powers would back away from confrontational approaches. On 21 February 1999 the two prime ministers signed the "Lahore Declaration", committing the two nations to peacefully resolving their differences.

Development continued on India's nuclear delivery systems - on 11 April 1999 India conducted a successful 14 minute test flight of the 2,500 kilometer Agni-II missile. "The entire process of achieving a minimum deterrent has been completed," Vajpayee announced following the test. "We are satisfied that we are now fully capable of defending our borders," he added. Pakistan responded with an eight-minute test flight of the Ghauri II three days later.

The promise of the Lahore Declaration proved to be stillborn. On 5 May 1999 two Indian army patrols in the snowy Yaldor area in Kargil, a border region next to Kashmir, were surprised to encounter a group of armed men, apparently from Pakistani Kashmir (known in India as "Pakistan-occupied Kashmir" or POK; in Pakistan they are called the Northern Areas or NA). This was the first contact with an infiltration operation from Pakistan to seize the mountain peaks inside India as an escalation of the long-standing Kashmir conflict, which would be become known as the Kargil War.

The "line of control", or LoC, between India and Pakistan runs across some of the harshest, most rugged, and highest territory in the world and consequently much of it consists of "unheld areas", territory so inhospitable that both sides abandon it during the brutal winters. It was because India had suspended patrol operations in the winter that made it possible for infiltrators to set up camp without being detected. The patrols that encountered them were the first of the season. Such areas had been opportunities for adventurousness in the past, as when the Siachen glacier was suddenly occupied by armed forces many years ago - becoming the highest and coldest battlefield on Earth. But this was the first time Pakistan had ever tried to exploit this particular region.It appears the infiltration operation was already underway during the signing of the Lahore Declaration. The larger of the two patrol parties went to check on the strangers, and found itself in an ambush and lost four soldiers. Firing continued for nearly a week before aerial surveillance on 12 May revealed to the army realized that the incursion was far more serious than it had assumed. Around 500 heavily armed guerillas had occupied at least 35 well-fortified positions atop the ridges facing Dras, Kargil, Batalik and the Mushko valley. Cover fire was being provided by the Pakistani artillery, which had begun a systematic bombardment of National Highway 1A that connects Leh to Srinagar in the Dras-Kargil region.

Within days the Indian army moved nearly 30,000 troops into the Kargil-Dras area along with special forces dropped on the high ridges by helicopter, and the battle was on in earnest; "Operation Vijay" (victory) to recapture the heights was launched in late May. Pakistan initially claimed not to be involved with the infiltration effort, a remarkable attempt at dissociation considering that the infiltrators were very well equipped and supplied, came from territory controlled by the Pakistani military, and were clearly in direct contact with the Pakistanis from which they were receiving direct artillery fire support. Eventually the continued direct involvement of regular Pakistani forces made the pretense an embarrassment for Pakistan, which dropped the attempt at evasion.

Over the next several weeks India outmaneuvered Pakistan both on the battlefield and in international diplomacy. Heavy Pakistani fire directed by the infiltrators from their commanding positions made the situation very difficult for India, but Pakistani positions on the Indian side were progressively captured or cut off from support as the superior weight of Indian forces made itself felt. By promising not to cross the LoC itself, India garnered nearly universal international support - and especially active Amercian support - for its position, while at the same time by mobilizing its forces along the entire Pakistani border it signalled that India was prepared to escalate and use its full military strength if necessary to prevent a Pakistani victory.

The objective of this operation seems to have been to try to obtain a limited gain on the ground - revising the LoC several kilometers in Pakistan's favor. The LoC has after all always been defined in de facto terms - it has no recognized status, it simply marks the effective zones of control of the two nations. The operation was calculated to circumvent India's military superiority - by picking the most difficult terrain possible for India's operations, and achieving the initial gain through stealth alone. Pakistan evidently hoped that international pressure would halt the conflict before India succeeded in driving the guerillas back.

By mid June the tide was turning, and by mid July the Kargil incursion had turned into a rout for Pakistan, both militarily and diplomatically. Pakistani forces retreated behind the LoC, and Pakistan suffered another severe blow to its international credibility, and in turn boosted India's prestige. After the end of the war Pakistani Prime Minister Nawaz Sharif asserted that the operation had been instigated without his knowledge - a claim, which whether true or not, was unfortunately all too plausible in Pakistan, with its tradition of the military operating free from civilian control.

The total depth of penetration across the LoC was no more than eight or nine kilometres at most. As intended by Pakistan, the operations for retaking the occupied areas were very difficult for India and this short, sharp war resulted in 474 killed and 1109 wounded on the Indian side (as of July 26, 1999).

A crucial but at the time unreported consequence of the Kargil War, tied in with the Indian mobilization along the Pakistani border, was the apparent deployment of at least five nuclear armed missiles. "Four nuclear armed Prithvis and one Agni were deployed for retaliatory strikes" according to Dr. Sanjay Badri-Maharaj, author of*The Armageddon Factor* (Indian Express, 18 June 2000).

This would have been a preproduction model of the Agni-II, the first deployable Agni version.

Sharif's demurral became even more plausible three months later when a showdown occurred between PM Sharif and army chief Gen. Pervez Musharraf on 13 October 1999. Acting while Musharraf was out of the country, Sharif fired him, but hours later Musharraf returned and overthrew Sharif in a coup (later to put Sharif on trial for his life).

Following the aggressive, destabilizing, and ill-conceived military operation of Kargil, the military coup in Pakistan did absolutely nothing to reassure India or the world regarding Pakistan's soundness and circumspection. The result was naturally even deeper isolation for Pakistan, on top of the sanctions that followed the 1998 tests, and the Kargil adventure.

Overt hostilities along the border continued to persist after the conclusion of the Kargil War. On 10 August 1999 an Indian fighter jet shot down a slow-moving Pakistani reconnaissance plane, killing all 16 aboard. The Indians said the plane had strayed across the border, though most of the wreckage landed in Pakistan.

On 17 August 1999, India took the major - though belated step - toward formalizing its declared status as a nuclear power by issuing a six-page document detailing a proposed doctrine governing its nuclear arsenal, entitled the "Draft Report of National Security Advisory Board on Indian Nuclear Doctrine". The report, which was prepared by a government-appointed advisory board, was made public Tuesday by National Security Advisor Brajesh Mishra.

The essential points of this doctrine were that India asserted a right to possess nuclear weapons, and would pursue a policy of credible "minimum" nuclear deterrence and use nuclear weapons only to retaliate against a first strike. According to the draft, "Any nuclear attack on India and its forces shall result in punitive retaliation with nuclear weapons to inflict damage unacceptable to the aggressor."

"India's peacetime posture aims at convincing any potential aggressor that any threat of use of nuclear weapons against India shall invoke measures to counter the threat," the draft said. It further stated that India would not use nuclear weapons against a state that does not have them or is not aligned with a nuclear-armed power, and that nuclear weapons would be tightly controlled and launched only with the authorization of the prime minister, or a designated successor.

The draft said the size, components, deployment and employment of nuclear forces would be decided in light of the strategic environment, economic imperatives and the needs of national security. But it took an expansive view of the concept of "minimum deterrence", recommending an arsenal that is able to deliver a nuclear blast from "a triad of aircraft, mobile land-based missiles and sea-based assets," one that can respond to an attack "in the shortest possible time" and employs a space-based early warning system. To raise the threshold for the outbreak of military conflict, India also would maintain highly effective conventional warfare capabilities, the draft document said.

The draft did not mention the Comprehensive Test Ban Treaty (CTBT) but it criticized the Nuclear Nonproliferation Treaty, saying it legitimized the possession of nuclear weapons by states that already had them.

The official U.S. State Department reaction given by Spokesman James P. Rubin was that India was "moving in the wrong direction" by trying to create a credible nuclear deterrence. Rubin said "We think it would be unwise to move in the direction of developing a nuclear deterrent and encouraging the other country to develop a nuclear deterrent and thereby creating an action-reaction cycle that will increase the risks to both countries."

China also condemned the document; and Pakistan, which 15 months ago matched India's nuclear tests with its own, said it would soon be matching India's doctrine with a published doctrine of its own.

Unlike from the U.S., the initial reaction from Europe was cautious. France welcomed the draft doctrine as a logical consequence of the decision to develop nuclear weapons.

The situation was cogently summarized by Tanvir Ahmad Khan in the Pakistani newspaper *The Dawn* on 24 August 1999:

The present draft is a landmark for three major reasons.

- First, it gathers together in a forceful single document elements that had surfaced disparately and with a certain air of tentativeness since the tests.
- Secondly, it relegates to history half-way concepts like existential deterrence and recessed deterrence that had been debated in both India and Pakistan. In doing so, it delivers a mighty blow to efforts aiming at freezing Indian and Pakistani capability at a non-weaponized level.
- Third, the nuclear doctrine as set forth in the text has hardly any meaning unless the weapons are manufactured and actually deployed in large numbers, and a sizable reserve of warheads and delivery vehicles is permanently maintained.

Tanvir Khan also observed that "the draft published at the moment does not add any transparency to the Indian targeting policy. Nor does it specify Pakistan or China as the principal zones of targeting." He also made some interesting assertions about Indian strategic literature:

Some analysts define the objective as the destruction of Pakistan as a social and economic entity. The targets considered in the relevant Indian literature include six to ten Pakistani metropolitan centres, four hydroelectric and thermal power stations, flooding of Punjab, obliteration of Pakistani railway system with attacks on Gujrat, Bahawalpur, Hyderabad and Dera Ghazi Khan, and disruption of all sea communications with nuclear attacks on Karachi and Gwadar. It has been calculated that a total of seventeen nuclear strikes will achieve all the objectives. If Pakistan also draws up a similar list of countervalue targets, breakdown of deterrence and the ensuing nuclear exchange would mark the end of a civilization.

Although a the time of its announcement, it was expected that the government in place following the elections in the autumn of 1999 would enact the draft doctrine formally, by early 2001 no action had been taken and the draft remained a proposal without official weight, except to the extent it reflected the thinking of Indian government officialdom.

In May 2000 the Atomic Energy Regulatory Board (AERB) which has been set up on 15 November 1983 by order of the President of India to exercise regulatory and safety functions for atomic energy in India was split off from the Bhabha Atomic Research Centre (BARC). According too an unnamed senior official of the Dept. of Atomic Energy (DAE) quoted by *Aviation Week & Space Technology* (19 June 2000), this split indicated that nuclear warheads for India's armed forces had entered series production. The separation "means the weaponization program at BARC is completed," explained the official. "It is a clear assertion that BARC does not want the AERB to look into its weaponization program." Instead, BARC will have an internal safety committee, which was set up by BARC Director, Anil Kakodkar.

The order for the split issued by Atomic Energy Commission (AEC) Chairman, Rajgopalan Chidambaram stated, "The regulatory and safety mechanism of BARC and its functions, hitherto exercised by the AERB, will henceforth be exercised through an internal safety committee structure to be constituted by the BARC director....

This is being done so as to ensure safety of the strategic nuclear program." Chidambaram added that the regulatory body is "always transparent" and has frequent interactions with the public. He said that BARC's internal committee will ensure compliance "wherever applicable" with the principles of good safety management as given in safety standards developed by the AERB. Despite the assertion of 'transparency' Chidambaram, speaking to a UNI reporter declined to give any details of the new committee saying that it was of strategic importance and details could not be revealed.

The DAE official said, "Most weapon laboratories have their internal checks systems, the Lawrence Livermore [Laboratories] in the U.S. being an example." However, he omitted to mention that in the U.S. the Department of Energy maintains independent oversight with the Defense Nuclear Facility Safety Board (DNFSB) which even includes reviewers outside of the DOE.

Further insight on the significance of this split was added in a *Times of India* article on 15 June 2000. S. Rajagopal, an expert on nuclear affairs and a professor of the Bangalore-based National

Institute of Advanced Studies, observed that this decision effectively reclassified BARC as a nuclear weapons laboratory. "This in turn will eliminate the need to place it under the International Atomic Energy Agency (IAEA) safeguards programme," he said.

Chidambaram's eight years in office as Chairman of the Atomic Energy Commission ended on 30 November 2000 when he was replaced by Dr. Anil Kakodkar today took charge as AEC Chairman, and as Secretary to the Government of India, Department of Atomic Energy in a brief ceremony held at Anushakti Bhavan, CSM Marg, Mumbai. Kakodkar This continued the tradition since Vikram Sarabhai's death in 1971 of having the top official in Atomic Energy be a leader of India's nuclear weapon program. As BARC director, Kakodkar had been the principal scientist involved in the May 1998 nuclear tests.

NUCLEAR POWER GROWTH IN INDIA

India now envisages to increase the contribution of nuclear power to overall electricity generation capacity from 2.8% to 9% within 25 years. By 2020, India's installed nuclear power generation capacity will increase to 20,000 MW (2.0×10 Watts, which is 20 GW). As of 2009, India stands 9th in the world in terms of number of operational nuclear power reactors. Indigenous atomic reactors include TAPS-3, and -4, both of which are 540 MW reactors. India's US$717 million fast breeder reactor project is expected to be operational by 2012-13.

The Indian nuclear power industry is expected to undergo a significant expansion in the coming years, in part due to the passing of theU.S.-India Civil Nuclear Agreement. This agreement will allow India to carry out trade of nuclear fuel and technologies with other countries and significantly enhance its power generation capacity. When the agreement goes through, India is expected to generate an additional 25,000 MW of nuclear power by 2020, bringing total estimated nuclear power generation to 45,000 MW.

India has already been using imported enriched uranium for light-water reactors that are currently under IAEA safeguards, but it has developed other aspects of the nuclear fuel cycle to support its reactors. Development of select technologies has been strongly affected by limited imports. Use of heavy water reactors has been particularly attractive for the nation because it allows Uranium to be burnt with little to no enrichment capabilities. India has also done a great amount of work in the development of a thorium centred fuel cycle. While uranium deposits in the nation are limited there are much greater reserves of thorium and it could provide hundreds of times the energy with the same mass of fuel. The fact that thorium can theoretically be utilised in heavy water reactors has tied the development of the two. A prototype reactor that would burn Uranium-Plutonium fuel while irradiating a thorium blanket is under construction at Kalpakkam by BHAVINI - another public sector enterprise like NPCIL

Uranium used for the weapons programme has been separated from the power programme, using uranium from indigenous reserves. This domestic reserve of 80,000 to 112,000 tons of uranium (approx 1% of global uranium reserves) is large enough to supply all of India's commercial and military reactors as well as supply all the needs of India's nuclear weapons arsenal. Currently, India's nuclear power reactors consume, at most, 478 tonnes of uranium per year. Even if India were quadruple its nuclear power output (and reactor base) to 20 GW by 2020, nuclear power generation would only consume 2000 tonnes of uranium per annum. Based on India's known commercially viable reserves of 80,000 to 112,000 tons of uranium, this represents a 40–50 years uranium supply for India's nuclear power reactors (note with reprocessing and breeder reactor technology, this supply could be stretched out many times over). Furthermore, the uranium requirements of India's Nuclear Arsenal are only a fifteenth (1/15) of that required for power generation (approx. 32 tonnes), meaning that India's domestic fissile material supply is more than enough to meet all needs for it strategic nuclear arsenal. Therefore, India has sufficient uranium resources to meet its strategic and power requirements for the foreseeable future.

Indian President A.P.J.Abdul Kalam, stated while he was in office, that "energy independence is India's first and highest priority. India has to go for nuclear power generation in a big way using thorium-based reactors. Thorium, a non fissile material is available in abundance in our country." India has vast thorium reserves and quite limited uranium reserves.

Nuclear Power Plants

Anti-nuclear Protests

Following the March 2011 Fukushima nuclear disaster in Japan, populations around proposed Indian NPP sites have launched protests that had found resonance around the country. There have been mass protests against the French-backed 9900 MW Jaitapur Nuclear Power Project in Maharashtra and the 2000 MW Koodankulam Nuclear Power Plant in Tamil Nadu. The Government of West Bengalrefused permission to a proposed 6000 MW facility near the town of Haripur that intended to host 6 Russian reactors. But that now is disputed: it's possible for Bengal to have its first nuclear power plant at Haripur despite resistance. A Public-interest litigation (PIL) has also been filed against the government's civil nuclear programme at the Supreme Court. The PIL specifically asks for the "staying of all proposed nuclear power plants till satisfactory safety measures and cost-benefit analyses are completed by independent agencies". But the Supreme Court said it was not an expert in the nuclear field to issue a direction to the government on the nuclear liability issue.

INDIAN NUCLEAR POWER

- India has a flourishing and largely indigenous nuclear power program and expects to have 14,600 MWe nuclear capacity on line by 2020. It aims to supply 25% of electricity from nuclear power by 2050.
- Because India is outside the Nuclear Non-Proliferation Treaty due to its weapons program, it was for 34 years largely excluded from trade in nuclear plant or materials, which has hampered its development of civil nuclear energy until 2009.
- Due to these trade bans and lack of indigenous uranium, India has uniquely been developing a nuclear fuel cycle to exploit its reserves of thorium.

- Now, foreign technology and fuel are expected to boost India's nuclear power plans considerably. All plants will have high indigenous engineering content.
- India has a vision of becoming a world leader in nuclear technology due to its expertise in fast reactors and thorium fuel cycle.

India's primary energy consumption more than doubled between 1990 and 2011 to nearly 25,000 PJ. India's dependence on imported energy resources and the inconsistent reform of the energy sector are challenges to satisfying rising demand.

Electricity demand in India is increasing rapidly, and the 1052 billion kilowatt hours gross produced in 2011 was more than triple the 1990 output, though still represented only some 750 kWh per capita for the year. With huge transmission losses – 222 TWh in 2011, this resulted in only about 774 billion kWh consumption. Gross generation comprised 836 TWh from fossil fuels, 33 TWh from nuclear, 131 TWh from hydro and 53 TWh from other renewables. Coal provides 68% of the electricity at present, but reserves are limited. Gas provides 15%, hydro 12%. The per capita electricity consumption figure is expected to double by 2020, with 6.3% annual growth, and reach 5000-6000 kWh by 2050, requiring about 8000 TWh/yr then. There is an acute demand for more and more reliable power supplies. One-third of the population is not connected to any grid.

At mid-2012, 203 GWe was on line with 20.5 GWe having been added in 12 months. In September 2012 it had 211 GWe. The government's 12th five-year plan for 2012-17 is targeting the addition of 94 GWe over the period, costing $247 billion. Three quarters of this would be coal- or lignite-fired, and only 3.4 GWe nuclear, including two imported 1000 MWe units planned at one site and two indigenous 700 MWe units at another. By 2032 total installed capacity of 700 GWe is planned to meet 7-9% GDP growth, and this was to include 63 GWe nuclear. The OECD's International Energy Agency predicts that India will need some $1600 billion investment in power generation, transmission and distribution to 2035. India has five electricity grids – Northern, Eastern, North-Eastern, Southern and Western. All of them are interconnected to some extent, except the Southern grid. All are run by the state-owned Power Grid Corporation of India Ltd (PGCI), which operates more than 95,000 circuit km of transmission lines. In July 2012 the Northern grid failed with 35,669 MWe load in the early morning, and the following day it plus parts of two other grids failed again so that over 600 million people in 22 states were without power for up to a day.

A KPMG report in 2007 said that India needed to spend US$ 120-150 billion on power infrastructure over the next five years, including transmission and distribution (T&D). It said that T&D losses were some 30-40%, worth more than $6 billion per year. A 2012 report costs the losses as $12.6 billion per year. A 2012 report costs the losses as $12.6 billion per year. A 2010 estimate shows big differences among states, with some very high, and a national average of 27% T&D loss, well above the target 15% set in 2001 when the average figure was 34%. Installed transmission capacity is only about 13% of generation capacity.

Nuclear power supplied 20 billion kWh (3.7%) of India's electricity in 2011 from 4.4 GWe (of 180 GWe total) capacity and after a dip in 2008-09 this is increasing as imported uranium becomes available and new plants come on line. Some 350 reactor-years of operation had been achieved by the end of 2011. India's fuel situation, with shortage of fossil fuels, is driving the nuclear investment for electricity, and 25% nuclear contribution is the ambition for 2050, when 1094 GWe of base-load capacity is expected to be required. Almost as much investment in the grid system as in power plants is necessary.

The target since about 2004 has been for nuclear power to provide 20 GWe by 2020, but in 2007 the Prime Minister referred to this as "modest" and capable of being "doubled with the opening up of international cooperation." However, it is evident that even the 20 GWe target would require substantial uranium imports. In June 2009 NPCIL said it aimed for 60 GWe nuclear by 2032, including 40 GWe of PWR capacity and 7 GWe of new PHWR capacity, all fuelled by imported uranium. This 2032 target was reiterated late in 2010 and increased to 63 GWe in 2011. But in December 2011 parliament was told that more realistic targets were 14,600 MWe by 2020-21 and 27,500 MWe by 2032, relative to present 4780 MWe and 10,080 MWe when reactors under construction were on line in 2017.*

* "the XII Plan proposals are being finalized which envisage start of work on eight indigenous 700 MW Pressurised Heavy Water Reactors (PHWRs), two 500 MW Fast Breeder Reactors (FBRs), one 300 MW Advanced Heavy Water Reactor (AHWR) and eight Light Water Reactors of 1000 MW or higher capacity with foreign technical cooperation. These nuclear power reactors are expected to be completed progressively in the XIII and XIV Plans."

The 16 PHWRS and LWRs are expected to cost $40 billion. The eight 700 MWe PHWRs would be built at Kaiga in Karnataka, Gorakhpur in Haryana's Fatehabad District, Banswada in Rajasthan, and Chutka(in Madhya Pradesh.

After liability legislation started to deter foreign reactor vendors, early in 2102 the government said it wanted to see coal production increase by 150 Mt/yr (from 440 Mt/yr) to support 60 GWe new coal-fired capacity to be built by 2015. This would involve Rs 56 billion new investment in rail infrastructure.

Longer term, the Atomic Energy Commission however envisages some 500 GWe nuclear on line by 2060, and has since speculated that the amount might be higher still: 600-700 GWe by 2050, providing half of all electricity. Another projection is for nuclear share to rise to 9% by 2037.

INDIAN NUCLEAR POWER INDUSTRY DEVELOPMENT

Nuclear power for civil use is well established in India. Its civil nuclear strategy has been directed towards complete independence in the nuclear fuel cycle, necessary because it is excluded from the 1970 Nuclear Non-Proliferation Treaty (NPT) due to it acquiring nuclear weapons capability after 1970. (Those five countries doing so before 1970 were accorded the status of Nuclear Weapons States under the NPT.)

As a result, India's nuclear power program has proceeded largely without fuel or technological assistance from other countries. Its power reactors to the mid-1990s had some of the world's lowest capacity factors, reflecting the technical difficulties of the country's isolation, but rose impressively from 60% in 1995 to 85% in 2001-02. Then in 2008-10 the load factors dropped due to shortage of uranium fuel.

India's nuclear energy self-sufficiency extended from uranium exploration and mining through fuel fabrication, heavy water production, reactor design and construction, to reprocessing and waste management. It has a small fast breeder reactor and is building a much larger one. It is also developing technology to utilise its abundant resources of thorium as a nuclear fuel.

The Atomic Energy Establishment was set up at Trombay, near Mumbai, in 1957 and renamed as Bhabha Atomic Research Centre (BARC) ten years later. Plans for building the first Pressurised Heavy Water Reactor (PHWR) were finalised in 1964, and this prototype – Rajasthan 1, which had Canada's Douglas Point reactor as a reference unit, was built as a collaborative venture between Atomic Energy of Canada Ltd (AECL) and NPCIL. It started up in 1972 and was duplicated Subsequent indigenous PHWR development has been based on these units, though several stages of evolution can be identified: PHWRs with dousing and single containment at Rajasthan 1-2, PHWRs with suppression pool and partial double containment at Madras, and later standardized PHWRs from Narora onwards having double containment, suppression pool, and calandria filled with heavy water, housed in a water-filled calandria vault.

The Indian Atomic Energy Commission (AEC) is the main policy body. The Nuclear Power Corporation of India Ltd (NPCIL) is responsible for design, construction, commissioning and operation of thermal nuclear power plants. At the start of 2010 it said it had enough cash on hand for 10,000 MWe of new plant. Its funding model is 70% equity and 30% debt financing. However, it is aiming to involve other public sector and private corporations in future nuclear power expansion, notably National Thermal Power Corporation (NTPC) – see subsection below. NTPC is very much larger than NPCIL and sees itself as the main power producer. NTPC is largely government-owned. The 1962 Atomic Energy Act prohibits private control of nuclear power generation, though it allows minority investment. As of late 2010 the government had no intention of changing this to allow greater private equity in nuclear plants.

NUCLEAR REACTORS DEPLOYED IN INDIA

The two Tarapur150 MWe Boiling Water Reactors (BWRs) built by GE on a turnkey contract before the advent of the Nuclear Non-Proliferation Treaty were originally 200 MWe. They were down-rated due to recurrent problems but have run well since. They have been using imported enriched uranium and are under International Atomic Energy Agency (IAEA) safeguards. However, late in 2004 Russia deferred to the Nuclear Suppliers' Group and declined to supply further uranium for them. They underwent six months refurbishment over 2005-06, and in March 2006 Russia agreed to resume fuel supply. In December 2008 a $700 million contract with Rosatom was announced for continued uranium supply to them.

The two small Canadian (Candu) PHWRs at Rajasthan nuclear power plant started up in 1972 & 1980, and are also under safeguards. Rajasthan 1 was down-rated early in its life and has operated very little since 2002 due to ongoing problems and has been shut down since 2004 as the government considers its future. Rajasthan 2 was restarted in September 2009 after major refurbishment, and running on imported uranium at full rated power.

The 220 MWe PHWRs(202 MWe net) were indigenously designed and constructed by NPCIL, based on a Canadian design. The only accident to an Indian nuclear plant was due to a turbine hall fire in 1993 at Narora, which resulted in a 17-hour total station blackout. There was no core damage or radiological impact and it was rated 3 on the INES scale – a 'serious incident'.

The Madras(MAPS) reactors were refurbished in 2002-03 and 2004-05 and their capacity restored to 220 MWe gross (from 170). Much of the core of each reactor was replaced, and the lifespans extended to 2033/36. Kakrapar unit 1 was fully refurbished and upgraded in 2009-10, after 16 years operation, as was Narora 2, with cooling channel (calandria tube) replacement. Following the Fukushima accident in March 2011, four NPCIL taskforces evaluated the situation in India and in an interim report in July made recommendations for safety improvements of the Tarapur BWRs and each PHWR type. The report of a high-level committee appointed by the Atomic Energy Regulatory Board (AERB) was submitted at the end of August 2011, saying that the Tarapur and Madras plants needed some supplementary provisions to cope with major disasters. The two Tarapur BWRs have already been upgraded to ensure continuous cooling of the reactor during prolonged station blackouts and to provide nitrogen injection to containment structures, but further work is recommended. Madras needs enhanced flood defences in case of tsunamis higher than that in 2004. The prototype fast breeder reactor (PFR) under construction next door at Kalpakkam has defences which are already sufficiently high, following some flooding of the site in 2004.

The Tarapur 3&4 reactors of 540 MWe gross (490 MWe net) were developed indigenously from the 220 MWe (gross) model PHWR and were built by NPCIL. The first – Tarapur 4 – was connected to the grid in June 2005 and started commercial operation in September. Tarapur 4's criticality came five years after pouring first concrete and seven months ahead of schedule. Its twin – unit 3 – was about a year behind it and was connected to the grid in June 2006 with commercial operation in August, five months ahead of schedule. Tarapur 3 & 4 cost about $1200/kW, and are competitive with imported coal. Future indigenous PHWR reactors will be 700 MWe gross (640 MWe net). The first four are being built at Kakrapar and Rajasthan. They are due on line by 2017 after 60 months construction from first concrete to criticality. Cost is quoted at about Rs 12,000 crore (120 billion rupees) each, or $1700/kW. Up to 40% of the fuel they use will be slightly enriched uranium (SEU) – about 1.1% U-235, to achieve higher fuel burn-up – about 21,000 MWd/t instead of one third of this. Initially this fuel will be imported as SEU.

Kudankulam 1&2: Russia's Atomstroyexport is supplying the country's first large nuclear power plant, comprising two VVER-

1000 (V-412) reactors, under a Russian-financed US$ 3 billion contract. A long-term credit facility covers about half the cost of the plant. The AES-92 units at Kudankulam in Tamil Nadu state have been built by NPCIL and also commissioned and operated by NPCIL under IAEA safeguards. The turbines are made by Leningrad Metal Works. Unlike other Atomstroyexport projects such as in Iran, there have been only about 80 Russian supervisory staff on the job. Construction started in March 2002.

Russia is supplying all the enriched fuel through the life of the plant, though India will reprocess it and keep the plutonium*. The first unit was due to start supplying power in March 2008 and go into commercial operation late in 2008, but this schedule has slipped by five years. In the latter part of 2011 and into 2012 completion and fuel loading was delayed by public protests, but in March 2012 the state government approved the plant's commissioning and said it would deal with any obstruction. Fuel loading was in September, and unit 1 started up in mid-July 2013, with unit 2 expected to do so early in 2014. Unit 1 was connected to the grid in October 2013 and is expected in commercial operation at full power early in 2014, with unit 2 following in October 2014. Each is 917 MWe net.

While the first core load of fuel was delivered early in 2008 there have been delays in supply of some equipment and documentation. Control system documentation was delivered late, and when reviewed by NPCIL it showed up the need for significant refining and even reworking some aspects. The design basis flood level is 5.44m, and the turbine hall floor is 8.1m above mean sea level. The 2004 tsunami was under 3m.

A small desalination plant is associated with the Kudankulam plant to produce 426 m^3/hr for it using four-stage multi-vacuum compression (MVC) technology. Another reverse osmosis (RO) plant is in operation to supply local township needs.

Kaiga 3 started up in February, was connected to the grid in April and went into commercial operation in May 2007. Unit 4 started up in November 2010 and was grid-connected in January 2011, but is about 30 months behind original schedule due to shortage of uranium. The Kaiga units are not under UN safeguards, so cannot use imported uranium. Rajasthan 5 started up in November 2009, using imported Russian fuel, and in December it was connected to the northern grid. RAPP 6 started up in January 2010 and was grid connected at the end of March. Both are now in commercial operation.

Under plans for the India-specific safeguards to be administered by the IAEA in relation to the civil-military separation plan, eight further reactors were to be safeguarded (beyond Tarapur 1&2, Rajasthan 1&2, and Kudankulam 1&2): Rajasthan 3&4 from 2010, Rajasthan 5&6 from 2008, Kakrapar 1&2 by 2012 and Narora 1&2 by 2014.

In mid-2008 Indian nuclear power plants were running at about half of capacity due to a chronic shortage of fuel. Average load factor for India's power reactors dipped below 60% over 2006-2010, reaching only 40% in 2008. Some easing after 2008 was due to the new Turamdih mill in Jharkhand state coming on line (the mine there was already operating). Political opposition has delayed new mines in Jharkhand, Meghalaya and Andhra Pradesh.

A 500 MWe prototype fast breeder reactor (PFBR) is under construction at Kalpakkam near Madras by BHAVINI (Bharatiya Nabhikiya Vidyut Nigam Ltd), a government enterprise set up under DAE to focus on FBRs. It was expected to start up about the end of 2010 and produce power in 2011, but this schedule is delayed significantly. Construction was reported 94% complete in February 2013. Four further oxide-fuel fast reactors are envisaged but slightly redesigned by the Indira Gandhi Centre to reduce capital cost. One pair will be at Kalpakkam, two more elsewhere.

In contrast to the situation in the 1990s, most reactors under construction more recently have been on schedule (apart from fuel shortages 2007-09), and the first two – Tarapur 3&4 – were slightly increased in capacity. These and future planned ones were 450 (now 490) MWe versions of the 202 MWe domestic products. Beyond them and the last three 202 MWe units, future units will be nominal 700 MWe.

The government envisages setting up about ten PHWRs of 700 MWe capacity to about 2023, fuelled by indigenous uranium, as stage 1 of its nuclear program. Stage 2 – four 500 MWe FBRs –

will be concurrent. Construction costs of reactors as reported by AEC are about $1200 per kilowatt for Tarapur 3&4 (540 MWe), $1300/kW for Kaiga 3 & 4 (220 MWe) and expected $1700/kW for the 700 MWe PHWRs with 60-year life expectancy.

INDIA'S NUCLEAR POWER PROBLEM

In January 2010, before the nuclear disaster in Fukushima, Japan, and before the anti-nuclear protests in India spread nationwide, Anuradha Talwar was tallying up a demographic survey of the people of Haripur, a rural coastal village in West Bengal. Sitting on a tiled veranda, alternating between using her cell phone and directing the small army of young women sifting through spreadsheets, Talwar was determined to count every man, woman, and child who would lose their homes to accommodate a 10,000 megawatt nuclear reactor complex, the largest on the subcontinent. According to a senior government official, Haripur is an inhospitable environment where "most of the land [has] a high saline content and cannot be used for agriculture." Talwar knows better. The nuclear power complex would in fact evict some two hundred thousand farmers and fishermen. She dismisses the government's claim that Haripur is a barren wasteland by recalling the sumptuous meal of home-grown vegetables and fragrant fish curry that villagers prepared for her the previous evening.

A plump, soft-faced, middle-aged woman with thinning grey hair and sizeable *bindi*, she does not come across as someone who would lead the opposition against the West Bengal state government's attempted land grab. But Talwar, whose surname means "sword" in Bengali, has spent decades fighting for human rights and sustainable development in sectors as diverse as health care, gender equality, labour practices, disaster relief, malnutrition, and starvation. To her and to the villagers in Haripur, nuclear power is nothing special. They are not impressed by the prospects of developing a carbon-free energy system that would mitigate climate change. Nor are they drawn into the debate over the risks and uncertainties of generating nuclear energy. To them, what matters is that livelihoods are in jeopardy.

Similar scenes of resistance are rippling throughout India as the government of Prime Minister Manmohan Singh undertakes a massive expansion of the nation's nuclear energy program. In communities affected by India's growing nuclear power infrastructure, activists like Talwar are conducting surveys, handing out pamphlets, forming committees, contacting journalists, and staging protests. In some places, including Haripur, resistance to nuclear energy plans has even turned violent.

What is noteworthy about the bourgeoning local activism is how often it differs from the campaigns led by established anti-nuclear groups, who typically focus on the morality of nuclear weapons or the risk of a cataclysmic nuclear power plant accident. Instead, India's new grassroots activists are struggling against the government's nuclear energy plans for a wider variety of reasons, ranging from ingrained distrust of the government due to corruption and lack of accountability, to tangible local concerns such as losing land rights and economic livelihoods. The affected communities, largely comprised of farmers, fisherman, and miners, are essentially concerned with the broad and deep issues of democracy, citizenship, and government responsibility. At its core, the resistance is challenging the distribution of power and how it governs relationships between the state, citizens, and private interests.

A dramatic case in point is the rising furor over the Koodankulam nuclear plant in the state of Tamil Nadu, at the southern tip of India. Protests that intensified after the Fukushima accident forced officials to delay the commissioning of the plant, scheduled to go critical last December. In March, hundreds of protesters from farming and fishing communities, many of them women, converged on the nearby village of Idinthakarai in an effort to halt construction activities at Koodankulam. Led by local resident and long-time anti-nuclear activist S. P. Udaykumar, they organized demonstrations and began a relay fast. In response, authorities placed Idinthakarai under martial law and arrested some two hundred protesters. Reports say that activists were beaten and subjected to religious profiling and open mob violence, while Singh apportioned the blame for the protests against

Koodankulam on foreign hands. The stirring of Indian unrest over a program ostensibly intended to boost India's broad economic fortunes and reduce the nation's contribution to global warming is a cautionary tale of what can go wrong when policies are formulated primarily around technological considerations at the expense of profound concerns related to community well-being, culture, and justice.

In undertaking a massive project destined to directly impact the lives of millions of citizens, the Indian lesson shows it is essential that governments bolster democratic institutions and foster a transparent airing of all concerns. These would include questions about whether and how land should be acquired for nuclear infrastructure development, what kinds of compensation and rehabilitation would be due to displaced communities, how the government should recognize tribal identity and sovereignty over resources, and what responsibilities the government has towards safeguarding the health of communities, such as uranium miners, who are embedded from the very start in the nuclear economy. The debate from the community to the national level should include the question whether nuclear energy is even the right choice for Indian energy security.

ONWARD TOWARD MODERNITY

Indian leaders grasped the significance of harnessing the atom after Independence in 1947. Nuclear technology was a potent sign of all things modern, synonymous with progress, self-reliance, and development. It would catapult India toward parity with the West by supplying the country's farthest reaches with energy as well as further securing its borders with nuclear weapons.

The government of Jawaharlal Nehru, tapping the nuclear physicist, Homi J. Bhabha, established the country's Atomic Energy Commission (AEC) in 1948 and then the Department of Atomic Energy (DAE) in 1954. From the outset, India's nuclear establishment operated with an obsession for secrecy. The government barred other public and private institutions from studying nuclear issues. The AEC and DAE were, and remain to this day, solely accountable to the prime minister.

After Independence, India decided that nuclear technology should be used to develop weapons for national security rather than to power economic growth. India refused to sign the 1968 Non-Proliferation Treaty (NPT), a pact designed to curb nuclear weapons that has now been joined by 190 nations and in 1974, ten years after neighbouring China conducted its first nuclear weapon test, India detonated a nuclear device at the Pokhran Test Range in Rajasthan. It was the first confirmed such test by a nation not serving as a permanent member of the United Nations Security Council, and was followed by another nuclear test in 1998 under the right-wing Bharatiya Janata Party. India's nuclear ambitions, though enhancing its military strength, risked isolating the country in international affairs and the nuclear establishment's culture of secrecy deepened.

India shifted course dramatically after Singh's election in 2004. His government now openly sought foreign assistance to develop nuclear energy, in sharp contrast with India's prior focus on creating a homegrown system that would exploit India's vast thorium reserves. Citing reasons such as combating climate change, galvanizing its innovation economy, and reducing dependence on coal energy, Singh promoted nuclear energy as a major component of India's future energy portfolio.

Political ostracism quickly turned into talk of partnership and new beginnings. The United States saw in India a strategic counterbalance to China, a partner in climate change mitigation, and a necessary foothold in a region characterized by turmoil in Pakistan and Afghanistan. In 2005, Singh and then-U.S. President George W. Bush initiated the U.S.-India Civil Nuclear Agreement, which was completed and signed in 2008. The bilateral accord for peaceful, civilian nuclear cooperation allows India to pursue nuclear commerce with the Nuclear Suppliers Group, without being required to sign the NPT. In exchange, India ceded oversight of self-identified civilian nuclear energy facilities to the International Atomic Energy Agency. In addition to the United States, nations such as Australia, France, Argentina, Mongolia, Kazakhstan, Russia, the United Kingdom, Canada, and South Korea pledged technological know-how and access to uranium reserves to help India achieve its nuclear energy ambitions. Currently, nuclear energy provides less than 3 percent of India's electricity needs. Since Apsara, India's first nuclear reactor and built from British plans, became operational in 1956, only twenty more reactors have been constructed and they all are operating well below capacity. India's nuclear endeavours have become notorious for cost overruns. Nonetheless, Singh has set his sights high. His target is to increase India's installed capacity more than sevenfold to 35,000 MWe by the year 2022, and to 60,000 MWe by 2032.[3]

India's 1998 nuclear weapons test galvanized the anti-nuclear movement, which has since greeted Singh's plans for developing nuclear energy with deep suspicion. Consisting of middle-class journalists, writers, scientists, and academics, the movement repeats a mantra that warns of the possibilities of nuclear war and of nuclear accidents like Three Mile Island, Chernobyl, and Fukushima. They also question the morality of nuclear weapons, the geopolitical downsides to being a nuclear power, the undemocratic nature of India's nuclear establishment, and the impact of radioactive waste on the environment and public health. The movement sees the need to mobilize political support and scientific expertise in the cause; it conducts its own studies, stages protests, publishes articles, and participates in national and international workshops and conferences.

What these vanguard anti-nuclear activists—not to mention the Indian government—have failed to fully appreciate, but are now rapidly taking seriously, is the stirring of unrest in local communities far removed from expert debates over technical pros and cons. Socio-economic as well as environmental grievances are being voiced in disparate regions of the country, from West Bengal and Tamil Nadu to the states of Haryana and Maharashtra, where new nuclear power plants are planned in primarily fertile farmlands near fishing grounds. Protests are also rising in the historically marginalized tribal communities in the states of Meghalaya and Andhra Pradesh, due to central government's redoubled efforts to open new mines in these regions, believed to contain large reserves of high-grade uranium needed in nuclear technology.

The Case of Haripur

In trying to build nuclear power plants in West Bengal, the state has been confronted by a number of legacies: the history of local Communist rule; a cultural memory of violent resistance to British colonialism; a movement against Special Economic Zones (SEZs) in response to neo-liberal economic policies in the 1990s; and a deep suspicion of the nuclear establishment. The Communist Party of India-Marxist (CPI-M) governed West Bengal from 1977 to 2011. It is a pro-peasant party that favors rural development over industrialization.

The neo-liberal policies that brought wealth to technopolises like Bangalore and Chennai sidestepped West Bengal, leaving it impoverished and economically stagnant. West Bengal Chief Minister Buddhadeb Bhattacharya defied the party line and attempted to usher in liberalization and industrialization through strong-arm tactics. In 2006, the state forcibly acquired land—via the colonial Land Acquisitions Act from 1894—in order to establish SEZs. These industrial enclaves bypass bureaucratic red tape and cumbersome legal technicalities, including labour laws, to rapidly create products for export and service markets.

Public uproar ensued. Anger boiled over when the West Bengal government sought to acquire the villages of Singur in 2006, and Nandigram in 2007, for a Tata Nano car plant and a chemical factory, respectively. The villages are located near Haripur in an area with a history of bloody violence around land rights during colonial rule. One morning in January 2007, without warning, the government posted public eviction notices in Nandigram. Thousands of villagers swarmed to the state police department in protest. West Bengal police and CPI-M thugs alike fired on a group of around four thousand villagers. Official estimates say that fourteen people were killed, but villagers place the number in the hundreds. Reports said that countless women and girls were raped, and hundreds of village homes were burnt although atrocities were committed on both sides. In the previous year, the state government suspended democratic rights in Singur amid bloodshed that included the rape and murder of an eighteen-year-old activist.

The SEZ violence, while not directly related to anti-nuclear protests, nevertheless helps illustrate how local political and social dynamics, rather than technological issues alone, have an important influence in the campaign against the government's nuclear energy ambitions. In Nandigram and Singur, community activism was spearheaded by Anuradha Talwar's organization, the West Bengal Agricultural Workers Union, also known by its Bengali acronym, PBKMS. For example, the group pursued an independent fact-finding mission to investigate police atrocities, violence committed by villagers, and Communist party infighting. Earlier, in 2006, PBKMS mobilized six thousand villagers to create a bamboo barricade to prevent scientists, engineers, and police from entering the village to perform soil tests for the Nuclear Power Corporation of India. Talwar and her colleagues opposed potential human displacement and the lack of transparency concerning its consequences.

FROM THE WEST KHASI HILLS TO JADUGODA

Protests against uranium mining have evolved as an integral part of the grassroots movement against India's nuclear energy program. Until the ban on nuclear trade with India was lifted, the lack of sufficient reserves of high-quality uranium was considered the Achilles' heel of India's nuclear program. After the U.S.-India nuclear deal, the central government set its sights on the West Khasi Hills in the state of Meghalaya to open a new uranium mine believed to contain some two hundred and seventy-five thousand tons of uranium. If the project does go through, as many as thirty thousand Khasi *adivasi*, or tribal people, may be displaced, and 351 hectares of land will be acquired from seventy-two villages. The Uranium Corporation of India Limited (UCIL), a public sector arm of the Department of Atomic Energy, built the first open cast uranium mine in Jadugoda in Jharkhand in 1967. (Jharkhand became India's first tribal state in 2000, carved from the state of Bihar.)

The Khasi opposition to uranium mining must be taken in the context of an ambivalent colonial and post-colonial tribal policy. Colonization was a force of economic, political, and cultural transformation that displaced and dispossessed *adivasi* communities. After an early history of violent and brutal repression, the British created protective enclaves for tribal groups, which were adopted by the post-colonial government after Independence, and are governed by the Fifth and Sixth Schedules of the Indian Constitution. The Schedules allow tribal regions to create self-governing, autonomous districts, to give tribes jurisdiction over land use, property inheritance, marriage, and social customs. The Khasis are protected under the Sixth Schedule.

The Khasi Students' Union (KSU), formed in 1978, has a slogan: "We are Khasi by blood, Indian by accident." The KSU's opposition to uranium mining stems partly from its history of xenophobic activities. Alleged KSU members killed a bus-load of non-tribals in 1979. The group has sought to ban non-tribals from the local economy unless they joined *adivasi* business partners. They have opposed the construction of railroads in the fear it would facilitate the influx of outsiders. In opposing uranium mining, the KSU's primary target is the intrusion of foreign technicians, engineers, and cheap labour. A KSU letter written to the state of Meghalaya's chief minister in 2004 stated: "We will not part with even an inch of our ancestral land to the foreigners who we consider our enemies."[8] A member of the Meghalaya People's Human Rights Council presents a more measured but no less alarmist view of the threat mining poses to the Khasi: "The illiterate and semi-literate indigenous Khasi will be forced to move out of their homes and landholdings to be supplanted by technologically advanced communities from outside the state. The mining township will become like military cantonment prohibited to all local people. This will upset the demographic structure of the areas, and ultimately of the entire state, thus not only rendering us a minority but also reducing us to the level of unwanted outsiders in our own land."

Other Khasi complaints derive from the rhetoric of identity politics. Khasis question why *adivasis* should be sacrificed for the greater good of India, an entity they see as a colonizing force. Why should the Khasis, activists ask, be forced to forfeit their rights to their land, subject themselves to grave health hazards, and face displacement to make room for uranium mines that will supply fuel for remote nuclear plants and a national nuclear weapons program? Furthermore, uranium mining exposes fault lines within Meghalaya, pitting landowners who want uranium mining for jobs and economic growth, against villagers who refuse to relinquish commonly-owned land, to which they have cultural, economic, and emotional attachments.

The Jharkhand Organization Against Radiation (JOAR) in Jadugoda frames its grievances quite differently. Although almost all of the Jadugoda uranium miners belong to the Santhal and Ho tribes, JOAR does not pitch the struggle in terms of identity politics, but as a shared experience of suffering related to health and occupational hazards. Those working and living in Jadugoda want to be seen as "radiated bodies" suffering at the hands of the nuclear economy. A villager tells a reporter from *Tehelka* magazine, "We have seen too many deaths due to cancer and tuberculosis, too many deformed children, too many miscarriages among women. Too much sorrow. Our lives are governed by radiation. There is no escape from it."

The origins of uranium mining in Jadugoda are murky. No one seems to know exactly how land in the village, protected under the Fifth Schedule, was transferred from the state to central government. Anecdotal accounts are infused with a sense of betrayal, loss of autonomy, and intrusion. Radiation awareness came gradually, only when people began to notice that "rashes, deformities on fellow beings, cows were born without tails, fish with unknown skin diseases were being discovered, small animals, including mice, monkeys and rabbits were disappearing from the area."

Activists established JOAR in 1979, more than a decade after the first local uranium mine was opened. The group stepped up its campaign in 1996 when the UCIL, with the help of the district police and paramilitary forces, razed thirty homes near Jadugoda to build a third tailing dam. JOAR stages rallies, sit-ins and marches, and calls attention to its cause in national and international forums. Shriprakash Prakash's 1999 documentary, *Buddha Weeps in Jadugoda*—a title that mocks the codename for India's first nuclear test, "Smiling Buddha"—explores the devastating impact of uranium mining on local villagers. JOAR also attempts to seek recourse through legal and scientific institutions. It has tried to produce policy-relevant science data through health surveys and studies that tested the effects of low-level radiation. None of its efforts, however, met the scientific rigor expected for epidemiological surveys, and as a result have not been taken seriously by UCIL. For example, in 1988, UCIL and the state conducted their own health surveys, but did not see enough evidence to establish a connection between leached uranium and adverse health and environmental impacts. The UCIL maintains that it has always followed proper, scientific protocols in monitoring uranium mining operations.

In response to the accusations of health hazards, the UCIL chairman said, "Cancer in this region is not beyond the national average. Illnesses are largely due to malnutrition and an unhealthy lifestyle." JOAR also filed a public interest lawsuit, accusing the DAE and UCIL of dumping nuclear waste from hospitals and other nuclear facilities into Jadugoda's tailing ponds. The UCIL and DAE denied the charges and the case was dismissed.

UCIL, in turn, accuses JOAR of working against national interests, spreading misinformation, and inciting fear. Its behaviour illustrates the monumental task that organizations like JOAR face in contesting the government's nuclear policies. UCIL held public hearings in 2004, 2005, and 2009 about opening new uranium mines in the Jadugoda area but the hearings were carefully staged. The UCIL was accused of providing villagers with placards that read, "We will die later of alpha, beta, gamma, but we are dying everyday of hunger," and "We are not afraid of pollution; those who give us food, clothing, and shelter are our own people." A video captured and posted on YouTube purports to show paramilitary forces flanking a UCIL official during a hearing in December 2005. The official threatened in Hindi that the hearing was only for listening and not for speaking, and anyone caught voicing their opinions would face severe penalties.

Democracy and Citizenship

The Indian government's handling of its nuclear energy plans highlights the flaws in Indian democracy and the deep distrust that citizens have for government institutions. Cases such as Haripur, Khasi Hills, and Jadugoda underscore the need for robust and responsive democratic institutions, such as courts of law and other policy instruments, to mediate the relationship between the government and citizens. Citizenship is fundamentally about the social contract between an individual and the state, with the implicit understanding that power over individuals will not be exercised arbitrarily. A social contract implies certain rights for an individual and a government responsible for protecting those rights. Citizens should have recourse through institutional channels and have sufficient trust in such institutions that a fair and impartial judgment will be passed. In India, the terms of the social contract seem up for grabs and, increasingly, the only language understood by both parties is one of public protest, whether through peaceful civil disobedience or violence.

Opposition to the Haripur nuclear power plant is part of an older, violent struggle against land acquisition in West Bengal and its newest manifestation, the SEZs. For the villagers of Haripur, citizenship, in the sense of having rights to property, land, and fair treatment by the law, is not automatic but something to be fought for, violently if necessary. Violence is understood as part of a common political repertoire by both sides. The West Bengal state, for its part, with its eventual capitulation to the violent protests against SEZs, implicitly views the use of force as an acceptable (but not desirable) form of voicing grievances.

In contrast, the KSU's fight against the decision to begin uranium mining in the West Khasi Hills enlists the politics of identity, and to an unsettling degree, of xenophobia, to reject the conventions of Indian citizenship. The most fundamental question of power raised by the KSU is who gets to decide who lives where. Khasi suspicion of "mainland" India stems from decades of policies that controlled and developed tribal regions in ways that damaged or destroyed communities. Khasis see economic development in general, and uranium mining in particular, as a ploy for further marginalization. Protecting Khasi identity and culture in a way that does not engender violent identity politics and allows the benefits of economic development to come to the region in a sustainable and socially just manner will require the coordination of policies in a host of areas beyond the narrow field of nuclear energy. Policies such as land use, tribal development, and rehabilitation of displaced people.

The struggle of JOAR to receive national and international recognition for the health and environmental damage experienced by the adivasi community is a story about knowledge: about who has it and whether it counts, and how it can be turned into policy-relevant knowledge. JOAR and the people of Jadugoda attempted several times to speak to the government and UCIL on their terms—in terms of science and law—and thus employ the tools granted to them through citizenship. But at every turn, they were prevented from entering the corridors of power and expertise because those were precisely the two qualities they did not possess. For the people of Jadugoda, the power, secrecy, and absolute unaccountability of the nuclear establishment closed down any options of dialogue.

Just, Sustainable, Feasible

More than 412 million Indians have no access to electricity, and 668 million depend on biomass for cooking but it remains to be seen whether nuclear energy will help alleviate poverty. The concerns that Indian citizens have about nuclear energy, however, cannot be addressed solely by nuclear energy policy. A myriad of other policies and accompanying institutions must also be involved in the process. Yet, the Indian government has aggressively pursued a nuclear future without sufficient deliberation about how to create an energy development strategy that goes beyond the narrow scope of technological tools and economic growth.

India's checkered history with development projects, such as its building of large dams, shows that the state tends to equate public debate with automatic opposition to any development plan the government puts forth. This approach sets up false and unhelpful dichotomies between progress and tradition, modernity and backwardness, science and superstition, government and citizens. In this stark view, victims and villains are easily created in the public consciousness. The adivasi, women, forest-dwellers and fishermen become the heroic defenders of culture and tradition; state officials, entrepreneurs, and the affluent elite are scorned as the agents of a neo-colonial order. The stories from Haripur, Khasi Hills, and Jadugoda, however, resist easy classification or stereotyping. Political mobilizations against Indian nuclear energy plans are diverse and throng with competing motivations and values.

With the demand for low-carbon energy sources in the fight against global climate change, India's nuclear establishment sees itself as a major player in de-carbonization efforts. It likes to claim that the world, especially the South, is on the cusp of a nuclear renaissance. But, due to public distrust, the activities of India's anti-nuclear movement, and technological breakdowns in other sectors, the establishment is having an increasingly difficult time communicating its message. In the wake of Fukushima, Indian nuclear officials are portrayed as laughably out of touch when they go on record stating that the nuclear disaster in Japan was "purely a chemical reaction and not a nuclear emergency" and that "there was no nuclear accident or incident."

The Indian government would be wise to reconsider its vision of nuclear energy so that it does not seem limited to simply getting its technology right. Creating robust policy debates across domains such as solar and wind power will benefit India's energy development as a whole. Sociological and anthropological perspectives must be integrated into policy discussions. Advancing the principles of democracy such as citizenship rights and government accountability will promote critical thinking about maximizing the public good beyond a simple cost-benefit analysis of market economics. That is the best approach, if India is to have a nuclear energy program that is socially just, environmentally sustainable, and economically feasible.

INDIA AND WEAPONS OF MASS DESTRUCTION

India possesses nuclear weapons and maintains short- and intermediate-range ballistic missiles, nuclear-capable aircraft, surface ships, and submarines under development as possible delivery systems and platforms. Although it lacks an operational ballistic missile submarine, India has ambitions of possessing a nuclear triad in the near future when INS Arihant the lead ship of India's *Arihant* class of nuclear-powered submarines formally joins the Indian Navy in 2011 after undergoing extensive sea-trials. Though India has not made any official statements about the size of its nuclear arsenal, recent estimates suggest that India has between 80 and 100 nuclear weapons, consistent with earlier estimates that it had produced enough weapons-grade plutonium for up to 75–110 nuclear weapons. Production of weapons-grade plutonium is believed to be taking place at the Bhabha Atomic Research Centre, which is home to the CIRUS reactor, acquired from Canada and shut down in 2010, to the indigenous Dhruva reactor, and to a plutonium separation facility.

India is not a signatory to the 1968 Nuclear Non-Proliferation Treaty (NPT), which India argues entrenches the status quo of the existing nuclear weapons states whilst preventing general nuclear disarmament. India tested a nuclear device in 1974 (code-named "Smiling Buddha"), which it called a "peaceful nuclear explosion." The test used plutonium produced in the Canadian-supplied CIRUS reactor, and raised concerns that nuclear technology supplied for peaceful purposes could be diverted to weapons purposes. This also stimulated the early work of the Nuclear Suppliers Group. India performed further nuclear tests in 1998 (code-named "Operation Shakti").

India has signed and ratified both the Biological Weapons Convention and the Chemical Weapons Convention.

Brief Historical Overview

As early as 26 June 1946, Jawaharlal Nehru, soon to be India's first Prime Minister, announced:

"As long as the world is constituted as it is, every country will have to devise and use the latest devices for its protection. I have no doubt India will develop her scientific researches and I hope Indian scientists will use the atomic force for constructive purposes. But if India is threatened, she will inevitably try to defend herself by all means at her disposal. "

India's first nuclear test occurred on 18 May 1974. Since then India has conducted another series of tests at the Pokhran test range in the state of Rajasthan in 1998.

India has an extensive civil and military nuclear program, which includes at least 10 nuclear reactors, uranium mining and milling sites, heavy water production facilities, a uranium enrichment plant, fuel fabrication facilities, and extensive nuclear research capabilities.

In 1998, as a response to the continuing tests, the United States and Japan imposed temporary economic sanctions on India. Some nuclear experts have speculated that India obtained nuclear enrichment from illicit proliferation through the A.Q. Khan Network from Pakistan.

Current arsenal and estimates of inventory

- In 2005, it was estimated that India had between 40 and 50 warheads.
- In November 2008, the Bulletin of the Atomic Scientists estimated that India has about 70 assembled nuclear warheads, with about 50 of them fully operational.
- A report by David Albright, published by the Institute for Science and International Security in 2000, estimated that India at end of 1999 had 310 kilograms of weapon grade plutonium, enough for 65 nuclear weapons. He also estimated that India had 4,200 kg of reactor grade plutonium which is enough to build 1,000 nuclear weapons. By the end of 2004, he estimates India had 445 kilograms of weapon grade plutonium which is enough for around 85 nuclear weapons considering 5 kg of plutonium required for each weapon.
- As of February 2011, the Federation of American Scientists estimated that India had a stockpile of 80-100 weapons.
- Former R&AW official J.K. Sinha, claimed that India is capable of producing 130 kilograms of weapon grade plutonium per year from six "unsafeguarded" reactors not included in the nuclear deal between India and the United States.

Doctrine

India has a declared nuclear no-first-use policy and is in the process of developing a nuclear doctrine based on "credible minimum deterrence." In August 1999, the Indian government released a draft of the doctrine which asserts that nuclear weapons are solely for deterrence and that India will pursue a policy of "retaliation only". The document also maintains that India "will not be the first to initiate a nuclear first strike, but will respond with punitive retaliation should deterrence fail" and that decisions to authorize the use of nuclear weapons would be made by the Prime Minister or his 'designated successor(s).'"

According to the NRDC, despite the escalation of tensions between India and Pakistan in 2001-2002, India remains committed to its nuclear no-first-use policy.

Indian National Security Advisor Shri Shivshankar Menon signaled a significant shift from "No first use" to "no first use against non-nuclear weapon states" in a speech on the occasion of Golden Jubilee celebrations of National Defence College in New Delhi on October 21, 2010, a doctrine Menon said reflected India's "strategic culture, with its emphasis on minimal deterrence."

Command and control

India's Strategic Nuclear Command was formally established in 2003, with an Air Force officer, Air Marshal Asthana, as the Commander-in-Chief. The joint services SNC is the custodian of all of India's nuclear weapons, missiles and assets. It is also responsible for executing all aspects of India's nuclear policy. However, the civil leadership, in the form of the CCS (Cabinet Committee on Security) is the only body authorized to order a nuclear strike against another offending strike: In effect, it is the Prime Minister who has his finger "on the button."

International treaties

India is not a signatory to either the Nuclear Non-Proliferation Treaty (NPT) or the Comprehensive Test Ban Treaty (CTBT), but did accede to the Partial Test Ban Treaty in October 1963. India is a member of the International Atomic Energy Agency (IAEA), and four of its 17 nuclear reactors are subject to IAEA safeguards. India announced its lack of intention to accede to the NPT as late as 1997 by voting against the paragraph of a General Assembly Resolution which urged all non-signatories of the treaty to accede to it at the earliest possible date.

India voted against the UN General Assembly resolution endorsing the CTBT, which was adopted on 10 September 1996. India objected to the lack of provision for universal nuclear disarmament "within a time-bound framework." India also demanded that the treaty ban laboratory simulations. In addition, India opposed the provision in Article XIV of the CTBT that requires India's ratification for the treaty to enter into force, which India argued was a violation of its sovereign right to choose whether it would sign the treaty. In early February 1997, Foreign Minister I.K.Gujral reiterated India's opposition to the treaty, saying that "India favors any step aimed at destroying nuclear weapons, but considers that the treaty in its current form is not comprehensive and bans only certain types of tests."

In August 2008, the International Atomic Energy Agency (IAEA) approved safeguards agreement with India under which the former will gradually gain access to India's civilian nuclear reactors. In September 2008, the Nuclear Suppliers Group granted India a waiver allowing it to access civilian nuclear technology and fuel from other countries. The implementation of this waiver makes India the only known country with nuclear weapons which is not a party to the NPT but is still allowed to carry out nuclear commerce with the rest of the world.

Since the implementation of NSG waiver, India has signed nuclear deals with several countries including France, United States, Mongolia, Namibia, and Kazakhstan while the framework for similar deals with Canada and United Kingdom are also being prepared.

Delivery systems

Below is the list of missiles currently in India's inventory or under development that can carry Nuclear Warheads. Information on the missiles is given below.

AAD and PAD

Under former president Dr. Abdul Kalam India pursued the Integrated Guided Missile Development Program (IGMDP) which was an Indian Ministry of Defense program for the development of a comprehensive range of missiles, including the intermediate range Agni missile (Surface to Surface), and short range missiles such as the Prithvi ballistic missile (Surface to Surface), Akash missile (Surface to Air), Trishul missile (Surface to Air) and Nag Missile (Anti Tank). Other projects such Indian Ballistic Missile Defense Program have derived from the IGMDP. In 2005, India became only the fourth country to have Anti Ballistic capability when India tested two systems the AAD and PAD.

India has methodically built an indigenous missile production capability, using its commercial space-launch program to develop the skills and infrastructure needed to support an offensive ballistic missile program. For example, during the 1980s, India conducted a series of space launches using the solid-fueled SLV-3 booster. Most of these launches put light satellites into near-earth orbit. Elements of the SLV-3 were subsequently incorporated into two new programs. In the first, the new polar-space launch vehicle (PSLV) was equipped with six SLV-3 motors strapped to the PSLV's first stage. The Agni IRBM technology demonstrator uses the SLV-3 booster as its first stage.

Prithvi

The Prithvi (Sanskrit: "Earth") I is mobile liquid-fueled 150 kilometer tactical missile currently deployed with army units. It is claimed that this missile is equipped only with various conventional warheads (which stay attached to the missile over the entire flight path).

The missile is of particular interest to the United States (and potential buyers) in that has the capability of maneuvering in flight so as to follow one of several different pre-programmed trajectories. Based on the same design, a modified Prithvi, the Prithvi II, is essentially a longer-ranged version of the Prithvi I except that it has a 250-kilometer range and a lighter payload. It is suspected that any nuclear missions will be executed by the

Prithvi II. Currently, the Prithvi II has completed development and is now in production. When fielded, it will be deployed with air force units for the purpose of deep target attacking maneuvers against objectives such as air fields.

- Prithvi I — Army Version (150 km range with a payload of 1,000 kg)
- Prithvi II — Air Force Version (250 km range with a payload of 500 kg)
- Prithvi III — Naval Version (350 km range with a payload of 500 kg)

The Prithvi missile project encompassed developing 3 variants for use by the Indian Army, Indian Air Force and the Indian Navy. The initial project framework of the Integrated Guided Missile Development Program outlines the variants in the following manner. in October 2009 India conducted 2 simultenous user trials of 350 km extended range Prithvi II to be used for strategic purposes.

Dhanush

Dhanush (Sanskrit: Bow) is a naval variant of the Prithvi missile. It can fire either the 250 km or the 350 km range missiles. Supposedly it is a customised version of the Prithvi and that the additional customizations in missile configuration are to certify it for seaworthiness. Dhanush has to be launched from a hydraulically stabilized launch pad. Its low range acts against it and thus it is seen a weapons either to be used to destroy an aircraft carrier or an enemy port. Indian Navy's K-15 Sagarika submarine-launched ballistic missile is reported to be a variant of the Dhanush missile. The ship launched Dhanush Ballistic Missile was tested from INS Subhadra of the Sukanya class patrol craft in 2000. INS Subhadra is a vessel which was modified and the missile was launched from the reinforced helicopter deck. The 250 km variant was tested but the tests were considered partially successful. In 2004, the missile was again tested from the INS Subhadra and was this time successful. Then the following year in December the missile's 350 km version was tested from the INS Rajput and hit the land based target.

Agni

The Agni (Sanskrit: Fire) missile system comprises five missiles:

- Agni I
- Agni II
- Agni III
- Agni IV
- Agni V

There are some reports about one other variant of Agni missile:

Agni VI

Agni-I uses the SLV-3 booster (from India's space program) for its first stage and a liquid-fueled Prithvi for its second stage.

Nuclear-capable Agni-II missiles have a range of up to 3,000 km and can carry a payload of 1,000 kg. Unlike the Agni-I, the Agni-II has a solid-fueled second stage.

In July 2006, India successfully test-fired Agni-III, a two-stage nuclear-capable ballistic missile with a range of 3,000 km. Both stages of the Agni-III utilizes solid-fuel propellants and its range can be extended to 4,000 km. The missile is capable of carrying a nuclear payload within the range of 600 to 1,800 kg including decoys and other anti-ballistic counter-measures.

India's DRDO is also working on a submarine-launched ballistic missile version of the Agni-III missile, known as the Agni-III SL. This missile is expected to provide India with a credible sea-based second strike capability. According to Indian defense sources, Agni-III SL will have a range of 3,500 km. In addition, the 5,000 km range Agni-V ICBM is expected to be tested by 2010-11.

Surya

The report of Surya ICBM (Sanskrit: Sun) has not been confirmed by officials of the Indian government and have repeatedly denied the existence of the project.The Surya ICBM is an ICBM program that has been mentioned repeatedly in the Indian press. Surya (meaning Sun in Sanskrit and many other Indian languages) is the codename for the first Intercontinental Ballistic Missile that India is reported to be developing. The DRDO is believed to have begun the project in 1994. As the missile is yet to be developed, the specifications of the missile are not known and the entire program continues to remain highly speculative. Estimates of the range of this missile vary from 5,000 km to 10,000 km.

It is believed to be a three-stage design, with the first two stages using solid propellants and the third-stage using liquid. In 2007, the *Times of India* reported that the DRDO is yet to reveal whether India's currently proposed ICBM will be called Agni-V (or Surya-1). As of 2009 it was reported that the government had not considered an 8,000-km range ICBM.

Four decades of investments in a missile-related design, development, and manufacturing infrastructure have also made this sector less vulnerable to long-term disruption by technology denial regimes. More significantly, India's sophisticated civilian satellite launch capability makes it one of the few developing states theoretically capable of building an intercontinental ballistic missile (ICBM).

Shaurya

The Shaurya missile (Sanskrit: Valour) is a short-range surface-to-surface ballistic missile developed by DRDO of India for use by the Indian Army. It has a range of 600 km and is capable of carrying a payload of one-tonne conventional or nuclear warhead. The Shaurya missile provides India with a significant second strike capability. Shaurya Missile is considered a land version of the Sagarika. This missile is stored in a composite canister just like the BrahMos supersonic cruise missile. The composite canister makes the missile much easier to store for long periods without maintenance as well as to handle and transport. It also houses the gas generator to eject the missile from the canister before its solid propellant motors take over to hurl it at the intended target. Shaurya missiles can remain hidden or camouflaged in underground silos from enemy surveillance or satellites till they are fired from the special storage-cum-launch canisters. DRDO Defence scientists admit that given Shaurya's limited range at present, either the silos will have to be constructed closer to India's borders or longer-range missiles will have to be developed. The Shaurya system will require some more tests before it becomes fully operational in two-three years. Moreover, defense scientists say the high-speed, two-stage Shaurya has *high maneuverability* which also makes it *less vulnerable* to existing anti-missile defense systems. When Anti-Ballistic Missile Systems Advanced Air Defence (AAD) and Prithvi Air Defence (PAD) are to be tested again, the Shaurya invulnerability to anti-missile systems will be tested. The DRDO scientists also have said that if Shaurya is successful and manages to avoid anti ballistic missile radars then the missile can even be used to improve the AAD and PAD systems.

Sagarika

Sagarika (Sanskrit: Wave / Born from the Ocean) is a nuclear capable submarine-launched ballistic missile with a range of 750 km. This missile has a length of 8.5 meters, weighs seven tonnes and can carry a pay load of up to 500 kg. The development of this missile started in 1991. The first confirmation about the missile came in 1998. The development of the underwater missile launcher known as the Project 78 (P78) was completed in 2001. This was handed over to the Indian Navy for trials. The missile was successfully test fired thrice. The Indian Navy plans to introduce the missile into service by the end of 2010. Sagarika missile is being integrated with the Arihant class submarine that is expected to begin sea trials by 2009. Sagarika will form part of the triad in India's nuclear deterrence and will provide with retaliatory nuclear strike capability.

Sagarika has already been test-fired from an underwater pontoon, but now DRDO is planning a full-fledged test of the missile from a submarine and for this purpose may use the services of a Russian sub-marine. Eventually it could be introduced into as many as 5 ballistic missile submarines.

CRUISE MISSILES

Nirbhay

Nirbhay (Sanskrit "Fearless") is a long range, subsonic cruise missile being developed in India. The missile will have a range of 1,000 km and will arm three services, the Indian Army, Indian Navy and the Indian Air Force.

The Nirbhay will be able to be launched from multiple platforms on land, sea and air. The first test flight of the missile is expected in the year 2009. Nirbhay will be a terrain hugging, stealth missile capable of delivering 24 different types of warheads depending on mission requirements and will use inertial navigation system for guidance. There are plans to arm the IL-76MDs with the aerial version of the missile.

3M-54 Klub

India has acquired around 200 3M-54 Klub for arming Talwar class frigate, Shivalik class frigate, Kolkata class destroyer and Sindhughosh class submarine. The Russian 3M-54 Klub is a multi-role missile system developed by the Novator Design Bureau (OKB-8) with a range of 250 km-300 km and an average speed of.8 Mach with a maximum of 2.9 Mach. India has both the Klub-N and Klub-S variant to be used for Ships and Submarines respectively. Both the Klub-N and Klub-S have been tested successfully. India currently has the 3M-54E, 3M-54E1, 91RE1 and 91RE2 variants. In addition the Navy has plans to arm the Tu-142 and Tu-22M with an air-launched version. Due to Klub's longer range than BrahMos it may also be used in the Mirage 2000 and Su-30 MKI too. The Navy has shown interest in buying more Klubs which would be incorporated on to the S-1000 submarine if bought by India. India is also keen on other Former Soviet cruise missile such as the P-700 Granit and P-500 Bazalt.

P-70 Ametist

India has Soviet P-70 Ametist submarine-launched cruise missiles. The missile were mostly probably bought in the early 90s and may be used today as canistered launched land based cruise missiles instead of submarine launched cruise missiles. The missiles can carry nuclear warheads and have a range of 50–65 km. Although they are extremely old and incompetent due to their low range and speed, there are still reports that they are kept in reserve and can still be used due to their upgrades in the late 90s.

Moskit

India has a number of operational Moskits. The P-270 Moskit is a Russian supersonic ramjet powered cruise missile capable of being launched from land and ships. India has most probably bought both land and ship variants which have a range of 120 km. India bought around 200 Klub missiles and now it is believed that the Moskit have been kept in reserve but can still be used.

Brahmos

BrahMos is a supersonic cruise missile that can be launched from submarines, ships, aircraft or land. It is a joint venture between India's Defence Research and Development Organisation (DRDO) and Russia's NPO Mashinostroeyenia who have together formed the BrahMos Aerospace Private Limited.

The acronym BrahMos is perceived as the confluence of the two nations represented by two rivers, the Brahmaputra of India and the Moskva of Russia. It travels at speeds of Mach 2.5 to 2.8 and is the world's fastest cruise missile. It is about three-and-a-half times faster than the U.S.A's subsonic Harpoon cruise missile. A hypersonic version of the missile is also presently under development (Lab Tested with 5.26 Mach Speed). BrahMos claims to have the capability of attacking surface targets as low as 10 meters in altitude. It can gain a speed of Mach 2.8, and has a maximum range of 290 km. The ship-launched and land-based missiles can carry a 200 kg warhead, whereas the aircraft-launched variant (BrahMos A) can carry a 300 kg warhead. It has a two-stage propulsion system, with a solid-propellant rocket for initial acceleration and a liquid-fueled ramjet responsible for sustained supersonic cruise. Air-breathing ramjet propulsion is much more fuel-efficient than rocket propulsion, giving the BrahMos a longer range than a pure rocket-powered missile would achieve.

The high speed of the BrahMos likely gives it better target-penetration characteristics than lighter subsonic cruise-missiles such as the Tomahawk. Being twice as heavy and almost four times faster than the Tomahawk, the BrahMos has almost 32 times the initial kinetic energy of a Tomahawk missile (although it pays for this by having only 3/5 the payload and a fraction of the range despite weighing twice as much, suggesting a different tactical paradigm to achieve the objective).

Although BrahMos is primarily an anti-ship missile, it can also engage land based targets. It can be launched either in a vertical or inclined position and is capable of covering targets over a 360 degree horizon. The BrahMos missile has an identical configuration for land, sea, and sub-sea platforms. The air-launched version has a smaller booster and additional tail fins for added stability during launch. The BrahMos is currently being configured for aerial deployment with the Su-30MKI as its carrier. India has produced more than 110 Brahmos by March 2011 as per SIPRI, inducted 1 regiment of Brahmos Type-I GLCM with 67 missiles.

SURFACE TO AIR MISSILE

Akash

Akash (Sanskrit: Sky) is India's medium range surface-to-air missile defense system The missile can target aircraft up to 30 km away, at altitudes up to 18,000 m. Akash can be fired from both tracked and wheeled platforms. Akash is said to be capable of both conventional and nuclear warheads, with a reported payload of 60 kg. A nuclear warhead could potentially give the missile the capability to destroy both aircraft and warheads from ballistic missiles. The missile is described as being able to strike several targets simultaneously, which could mean either separate, independently targetable warheads, or a sufficient blast to destroy a number of them.

Along with India, a limited number of other countries including the US and Russia have developed operational multi-target handling surface-to-air missile systems capable of carrying a nuclear warhead.

Delivery Mechanisms

Nuclear Submarines

According to some accounts, India plans to have as many as 25 nuclear submarines capable of carrying missiles with nuclear warheads. Currently, India has built one and is building two more nuclear submarines under the Arihant class submarine plan. India currently maintains six submarines of the Sindhughosh Class that can launch the nuclear-capable 3M-54 Klub cruise missiles.

- Former Leasing of Soviet submarines: In 1988 INS *Chakra* (Sanskrit: Wheel), a Charlie-class submarine was leased by the Indian Navy for three years from the Soviet Union, until 1991. The submarine was leased to India between 1988 and 1991 mainly for India to gain experience in the operations of a nuclear submarine. It was later decommissioned in 1991.
- Arihant class submarine: The Arihant class submarines (Sanskrit: Slayer of Enemies) are a class of nuclear-powered Ballistic Missile submarines being constructed for the Indian Navy at Visakhapatnam, India under the Advanced Technology Vessel (ATV) Project The ATV is an SSBN and will be armed with ballistic missiles.

The first of these, INS Arihant was launched on 26 July 2009. The vessel, which will undergo sea-trials for up to two years, will then be equipped with an unknown number of K-15 Sagarika SLBMs.

The second and third submarines of the class may incorporate the Nirbhay as well. As of July 2007, the Sagarika missile as well as Dhanush had undergone three successful tests each.

- INS Cruise Missile Submarines: The INS Sindhuraj (Sanskrit: King of the Ocean), INS Sindhuvir(Sanskrit: Warrior of the Ocean), INS Sindhuratna(Sanskrit: Gem of the Ocean), INS Sindhushastra (Sanskrit: Weapon of the Ocean), INS Sindhukesari(Sanskrit: Lion of the Ocean) and INS Sindhuvijay(Sanskrit: Conqueror of the Ocean) are capable of launching 3M-54 Klub and BrahMos nuclear-capable cruise missiles. India bought 10 Kilo class (in India known as Sindhughosh Class) submarine of which 6 have been refitted by the Russian Navy so that the they can launch cruise missiles such as nuclear capable 3M-54 Klub.
- Leasing of Russian Akula and Amur submarines: In 2000, negotiations between India and Russia were conducted into the leasing of two incomplete *Akula* class. The Akulas

were to be delivered to the Indian Navy in 2008 on a lease of at least seven years and up to ten years, in which at the end of the lease, it has an option to buy them. The acquisition was to help the Indian Navy prepare for the introduction of the ATV. The cost to India of acquiring two Akula submarines and their support infrastructure along with training of the crews had been estimated at $2 billion. The Indian version was reportedly armed with the 300 km range 3M-54 Klub nuclear-capable missiles. Supposedly on 9 November 2008 one of the two submarines was conducting tests, when an accident on board killed 20 sailors but no damage occurred to the submarine. Though this deal fell apart for some time due to the Indians demanding an upgrade/improvement in some of its safety features, Russia's President Dmitry Medvedev on his official trip to New Delhi said that the deal was back on track and that "The talk is not about selling submarines into India's property, but about their rent by India's navy". However, unlike the earlier deal the modified deal states that India can only rent and not buy the subs, but defence experts state that the so-called lease agreement is only to divert international attention and that it would be eventually modified and India would inevitably keep the subs. The first submarine will be named INS Chakra.. Home voyage under Indian control from the Russian port of Vladivostok to its Indian base Visakhapatnam commenced January, 2012.

Russia has also offered the advanced Amur Class Submarine, known as the S1000. According to GlobalSecurity India is already building the S1000 cruise missile submarines in Mazagaon Docks. The Amur will be most probably fitted with P-700 Granit or the Klub cruise missile capable of carrying nuclear warheads.

Frigates, destroyers and aircraft carriers

Other than submarines, India also maintains ships such as destroyers, modified patrol crafts and frigates which can launch nuclear capable ballistic and cruise missiles.

Talwar class frigate and Shivalik class frigate are frigates of the Indian Navy that can fire nuclear capable cruise missiles. INS Tabar and INS Trishul are Talwar class vessel armed with supersonic nuclear 3M-54 Klub cruise missiles while INS Shivalik was the first vessel of the Shivalik class to incorporate the 3M-54 Klub. Other vessels of the Shivalik Class and Talwar Class are to be armed with the BrahMos and 3M-54 Klub missiles by 2009 and 2010 respectively. All these frigates are also equipped with Barak 1 missiles or other SAMs and harbour helicopters such as the HAL Dhruv. In years to come, the Nirbhay missile is also to be incorporated into Talwar class frigates and Shivalik class frigates.

Rajput Class, Kolkata Class and Delhi Class are Destroyers of the Indian Navy that may be armed with nuclear capable missile-Nirbhay. In addition Kolkata Class will also incorporate the Russian nuclear 3M-54 Klub cruise missile.

The ship launched Dhanush Ballistic Missile was tested from INS Subhadra of the Sukanya class patrol craft in 2000. INS Subhadra is a patrol vessel which was modified and the missile was launched from the reinforced helicopter deck. The 250 km variant was tested but the tests were considered partially successful. In 2004, the missile was again tested from the INS Subhadra and was this time successful. Then the following year in December the missile's 350 km version was tested from the INS Rajput and hit the land based target.

INS Vikramaditya Aircraft Carrier (formerly known as Admiral Gorshkov) was fitted with P-500 Bazalt nuclear capable cruise missiles of the range of 550 km. The Vikramaditya could still be armed with this after its refit. India is also a potential customer for a Slava class cruiser which also incorporates the P-500 Bazalt.

Nuclear-capable aircraft

India currently has fourth generation jet fighters capable of launching nuclear weapons. Nuclear-capable aircraft are also seen as a less expensive way of dropping nuclear warheads as well as being as effective.

- Fighter jets: The Sukhoi Su-30MKI, Dassault Mirage 2000, and MiG-29 serve in the Indian Air Force and are also seen as a means to deliver nuclear weapons. In addition India maintains SEPECAT Jaguar and MiG-27M which can be used to drop gravity bombs. On the other hand, the Su-30MKI, capable of carrying nuclear weapons and tailor-made for Indian specifications, integrates Indian systems and avionics. is one of the best air superiority fighters and also consists of French and Israeli subsystems. The MKI variant features several improvements over the basic K and MK variants and is classified as a 4.5 generation fighter. Due to similar features and components, the MKI variant is often considered to be a customized Indian variant of the Sukhoi Su-35. The Mirage 2000Hs were heavily customised during the Kargil War and is the only other version, other than the French 2000N, to be able to be armed with nuclear weapons. Though the MiG-29 like the HAL Tejas after many test flights have not been tested to use nuclear weapons, they have the capacity to be armed with them. Both the HAL Tejas and Su-30MKI can travel excess of 3,000 km without refueling; this allows India to attack targets far away in an effective manner only using planes rather than delivery systems such as the Agni. The HAL Tejas is India's only indigenous plane to be armed with nuclear weapons, thus making India less dependent on Russia.

India has leased four Russian Tupolev Tu-22M3 bombers, which could carry air-launched cruise missiles. India has reportedly upgraded its Russian-built Tu-142 maritime patrol aircraft to carry air-launched cruise missiles. India is expected to buy up to 200 Sukhoi T-50 stealth fighter jets, developed jointly by Russia and India.

Ballistic missile defense

India has an active ABM development effort using indigenously developed and integrated radars and locally designed missiles. In November 2006, India successfully conducted the PADE (Prithvi Air Defence Exercise) in which an Anti-ballistic missile, called the Prithvi Air Defense (PAD) an *Exoatmospheric* (outside the atmosphere) interceptor system intercepted a Prithvi-II ballistic missile. The PAD missile has the secondary stage of the Prithvi missile and can reach altitude of 80 km. During the test the target missile was intercepted at an 50 km altitude. India became the fourth nation in the world to acquire such a capability and the third nation to develop it through indigenous effort. On 6 December 2007 the Advanced Air Defence (AAD) missile system was tested successfully. This missile is an Endo atmospheric interceptor with an altitude of 30 km. According to scientist V K Saraswat of DRDO the missiles will work in tandem to ensure a hit probability of 99.8 percent. Induction of the system into services is expected to be in 2010. Two new anti ballistic missiles that can intercept IRBM/ ICBMs are being developed. These high speed missiles (AD-1 and AD-2) are being developed to intercept ballistic missiles with the range of 5,000 km.

India also has Russian S300 PMU-2 and it is used as an interceptor for ballistic missiles. An indigenous nuclear tipped surface to air missile, Akash Missile is used to destroy low range missiles and is capable of destroying various targets and is one of the few of its kind systems in the world. India has also shown interest in the Russian S-400, the most advanced anti-ballistic missile.

Chemical weapons

In 1992 India signed the Chemical Weapons Convention (CWC), stating that it did not have chemical weapons and the capacity or capability to manufacture chemical weapons. By doing this India became one of the original signatories of the Chemical Weapons Convention [CWC] in 1993, and ratified it on 2 September 1996.

According to India's ex-Army Chief General Sunderji, a country having the capability of making nuclear weapons does not need to have chemical weapons, since the dread of chemical weapons could be created only in those countries that do not have nuclear weapons. Others suggested that the fact that India has found chemical weapons dispensable highlighted its confidence in the conventional weapons system at its command. In June 1997, India declared its stock of chemical weapons(stockpile of 1044 tonnes of sulphur mustard). By the end of 2006, India had destroyed more than 75 percent of its chemical weapons/material stockpile and was granted extension for destroying (the remaining stocks by April 2009) and was expected to achieve 100 percent destruction within that timeframe. India informed the United Nations in May, 2009 that it had destroyed its stockpile of chemical weapons in compliance with the international Chemical Weapons Convention. With this India has become third country after South Korea and Albania to do so. This was cross-checked by inspectors of the United Nations.

India has an advanced commercial chemical industry, and produces the bulk of its own chemicals for domestic consumption. It is also widely acknowledged that India has an extensive civilian chemical and pharmaceutical industry and annually exports considerable quantities of chemicals to countries such as the United Kingdom, United States, and Taiwan.

Biological Warfare

India has a well-developed biotechnology infrastructure that includes numerous pharmaceutical production facilities bio-containment laboratories (including BSL-3 and BSL-4) for working with lethal pathogens. It also has highly qualified scientists with expertise in infectious diseases. Some of India's facilities are being used to support research and development for BW defense purposes. India has ratified the BWC and pledges to abide by its obligations. There is no clear evidence, circumstantial or otherwise, that directly points toward an offensive BW program. New Delhi does possess the scientific capability and infrastructure to launch an offensive BW program, but has chosen not to do so. In terms of delivery, India also possesses the capability to produce aerosols and has numerous potential delivery systems ranging from crop dusters to sophisticated ballistic missiles.

No information exists in the public domain suggesting interest by the Indian government in delivery of biological agents by these or any other means. To reiterate the latter point, in October 2002, Indian President A.P.J. Abdul Kalam asserted that "we [India] will not make biological weapons. It is cruel to human beings..."

6

India's Draft Nuclear Doctrine

The use of nuclear weapons in particular as well as other weapons of mass destruction constitutes the gravest threat to humanity and to peace and stability in the international system. Unlike the other two categories of weapons of mass destruction, biological and chemical weapons which have been outlawed by international treaties, nuclear weapons remain instruments for national and collective security, the possession of which on a selective basis has been sought to be legitimised through permanent extension of the Nuclear Non-proliferation Treaty (NPT) in May 1995. Nuclear weapon states have asserted that they will continue to rely on nuclear weapons with some of them adopting policies to use them even in a non-nuclear context. These developments amount to virtual abandonment of nuclear disarmament. This is a serious setback to the struggle of the international community to abolish weapons of mass destruction.

India's primary objective is to achieve economic, political, social, scientific and technological development within a peaceful and democratic framework. This requires an environment of durable peace and insurance against potential risks to peace and stability. It will be India's endeavour to proceed towards this overall objective in cooperation with the global democratic trends and to play a constructive role in advancing the international system toward a just, peaceful and equitable order.

Autonomy of decision making in the developmental process and in strategic matters is an inalienable democratic right of the

Indian people. India will strenuously guard this right in a world where nuclear weapons for a select few are sought to be legitimised for an indefinite future, and where there is growing complexity and frequency in the use of force for political purposes.

India's security is an integral component of its development process. India continuously aims at promoting an ever-expanding area of peace and stability around it so that developmental priorities can be pursued without disruption.

However, the very existence of offensive doctrine pertaining to the first use of nuclear weapons and the insistence of some nuclear weapons states on the legitimacy of their use even against non-nuclear weapon countries constitute a threat to peace, stability and sovereignty of states.

This document outlines the broad principles for the development, deployment and employment of India's nuclear forces. Details of policy and strategy concerning force structures, deployment and employment of nuclear forces will flow from this framework and will be laid down separately and kept under constant review.

OBJECTIVES OF GLOBAL NUCLEAR DISARMAMENT

In the absence of global nuclear disarmament India's strategic interests require effective, credible nuclear deterrence and adequate retaliatory capability should deterrence fail. This is consistent with the UN Charter, which sanctions the right of self-defence. The requirements of deterrence should be carefully weighed in the design of Indian nuclear forces and in the strategy to provide for a level of capability consistent with maximum credibility, survivability, effectiveness, safety and security.

India shall pursue a doctrine of credible minimum nuclear deterrence. In this policy of "retaliation only", the survivability of our arsenal is critical. This is a dynamic concept related to the strategic environment, technological imperatives and the needs of national security. The actual size components, deployment and employment of nuclear forces will be decided in the light of these factors. India's peacetime posture aims at convincing any potential aggressor that :

(a) any threat of use of nuclear weapons against India shall invoke measures to counter the threat: and

(b) any nuclear attack on India and its forces shall result in punitive retaliation with nuclear weapons to inflict damage unacceptable to the aggressor.

The fundamental purpose of Indian nuclear weapons is to deter the use and threat of use of nuclear weapons by any State or entity against India and its forces. India will not be the first to initiate a nuclear strike, but will respond with punitive retaliation should deterrence fail. India will not resort to the use or threat of use of nuclear weapons against States which do not possess nuclear weapons, or are not aligned with nuclear weapon powers.

Deterrence requires that India maintain:

(a) Sufficient, survivable and operationally prepared nuclear forces,

(b) a robust command and control system,

(c) effective intelligence and early warning capabilities, and

(d) comprehensive planning and training for operations in line with the strategy, and

(e) the will to employ nuclear forces and weapons.

Highly effective conventional military capabilities shall be maintained to raise the threshold of outbreak both of conventional military conflict as well as that of threat or use of nuclear weapons.

INDIA'S DRAFT NUCLEAR DOCTRINE AND SECURITY

In April 1998, the Indian government had constituted a Task Force to recommend the establishment of a National Security Council (NSC). The Task Force submitted its report in June 1998 and, in November 1998, the government constituted a three-tier NSC with a full time National Security Advisor and a National Security Advisory Board (NSAB). Although the first task that was planned to be originally entrusted to the NSAB was to conduct a strategic defence review, because of post-Pokhran II compulsions, the NSAB was asked to first formulate India's nuclear doctrine. The NSAB submitted a draft nuclear doctrine paper to the government that was released to the public for wider debate on August 17, 1999. The key features of the proposed nuclear doctrine are reproduced below:

India shall pursue a doctrine of credible minimum deterrence. In this policy of 'retaliation only', the survivability of our arsenal is critical. This is a dynamic concept related to our strategic environment, technological imperatives and the needs of national security. The actual size, components, deployment and employment of nuclear forces will be decided in the light of these factors. India's peacetime posture aims at convincing any potential aggressor that:

- Any threat of use of nuclear weapons against India shall invoke measures to counter the threat; and
- Any nuclear attack on India and its forces shall result in punitive retaliation with nuclear weapons to inflict damage unacceptable to the aggressor.

The fundamental purpose of Indian nuclear weapons is to deter the use and threat of use of nuclear weapons by any state or entity against India and its forces. India will not be the first to initiate a nuclear strike but will respond with punitive retaliation should deterrence fail. India will not resort to the use or threat of use of nuclear weapons against states that do not possess nuclear weapons, or are not aligned with nuclear weapons powers.

The draft nuclear doctrine, while generally following the policy guidelines enunciated by the Prime Minister in Parliament, fleshed out his pronouncements and "provides a broad framework for the development, deployment and employment of India's nuclear forces." The draft paper proposes that India should establish a credible, minimum nuclear deterrent capability comprising sufficient, survivable and operationally ready nuclear forces based on the principle of no first use of nuclear weapons. It emphasises that the level of India's nuclear capability should be consistent with maximum credibility, survivability, effectiveness, safety and security. It provides for the establishment of effective intelligence and early warning systems. It recommends that India's nuclear forces be based on a triad of strategic bombers, land-based ballistic missiles and submarine launched ballistic missiles (SLBMs).

Though a sea-based nuclear capability will take many decades to develop, the requirement of SLBMs is considered inescapable due to their relatively lower vulnerability. Nuclear forces that need to survive a first strike have no option but to ensure that at least 50 to 60 per cent of the arsenal is made comparatively invulnerable by being maintained as SLBMs. The draft paper proposes that India's nuclear strike capability be configured to inflict punitive retaliation the consequences of which would be unacceptable to a potential adversary who will therefore be deterred from doing the unthinkable. The doctrine highlights the cardinal supremacy of civilian control over India's nuclear weapons and proposes that the final authority for the release of nuclear weapons must vest with the Prime Minister or his designated successor(s).

The proposed doctrine also rejects the concept of nuclear warfighting and does not, hence, consider it necessary for India to match its nuclear warheads and delivery systems with those of its potential nuclear adversaries. A small number of survivable nuclear warheads and delivery systems that can inflict damage which would be unacceptable to the adversary are considered adequate for the purposes of deterrence. Although the paper has left some ambiguity by not clearly rejecting the need for tactical or battlefield nuclear weapons in India's context, the tenor of the paper and its emphasis on a retaliatory policy appear to rule out any thinking towards tactical nuclear weapons. However, the real distinguishing feature of India's nuclear doctrine is that it is "... anchored in India's continued commitment to global, verifiable and non-discriminating nuclear disarmament..." that has been described as India's national security objective. The use of nuclear weapons is considered "the gravest threat to humanity and to peace and stability in the international system." The doctrine paper clearly points out India's desire to see the world completely rid of nuclear weapons.

As expected, the draft doctrine initiated a major debate in the country about its nuclear policies. Amitabh Mattoo called it "an unapologetic realpolitik articulation of the principal raison d'être of India's nuclear weapons and the requirements needed to lend credibility to the country's deterrent posture." While agreeing with the thrust of India's nuclear policy, he wrote that India's primary quest appeared to be to acquire the strategic autonomy necessary for making independent decisions in an often unfriendly world and to pursue economic and political development without fear of external threats. R. Prasannan called the draft doctrine a wish list attached to the collective speeches of the Prime Minister and his Cabinet colleagues. Bharat Wariavwalla criticised the draft doctrine on the grounds that the definition of minimum deterrence would be very different vis a vis China and Pakistan and, hence, the term is much too loose to pass off as doctrine.

Many analysts and even foreign governments have sought to raise doubts about India's draft nuclear doctrine. It did not help matters that the doctrine was unveiled the week after the Indian Air Force had shot down a Pakistani Atlantique reconnaissance aircraft that had intruded into Indian territory. The US government rejected the Indian desire to develop a nuclear arsenal." The Indian tests also spurred fears of a new Middle East arms race. However, not all Western powers denounced India's attempts to establish a credible weaponised nuclear deterrent. France welcomed the release of India's draft nuclear doctrine as a "logical and indeed wanted step". The most surprising criticism of the draft doctrine is that it conjures up dark visions of a nuclear arms race in Southern Asia. If all nuclear weapons states were to follow a no first use policy, it would be logical to assume that there would gradually be a net reduction in the size of nuclear arsenals - an arms race in reverse! Jasjit Singh offers the following explanation:

The concerns about a potential arms race reflect a perception arising out of the prism of Cold War mind-sets where first strike (and even "launch on warning") was the order of the day. This necessitated large arsenals and potentially pre-emptive strikes with nuclear weapons. The result was the peak of 67,000 nuclear warheads. But China did not follow the same route and relied on minimum deterrence concept with a no first use commitment. There is no evidence that China's nuclear posture led to any arms race. Even in future, China's nuclear arsenal is likely to be dictated by the size of US/Russian arsenals and issues like ballistic missile defences etc. rather than the defensive doctrine of India.

The worst criticism of the draft doctrine has been that opting for a triad of nuclear forces is not indicative of a minimalist posture but of a maximalist one, particularly as sea-based nuclear weapons have been envisaged to form part of the nuclear force. This criticism fails to take into account the fact that the credibility of a nuclear deterrent that is limited to retaliatory strikes only hinges around the ability of the nuclear force to survive a first strike in sufficient numbers to inflict unacceptable punishment in retaliation. Since submarines offer the best survival potential, India has to rely on a small number of SLBMs for credible deterrence. Raja Menon has also criticised the proposed doctrine: "...There is a serious dysfunction between 'minimum deterrence' and a tri-Service arsenal. The two cannot go together, and is (sic) akin to yoking a horse and camel together." However, surprisingly, he finds no use for aircraft-delivered nuclear bombs and states that "to even consider the role of the army in nuclear deterrence, minimum at that, is truly distressing." His hypothesis is that an arsenal for minimum deterrence requires only second-strike weapons, which can only be based on SSBNs.

Some critics have averred that the nuclear threats have not been enunciated and that the draft document does not define the nuclear force levels that India considers "minimum". Others have protested that the costs of India's nuclear deterrent have not been spelt out. The critics of the draft document forget that doctrine defines only a set of beliefs and guidelines on which policy and strategy is based. In the Preamble of the draft paper it is clearly stated in Para 1.6 that "this document outlines the broad principles for the development, deployment and employment of India's nuclear forces." Details regarding the targeting philosophy, nuclear force structures and the finer nuances of command and control cannot be expected to appear in a paper on nuclear doctrine.

The exception in the draft doctrine that India's non-use of nuclear weapons policy against countries that are not nuclear weapons states does not apply if they are militarily aligned with nuclear weapons states, has also been criticised. This exception would include non-nuclear members of NATO and the military allies of the US such as Japan. Rajesh Rajagopalan explains the reasons behind such exceptions: Two reasons could be suggested for this exception, one practical and the other strategic. The practical reason is that the Negative Security Assurance (NSA) of various nuclear weapons states, around which this non-use policy is based, makes similar exceptions. In fact, the exceptions there are broader and the NSA does not apply to countries that have refused to sign the NPT or are suspected of nuclear weapons ambitions...

The strategic reason... (is that) a good number of non-nuclear countries still host the nuclear arms of nuclear weapons states and share in the command and control infrastructure of nuclear powers. Theoretically, a nuclear attack on India could be mounted by the nuclear forces hosted in third countries. Excluding these countries would mean that no retaliation could be mounted on the bases from where such attacks are launched...

Rajesh Rajagopalan points out that 'minimum deterrence' is mistakenly characterised as doctrine whereas it actually refers to the nuclear force structure. He states that the Indian doctrine is one of 'assured retaliation' and this is to be given effect by a minimalist nuclear force as "an assured retaliation posture is premised on the belief that no one will start a nuclear war if they are assured of a nuclear retaliation, even if it is a weak retaliation. In other words, for an Indian nuclear deterrent to work effectively against China or Pakistan, it is not necessary to threaten them with complete destruction: even retaliating with a few nuclear warheads will create unacceptable costs to both." While the interpretation is no doubt technically correct, it is also true that a policy of assured retaliation, combined with a small nuclear force built on the principle of sufficiency, could overall be characterised as minimum deterrence. However, it is a finely nuanced distinction that must be noted.

Pakistani government spokesmen and scholars have been particularly critical of India's no first use doctrine on the grounds that it is only a declaratory policy and can be easily changed when the need arises. They have failed to take note of the fact that a country's nuclear force structure, command and control system, alert status and its deployment posture are based on its nuclear doctrine. First use doctrines require hair trigger alerts, launch-on-warning and launch-through-attack strategies and elaborate surveillance, early warning and intelligence systems with nuclear warheads loaded on launchers and ready to fire. Nuclear armed aircraft would need to be ready on runway alert, if not constantly airborne as in the case of the erstwhile US Strategic Air Command. India cannot ever resort to any of these measures without Pakistan learning about them almost immediately. What the Pakistanis also forget, or deliberately ignore, is that India has offered to negotiate a mutual no first use treaty with Pakistan that would be binding and verifiable. India's track record of adherence to international treaties has been exemplary. Unfortunately, the same cannot be said of India's neighbours who have violated numerous treaties with impunity, including the NPT and the MTCR.

The charge that India's nuclear doctrine would initiate an arms race in the Southern Asian region is specious and unjustified. China's gradual moves towards a nuclear triad over a period of three and a half decades have not forced India to play "catch up". Even now India does not feel it necessary to match China's 400-plus nuclear warheads, or to follow China and develop multiple independently targetable re-entry vehicles (MIRVs). India has decided to base its deterrent on a small force of survivable nuclear warheads and delivery systems for a retaliatory strike that can inflict punitive damage on a handful of value targets.

There is no reason why Pakistan should feel compelled to match India's nuclear warheads and missiles, particularly as it has opted for a first strike doctrine and does not have to worry about the survival of its nuclear forces. With a first use doctrine, even for deterring conventional war Pakistan does not need to match India warhead for warhead and missile for missile. Kenneth Waltz has argued that the distinction between nuclear forces designed for war fighting, that need to be compared with one another, and those designed to deter the use of nuclear weapons, must be clearly understood. Forces designed for deterrence need not match the adversary's nuclear forces as long as they can do unacceptable damage to the adversary with unacceptable damage sensibly defined. Putting it most appropriately, he has said that "more is not better, if less is enough." Hence, those who are raising the bogey of a nuclear arms race in Southern Asia need to review their alarmist views.

It emerges quite clearly that most of the criticism of the proposed nuclear doctrine stems not from any genuine disagreement with India's no first use doctrine and its professed need to establish a credible minimum nuclear deterrent, but from the desire of many Western countries that India should "cap, reduce and eliminate" its nuclear capability and sign the NPT and the CTBT as a non-nuclear weapons state. Since India's nuclear tests and its declaration of the weaponisation of its nuclear deterrent were based on substantial national security interests, the cap, reduce, eliminate mantra is unlikely to now get anywhere.

Efficacy of No First Use

The concept of no first use logically flows out of the current conventional wisdom that the sole purpose of nuclear weapons, if they have a purpose at all, is to deter the use of nuclear weapons. As is well known in nuclear theology, Bernard Brodie had argued many decades ago that the advent of nuclear weapons had fundamentally altered the relationship between war and national policy and that nuclear weapons were so destructive that their only real purpose could be the avoidance of war itself. On the other hand, many other strategists saw nuclear weapons as simply one more addition to a nation's or even a military commander's arsenal, though a very destructive one, and convinced themselves that the use of nuclear weapons could be incorporated into warfighting strategies. Those who saw nuclear weapons as serving a military purpose in real combat naturally opted for first use and pre-emptive nuclear strategies and developed complex warfighting doctrines while the others saw no real purpose except that of deterrence and adopted deterrence strategies, including no first use.

India's declaration of its no first use doctrine has once again focussed international debate on the efficacy of no first use policies, even though India has repeatedly re-iterated that it is willing to negotiate no first use treaties bilaterally or multilaterally with all nuclear weapons states including China and Pakistan. It is often mistakenly believed that the concept of no first use is China's contribution to international peace and stability. In fact, the no first use formulation goes back to 1925 when the international community concluded a no first use treaty on chemical weapons and toxins in the Geneva Protocol. Though enormous stockpiles of chemical weapons were produced during the Second World War, neither side used them. This was because mutual deterrence continued to operate among the nations that had chemical weapons stockpiles till these were finally delegitimised by the 1993 Chemical Weapons Convention. However, in situations of asymmetry, deterrence did not operate and chemical weapons were used on several occasions: "By the Italians in Ethiopia, by the Japanese against the Chinese and finally by Saddam Hussain against the Iranians." It could be concluded that a no first use policy works best during conditions of mutual deterrence.

A no first use commitment is not merely a verbal or even a negotiated assurance, it can and must be seen to be reflected in the nuclear force structure, the deployment patterns, the types of surveillance assets in place and the state of readiness of a country's nuclear forces. China announced a no first use commitment immediately after its nuclear test in October 1964. In recent years it has diluted this policy by emphasising that such a declaration does not apply to territories that belong to China. While Taiwan falls in this category, so does Arunachal Pradesh in India which China still claims as its own territory. Hence, it can be plausibly stated that China could contemplate the use of nuclear weapons during a war over Taiwan or a border conflict with India in Arunachal Pradesh. The former Soviet Union had also subscribed to the no first use policy. As far back as 1955, the Soviet Union had proposed a no first use pledge by all nuclear weapons states. However, Russia's recently declared military doctrine has withdrawn that pledge and Russia is now committed to a first use nuclear policy even against conventional military threats. Several US thinkers, some of them important former members of the US military establishment such as Robert McNamara and George Kennan, have repeatedly called for a no first use pledge. Despite the end of the Cold War, the US and its NATO allies and friends, including the United Kingdom and France have refused to heed such wise counsel. In fact, the US has said that it would consider the use of its nuclear weapons against chemical and biological weapons and NATO, under US leadership, has developed an "out of area" strategic concept that undermines peace and stability in the international order.

Rooted in its strategic culture as it is, India's no first use doctrine is not a hastily formulated policy designed to win brownie points from the international community after upsetting the non-proliferation apple cart. It is a carefully thought through policy that has taken decades to mature, even if it was not publicly well articulated. Jaswant Singh has written: "No other country has debated so carefully and, at times, torturously over the dichotomy between its sovereign security needs and global disarmament instincts, between a moralistic approach and a realistic one, and between a covert nuclear policy and an overt one." K. Subrahmanyam had written in 1986: "Today the international system is dominated by nuclear dacoits who are refusing to disarm and there is nothing unethical if India were to secure for itself necessary self-protection capabilities to ward off coercive use of nuclear diplomacy... If India is to make a serious intervention in the disarmament debate and contribute to nuclear disarmament, acquiring nuclear capability is a fee that has to be paid." Even during the mid-1980s, defence analysts like General K. Sundarji and K. Subrahmanyam were advocating a minimum deterrent capability for India and had ruled out the need for tactical nuclear weapons as these were meant for nuclear warfighting - a concept that India did not subscribe to. Hence, minimum deterrence is not a new concept in the Indian context that has been thrust on an unsuspecting nation by the government and the NSAB.

NUCLEAR EXPLOSIONS AND THE INDIAN GOVERNMENT'S ADVOCACY

Ever since the May 1998 nuclear explosions and the Indian government's advocacy of the doctrine of no first use and a minimum credible deterrent, a major debate has been raging in the strategic community in India on the issue of no first use of nuclear weapons. Many analysts have averred that India has gained nothing and has unnecessarily elected to bear the horrendous costs of a nuclear strike by choosing to adopt a purely retaliatory nuclear policy. Rear Admiral Raja Menon asks: "Will India... be committed to absorbing a nuclear strike in case deterrence fails?" And answers: "Hardly, because in the event that an intelligence warning of a 'definite' nuclear strike is received, the NCP (National Command Post) will have to consider, among other options, a first launch." To advocate no first use and then consider first use as soon as the alarm bells are sounded would be duplicitous and worthy of the strongest possible condemnation. It is argued that after all India's no first use doctrine is only a declaratory doctrine and if other nuclear powers are not willing to accept India's offer of a negotiated no first use treaty, why should India subject itself to the ravages of nuclear destruction? It is likely that eventually one or more NWS (including Pakistan) will come around to accepting India's offer of a negotiated bilateral or multilateral no-first-use treaty. Given the groundswell of public opinion against the continuation of nuclear weapons almost all over the world, it may happen sooner rather than later. Meanwhile, some hard questions need to be asked. Is India likely to be faced by situations occasioned by operational realities when it might become necessary for the Indian political leadership to order the first use of nuclear weapons? When will the situation become operationally so critical that India might be forced to do the unthinkable? So, is India's no first use doctrine merely rhetorical nonsense or is it based on sound operational reasoning? These issues pose a strategic dilemma and present a complex challenge that is not at all easy to rationalise.

It is now universally accepted that nuclear weapons are political weapons and not weapons of 'warfighting'. However, the close link between nuclear weapons and a nation's conventional military capabilities is undeniable. If a nation's conventional capability is extremely low vis a vis a nuclear armed adversary, it may be necessary for that nation to adopt an in extremis 'first use' strategy to thwart a conventional military offensive that may threaten to undermine its territorial integrity and lead to its break up. This is the situation that Pakistan finds itself in at present. While India may have no intentions of launching a major conventional offensive into Pakistan, given India's conventional superiority (no matter how slender the edge may be), Pakistan has based its national security strategy on the first use of nuclear weapons to prevent its comprehensive military defeat like in 1971 and, consequently, its disintegration as a nation. It is for this reason that Pakistan does not accept India's offer of a bilateral no first use treaty as a nuclear confidence building and risk reduction measure.

Though overall China's conventional military forces far outnumber India's, due to China's problems in inducting, deploying and logistically sustaining large forces in Tibet, India enjoys a reasonable defensive capability at present and therefore does not need a 'first use' nuclear strategy to deter a conventional Chinese offensive backed by nuclear-tipped ballistic missiles deployed in Tibet. However, India's existing defensive capability is being quickly eroded as China is rapidly modernising its armed forces, raising rapid deployment divisions and improving the logistics infrastructure in Tibet while exhibiting extreme intransigence in resolving the outstanding territorial and boundary dispute with India. If India continues to neglect the upgradation of its conventional military capability and military modernisation by investing the grossly inadequate sum of less than 2.5 percent of its GDP for defence, as it is doing at present, the nation may again have to suffer the ignominy of large-scale military reverses, should China choose to fight even a limited border war after completing its military modernisation by 2005-2010.

While nuclear doctrine must undoubtedly be based on sound theoretical underpinnings, it has to be ultimately tested in the crucible of operational reality. The proponents of a first use strategy for India need to more deliberately ponder the threat scenarios that might justify the unthinkable. Some plausible scenarios are worth considering in this context. Starting at the lower end of conventional conflict with low intensity conflict (LIC) and Pakistan's ongoing proxy war with India, would the use of a Stinger or Unza surface-to-air (SAM) missile by Pakistan-supported mercenary Islamists to bring down an Indian Airlines aircraft over Kashmir Valley justify an Indian nuclear strike? Or, would a pro-active punitive response across the Line of Control (LoC) with massive artillery and air power sustained over a few weeks be more desirable? In another scenario, would a battalion or even a brigade size attack by the Pakistan army across the LoC, or even Kargil-type intrusions on the Indian side of the LoC, that result in major gains for Pakistan, justify the first use of nuclear weapons by India when their retaliatory use by Pakistan would be a certainty? Or, would a punitive ground and air forces conventional response across the LoC (and perhaps across the international boundary by the IAF) in another sector yield better dividends? After all, it is well known that there are areas on the LoC where Indian forces could be heading for key value objectives in Pakistan Occupied Kashmir (POK) within days of the outbreak of hostilities in Jammu and Kashmir (J&K).

In case such exchanges across the LoC escalate to a larger conventional conflict, as they well might, Pakistan may launch its Army Reserve North (ARN) through the Shakargarh Bulge in the Sialkot sector and threaten to cut off Kashmir's lifeline NH-1A between Pathankot and Jammu. If Pakistan achieved initial success, such an offensive would pose a grave danger to the security of J&K. Would the first use of nuclear weapons be a rational choice for India under such circumstances? Or would it perhaps be more prudent to launch one or more Indian Strike Corps counter-offensives across the International Boundary in Punjab, Rajasthan and Gujarat, as General Harbaksh Singh did in 1965 with Lal Bahadur Shastri as Prime Minister, to make the Pakistanis recoil from their offensive in the Jammu sector? Surely, the launching of sizeable counter offensives into Pakistan's heartland would be a better way to relieve pressure on J&K.

Another option favoured by military analysts is the "zero warning" option in which Pakistan is given the credible capability of launching what may be termed as a "cold start" conventional war due to the proximity of its cantonments to the International Boundary, or by concentrating strike formations under the garb of training exercises. While there may be some merit in the initial military viability of such an option, unless India strengthens its technological intelligence and humint capabilities, what needs to be considered is the "day after" impact of India's counter moves to checkmate such a Pakistani offensive. With the IAF in full flow within hours and army formations closing in rapidly on the ingressing Pakistani units, while also simultaneously sealing the border behind them, the invaders would be hard pressed to ensure their own security and would eventually be destroyed in detail. International opinion would also be firmly on India's side. Any well prepared army or air force can achieve tactical surprise, as the Egyptians did during the Yom Kippur war against the Israelis in 1973; the acme of military skill lies in being able to sustain the offensive logistically beyond 48 hours and holding on to the initial gains in the face of the adversary's reaction. It should be clear to perceptive observers that Pakistan has learnt the right lessons from its strategic blunder in Kargil during the summer months of 1999 and is unlikely to repeat such hara-kiri in a hurry.

Inherent in an Indian nuclear first strike option, as advocated by the opponents of no first use, is the Pakistani nuclear retaliation that would inevitably follow on Indian cities and military targets. Cities like Jodhpur, Bikaner, Ahmedabad, Jalandhar, Ludhiana and perhaps even New Delhi and Mumbai would be the likely targets of a retaliatory Pakistani nuclear strike. In all the above scenarios, given the limited gains that an Indian first strike may achieve and the real possibility of successful Pakistani nuclear retaliation, the resounding answer to the first use nuclear option by India is no. An Indian nuclear first strike would not be justified as the costs of Pakistani retaliation would be prohibitive. Nor would it be operationally expedient. In none of the above scenarios India's survival as a nation-state is likely to be seriously threatened. Various other even more pessimistic scenarios could be considered but the result would be the same.

It clearly emerges that across the entire spectrum of conventional conflict, the first use of nuclear weapons by India does not make sound strategic sense. Besides, a first use doctrine would invite international opprobrium, seriously undermine India's efforts towards total nuclear disarmament and be prohibitively costly to implement. It is not generally well appreciated that a first use doctrine requires a massive investment in surveillance and target acquisition infrastructure by way of satellite and aerial reconnaissance and human intelligence to execute 'launch on warning' and 'launch through attack' strategies, with the nuclear forces being maintained on permanent hair trigger alerts. A first use doctrine also requires quick political decision-making and decentralisation of the control of nuclear weapons to theatre commanders in the armed forces. Hence, such a doctrine is inherently more risky and more likely to lead to the accidental, even unauthorised, use of nuclear weapons.

It would, of course, be far better to mutually negotiate a no first use treaty with adversarial nuclear armed states as that would be the best nuclear risk reduction measure. Russia and China have signed a mutual no first use treaty. In case India's nuclear-armed adversaries continue to be recalcitrant in signing a binding no first use pact, it would be worthwhile for India to consider some essential qualifications to India's unilateral no first use doctrine. The first is to clearly spell out that a nuclear strike on Indian soldiers even within Pakistani territory would be deemed to be a nuclear strike on India and would invite massive punitive nuclear retaliation. The absence of this rider would negate India's conventional edge over Pakistan as the army would be forced to plan on launching only shallow limited objective offensives to avoid risking nuclear strikes on the mechanised spearheads leading India's advance. Only the capability of executing deep offensive strikes can ensure conventional deterrence and present viable policy options to prevent Pakistan's predilection for attempting salami slicing in J&K. The second caveat should be that even a conventional bombing or missile attack on India's nuclear establishments and nuclear weapons storage sites during war, that results in casualties due to a nuclear explosion or even radiation leaks, would invite a nuclear response. Though India and Pakistan have signed an agreement on not targeting each other's nuclear facilities, such agreements have little value when war is declared. Also, state-sponsored acts of terrorism or sabotage of India's nuclear establishments and storage sites should also result in nuclear retribution against the sponsoring country. With better surveillance systems and improvements in the intelligence gathering apparatus, it should be possible to accurately determine the identity of the originator of such heinous crimes. Without these inescapable qualifications, with others to be added when necessary, it would be extremely difficult for India to implement a credible no first use doctrine.

Key Features of Nuclear Doctrine

Even though the draft nuclear doctrine formulated by the NSAB is yet to be formally debated in Parliament, there is a broad national consensus on its central facets. According to Jasjit Singh, the following essential elements constitute the key features of India's nuclear doctrine:

Firstly, India's nuclear weapons are meant to deter the use and threat of use of nuclear weapons against India. "But unlike most other nuclear weapon states, India's nuclear weapons are not meant to deter the use and threat of use of conventional weapons, chemical weapons, biological weapons or a generalised formulation of protecting national interests any time anywhere. The doctrine requires that the nuclear policy should seek to deter rather than fight a war with nuclear weapons. The orientation of the doctrine is thus quite narrowly focused on the need to defend India through deterrence against nuclear weapons threat." However, India recognises that nuclear weapons cannot provide deterrence in all circumstances and limited conventional conflict remains possible even under the overhang of nuclear weapons. This was borne out by the 1999 Kargil conflict between India and Pakistan.

Secondly, India's nuclear doctrine is firmly anchored on the principle of "no first use" even against nuclear threat or use. "India's use of its nuclear weapons would be predicated on failure of deterrence, that is, if and when an adversary uses nuclear weapons against India. This severely circumscribes the potential development, deployment and employment of the nuclear arsenal." Thirdly, India's no first use doctrine is a defensive doctrine that limits the use of nuclear weapons to retaliation only. Hence, it is only a precaution against the use of nuclear weapons against India and is in total harmony with the UN Charter. "Article 51 of the Charter under Chapter VII clearly endorses 'the inherent right of individual or collective self-defence if an armed attack occurs against a Member of the United Nations' (emphasis added)... In fact, UN Security Council Resolution 1172 is a gross violation of the UN Charter since it seeks to deny India the right enshrined in the Charter (by seeking) elimination of the capabilities that the permanent members of the Security Council themselves possess and jealously guard by disregarding their treaty obligations of nuclear disarmament."

Fourthly, the doctrine is based on the concept of minimum deterrence that implies that India's nuclear policy, strategy and posture would be guided by the minimalist principle. "The emphasis on "minimum" deterrence clearly defines this principle in relation to the capability sought, the size of the arsenal, costs involved, the level of retaliation required and the nuclear posture in peace time and in times of crisis and active threat."

Finally, "India's nuclear doctrine emphasises that global, verifiable and non-discriminatory nuclear disarmament is a national security objective. This is to be expected from a country that has pursued the goal of complete abolition of nuclear weapons for decades in order to remove its own security dilemma as well as ensure greater prospects for international peace and security."

India's desire to develop a credible minimum nuclear deterrent against nuclear blackmail and the threat of use of nuclear weapons, is an eminently justifiable national security imperative. India's no first use, retaliation-only nuclear doctrine is not only morally befitting and worthy of India's civilisational heritage, it is also operationally sound strategy. However, deterrence hinges on credibility and India is still far from demonstrating strong political resolve to execute a massive retaliatory nuclear strike. Only when India's adversaries are convinced that India has both the necessary political and military will and the hardware wherewithal to respond to a nuclear strike with punitive retaliation that will inflict unacceptable loss of human life and unprecedented material damage, will they be deterred. Only then will the nuclear monster remain tightly leashed in and around India's neighbourhood. The adoption of graduated or flexible response strategies will weaken the quality of India's deterrence and may tempt its adversaries to test India's resolve and capabilities. As long as offensive nuclear deterrence continues to be so unabashedly practised by most of the other NWS, India's defensive nuclear deterrence policies are totally justified.

DEAL OF INDIAN DRAFT NUCLEAR DOCTRINE

The draft has naturally attracted a great deal of comment which was the stated purpose of releasing it to public. Two basic points need attention. Firstly, this is NOT the doctrine accepted or endorsed by the Government of India as yet. It is, as the document says, a draft proposal of the National Security Advisory Board. Secondly, many comments in India and abroad have confused the very concept of a "doctrine" in spite of a clear statement in Preamble of the paper where in para 1.6 the document states that "this document *outlines the broad principles* for the development, deployment and employment of India's nuclear forces.? (Emphasis added) A doctrine is expected to define broad principles and concepts for the guidance of policy makers after it has been approved by duly constituted authorities. It must not be confused with policy, strategy or even posture which no doubt may be expected to flow from it. This elementary fact seems to have been missed by most critics. For example, many people complain that the doctrine does not indicate the ?cost? of India's proposed doctrine. The issue of costs is very important. But should a doctrine paper go into costs? If it does, would it remain a document that outlines ?broad principles?? On the other hand the document consistently states that India would pursue a doctrine of credible ?minimum? deterrence. The concept of minimum is not merely related to a single aspect of, say, numbers, but also to costs and posture.

Much of the critique of the document has risen from two factors. The first is the rather unique approach of making the proposal public for discussion and debate. Unlike conventional weapons whose development, deployment and employment would remain restricted to military and defence establishments, nuclear weapons concern all citizens. In an established democracy the people have a right to know what principles will govern the nuclear policy. The second is even more important. The doctrine does not adopt the conventional wisdom of other nuclear weapon states. To that extent this is not only in contrast to the acknowledged wisdom of the main nuclear powers but seeks to chart a new path.

The central foundation of the doctrine is built on four principles: India's nuclear weapons are meant to deter nuclear weapons threat/ use. Unlike most other nuclear weapon states, India's nuclear weapons are NOT meant to deter the use and threat of use of conventional weapons, chemical weapons, biological weapons or a generalised formulation of protecting national interests any time anywhere. The doctrine requires that the nuclear policy should seek to deter rather than fight a war with nuclear weapons. The orientation of the doctrine is thus completely defensive in philosophy. This also logically severely limits the potential development, deployment and employment of the nuclear arsenal. And hence the emphasis on "minimum." It is unfortunate that in spite of repeated emphasis on minimum deterrence and even simple statements of intent to respond to a nuclear attack with punitive retaliation are interpreted as "massive retaliation" by reputed organisations well versed in the lexicon and concepts of nuclear strategy.

The doctrine rests on the principle of "No First Use? even against nuclear threat or use. It commits Indian nuclear policy to one of retaliation only. Para 2.4 of the draft paper expresses it in the following terms: The fundamental purpose of Indian nuclear weapons is to deter the use and threat of use of nuclear weapons by any State or entity against India and its forces. India will not be the first to initiate a nuclear strike, but will respond with punitive retaliation should deterrence fail.?

The only country to adopt a similar commitment is China although uncertainties have grown in recent years whether China" commitment is a political statement or a doctrinal precept. A retaliation only doctrine accepts the fact that India will not initiate a nuclear strike under any circumstance. On the other hand, in order to reduce the risk of an attack on India it promises in unequivocal terms that sure and certain retaliation will follow. Assuming that rationality operates, as indeed it is expected to in any deterrence equation, this prospect which would lead to unacceptable punishment to the aggressor is expected to function as a deterrent. This no doubt seeks to ensure security of India based on the promise of assured retaliation.

As a defensive doctrine of no-first-use and limiting the use of nuclear weapons to retaliation only, India's draft doctrine is in total harmony with the UN Charter. Article 51 of the Charter under Chapter VII clearly endorses "the inherent right of individual or collective self-defence if an armed attack occurs against a Member of the United States.

The doctrine emphasizes that global, verifiable and non-discriminatory nuclear disarmament is a national security objective. This is to be expected from a country that has pursued the goal of complete abolition of nuclear weapons for decades. In fact the doctrine clearly states that the absence of nuclear disarmament has created the need for India to acquire its nuclear deterrent. It also makes it clear that India's nuclearisation has emerged out of the failure of the international community to institute disarmament half a century after nuclear weapons came into use and more than three decades after the five nuclear weapons states were bound by treaty obligations to do so. The draft doctrine makes it clear that India will not follow the disastrous route of the first tier nuclear weapon states who built up tens of thousands of nuclear weapons in a mindless arms race which they find difficult to even reverse. On the other hand, questions have been raised on the doctrine which needed to be addressed.

Apprehensions have been expressed that this doctrine would set off a nuclear arms race. It is indeed surprising that a doctrine that repeatedly affirms the principle of no-first-use and use in retaliation only is considered by some people to trigger an arms race! Any objective examination of the concept would reveal the reverse to be the case. For a moment let us assume that all nuclear weapon states follow the principle of no-first-use enshrined in the draft doctrine. In that case no country will initiate a nuclear strike. Logically this should trigger an arms race in reverse reducing arsenals to minimum levels and under-cut the necessity for deterrence if the doctrine is implemented honestly. The doctrine promises that India will work for an international treaty banning the first use of nuclear weapons.

The concerns about a potential arms race reflect a perception arising out of the prism of cold War mind-sets where first strike (and even ?launch on warning?) was the order of the day. This necessitated large arsenals and potentially pre-emptive strikes with nuclear weapons.

The result was the peak of 67,000 nuclear warheads. But China did not follow the same route and relied on minimum deterrence concept with a no-first-use commitment. There is no evidence that China's nuclear posture led to any arms race. Even in future China's nuclear arsenal is likely to be dictated by the size of US/ Russian arsenals and issues like ballistic missile defences etc. rather than the defensive doctrine of India.

There is no doubt that India's nuclear doctrine poses a serious challenge to the prevailing doctrines of offensive orientation and first strike strategic doctrines of the US/NATO and Russia. China has been demanding a treaty on no-first-use among the weapon states. The Chinese and Indian doctrines now indicate a counter view to the traditional aggressive doctrines of other nuclear weapon states who visualise use of nuclear weapons against non-nuclear threats. It is not surprising therefore that the US responded to the draft doctrine by saying that India is "moving in the wrong direction."? But since the State Department spokesman acknowledged that the US had yet to examine the document, this appears to have been a reflect action to a doctrine which reflected thinking in total contrast to the US doctrine and belief system.

In conclusion it can be stated with a high level of confidence that the proposed doctrine denotes a serious effort at restraint in the principles for the development, deployment and employment of nuclear weapons. India exercised restraint for decades through its policy of keeping the nuclear option open.

Unfortunately this was not adequately recognised and the noose of non-proliferation without disarmament was pursued by the nuclear weapon states and their allies who themselves are nuclear weapon states in security terms if not in legal terms. The draft doctrine promises restraint within the new framework of a state with nuclear weapons that only seeks to deter a nuclear attack rather than exercise nuclear hegemony. In the final analysis we have to ask a question of our own. There would remain many in this world who for some reason or the other are opposed to India acquiring nuclear weapons. Their views must be respected.

But now that India has declared itself to be a state with nuclear weapons and possesses an efficient nuclear arsenal, the proposed doctrine must be judged from the point whether a defensive doctrine of credible minimum deterrence which relies on no-first-use and use in retaliation only enhances peace and stability or an aggressive doctrine of first use seeking to use nuclear weapons even against non-nuclear threats would be preferred?

MAJOR POINTS MADE IN THE DRAFT DOCTRINE

- India's DND is based on the principle of pursuing security through reliance on the presumed efficacy of nuclear deterrence. The DND, however, admits that such deterrence can fail, in which case India promises adequate punitive retaliation.
- India's nuclear arsenal must be such that it will always provide maximum credibility, effectiveness and survivability. Therefore, the size of the arsenal cannot be fixed but its nature must be dynamic and flexible enough to respond to changes in the security environment (such as changes in the weapons postures of perceived rivals), to changing security needs (as defined by state elites), and to technology advances.
- India's nuclear might must deter any state with nuclear weapons.
- India will pursue triadic deployment and have multiple redundant systems, that is, more than just a 'bare minimum'.
- India will not strike first but will carry out the promptest possible retaliation which will also be punitive, meaning massive enough to be unacceptably damaging to the opponent.
- The nuclear arsenal will be tightly controlled by the political centre, namely the Prime Minister, but will also be of a highly mobile and dispersed nature.

- The safety and security of the weapons system is of paramount importance, and all precautions will be taken to ensure against sabotage, theft and unauthorized or inadvertent use of nuclear weapons (the DND says nothing on how this is to be achieved or ensured).
- India will not accept any restriction whatsoever on its research and development capabilities or activities in regard to nuclear weapons and related areas.
- India promises No-First-Use (NFU) against nuclear weapons states and No-Use against non-nuclear weapons states except where the latter are aligned to nuclear weapons states.
- India will pursue arms control measures and believes in the goal of complete, global disarmament, which it will also pursue.

Nuclear Legitimisation

A major motive of the government was the attempted legitimisation of India's nuclear weapons through the DND. One component of this attempt is the desire to divert public concern and discussion away from the issue of the rights and wrongs of 'going nuclear', i.e., actually manufacturing and deploying such weapons. It is incredible that a first-ever national nuclear doctrine draft does not even attempt to discuss the relative merits and demerits of a non-nuclear weaponised stance in any depth. Instead, it assumes that India has to have nuclear weapons, and proceeds to lay out the kind of weapons systems it feels are required. This omission makes the DND part of the ongoing cosmetic cover-up to treat the Indian nuclear arsenal as a legitimate *fait accompli*. By focusing public awareness mainly on the 'issue' of what kind of weapons system India should have, the DND deliberately makes it more difficult for people to think of reversing India's nuclear weapon-related direction at a time when this is very feasible, as well as desirable and necessary. A second dimension of this attempt to achieve legitimisation is international. The political climate worldwide about nuclear weapons has changed during the decades-long gap in nuclear proliferation prior to May 1998. International opinion against nuclear weapons is now far stronger and more widespread than in the sixties, leaving India (and Pakistan) in considerable diplomatic-political isolation on the issue. In this context, releasing the DND in the name of 'democratic debate' and offering to discuss the DND with other nuclear weapons powers is a way of working around international pressure to further develop and eventually deploy nuclear weapons under the guise of a 'responsible', 'open-minded' and 'consultative' process.

This symbolic value of the DND has nothing to do with its actual contents, which are far more adventurist than would have been expected from government spokespeople making so-called reasonable calls for 'minimum nuclear deterrence'.

India's DND is open to two major levels of criticism. The first and most important level is the fundamental flaw embodied in all nuclear doctrines. This has to do with the inescapable and irreconcilable dilemma of deterrence. At the second level lies a more detailed criticism of specific proposals made within the DND. The first flaw is addressed here, while the actual provisions of the Indian DND are addressed later.

Deterrence is an attempt to achieve security by threatening someone else's security. It is an attempt to avoid war by preparing to fight a war. It seeks security for one country by generating fear and hostility in the other. Not surprisingly, deterrence frequently breaks down and there are actual wars. In non-nuclear confrontations, life carries on despite conventional wars, even for the loser. However, in the case of nuclear deterrence, this cannot be, since there is no way of maintaining civil society for the losers (and even for the winners) after a nuclear exchange. Therefore, unlike for non-nuclear deterrence, the only purpose of preparing for a nuclear war is to avoid it. If nuclear deterrence breaks down (and it is illogical and irrational to believe that it cannot break down, especially since non-nuclear deterrence clearly can, and does) all security collapses, as does most life.

Why can nuclear deterrence break down? It can because it is based on a limited, frequently uninformed, erroneous, and changing perception of how opponents will think about and respond to the threat of nuclear war. In fact, mutually hostile countries would always be tempted to strike first, regardless of commitments given, because it is easy to believe that to do so confers 'great advantage' over a hostile opponent. In the nuclear deterrence framework, the initiator can hope to knock out most of the nuclear might of its opponent especially if it also tries to 'decapitate' the political leadership of the 'enemy'. The country that strikes second is no longer acting to enhance its security, so that nuclear retaliation is an act of revenge, not of security.

In sum, nuclear deterrence, the most 'reasonable' foundation of all nuclear doctrines aiming at security, is nothing but the irrational hope that a terrible fear of the consequences of nuclear war will continuously promote wise decisions by fallible human beings operating under intense pressure in changing circumstances they can never fully control. All nuclear doctrines are thus basically nothing but hope masquerading as operative strategies. The Indian DND is no exception.

SPECIFIC FEATURES OF THE INDIAN DND

As noted earlier, the DND is an attempt to serve as a framework for the limited debate about what kind of nuclear weapons India is to have. The DND is thus a statement of intent and will be treated as such for the moment, although the issue of the lack of India's capacity to build what the DND claims is necessary is itself a major point of concern.

An inconsistent stance: The DND (Paragraph 2.1) says that building a deterrent force is "consistent with the UN Charter, which sanctions the right of self-defence". This extension of the cover of the UN charter to nuclear weapons is illegitimate and hypocritical.

This is especially so, given the ruling of the International Court of Justice (ICJ) which has rejected any such right in regard to nuclear weapons except in the case of the most "extreme circumstance of self-defence" on which it has given no ruling at all. Nuclear weapons are instruments of revenge or offence, not defence. In fact, in 1995, the Indian government had submitted its own memorandum to the ICJ insisting that the use of nuclear weapons, the threat of their use (deterrence), their development and deployment, and even preparations to build such weapons were immoral, illegal and unacceptable "in all circumstances"!

Punitive Retaliation and Potential Targets

The draft admits that deterrence can fail but say that in that case there will be "punitive retaliation". Punitive retaliation comes when 'nuclear security' has failed. But the DND fails to acknowledge the basic insoluble dilemma of nuclear deterrence. Of course, the DND also does not admit that such retaliation, even if possible, is simply a senseless and suicidal act of revenge since it will lead to continuing nuclear exchanges. Given this context of punitive retaliation, the DND is covering up the fact that once deterrence fails there is permanent collapse of security.

Further, the draft says "Indian nuclear weapons are to deter use and threat of use of nuclear weapons by any State or entity against India". Paragraph 4.1 says "Any adversary must know that India can and will retaliate to inflict destruction that the aggressor will find unacceptable". These stances are so open-ended that they can assert a need for nuclear deterrence against almost anybody, including major nuclear weapons states such as the USA as well as entities such as NATO. This would require a huge weapons system for 'credible' second-strike capacity. These stances effectively commit India to an arms race with the major nuclear weapons states — an economically, politically and socially suicidal policy.

In paragraph 2.5, the DND says there will be no use of nuclear weapons against non-nuclear states if they "are not aligned with nuclear weapons powers". So Japan, for example, may not get an assurance of non-use, only of no-first-use (NFU). This ambiguity not only dilutes India's earlier NFU commitment but is more objectionable than, say, China's NFU commitment which specifically excludes use against any non-nuclear state regardless of whether or not it is allied to a nuclear state.

This paragraph also flatly contradicts paragraph 8.3 in the same document which says, "Having provided negative security assurances, India shall work for internationally binding negative security assurances by nuclear weapons states to non-nuclear weapons states."

Paragraph 5.2 talks of "sequential plans", "flexibility and responsiveness", an "integrated operational plan" and "a targeting policy". These make sense only in relation to identified, actual opponents. This flatly contradicts the government claim that India's weapons are "not country-specific". Such a posture in practice will clearly vitiate India's immediate security environment further rather than improving it.

The Notion of 'Minimum' Deterrence

The draft doctrine talks of triadic deployment and "sea-based assets", "multiple redundant systems, mobility, dispersion and deception". Paragraph 2.2 talks of developing a capability of "maximum (our emphasis) credibility, survivability, effectiveness". What all this means is simple. In defining its 'minimum deterrent', the DND is so ambitious and open-ended that it makes a mockery of any even remotely reasonable notion of 'minimum'. Britain has moved towards a single system of deployment; France is moving towards it and NATO in practice no longer has triadic deployment (it has some airborne and submarine deployment). In this background, India's idea of triadic deployment as a 'minimum deterrent' appears especially bizarre. The DND also talks of "sea-based" rather than strictly submarine-based nuclear weapons, which leaves open the option of tactical nuclear missiles on surface vessels. 'Tactical' nuclear weapons are not, incidentally, explicitly repudiated anywhere in the DND. Since such weapons are irrelevant even to the notion of nuclear deterrence, there is ground for legitimate concern that the DND has a hidden agenda extending beyond even 'minimum nuclear deterrence' to nuclear weapon-based attempts at hegemony.

Paragraph 3.2 commits India to shift from "peacetime deployment to fully employable forces in the shortest possible time". When this is linked with the requirement for "mobility, dispersion and deception", and with paragraph 5.5 which talks of executing "operations in an NBC environment" ('NBC' refers to 'nuclear, biological and chemical' weapons) what emerges is a rationalization of two actions.

Firstly, it implies possible delegation of authority to use nuclear weapons, which contradicts talk of centralizing such a decision at one point (the Prime Minister). Certainly, all nuclear weapons systems and nuclear deterrence ideologies suffer from this inescapable and unresolvable contradiction, and it would have been astounding if the Indian DND, with its far-beyond-'minimum' stances, were to be any exception. If there is a 'decapitating first strike' which is even partially successful, who will decide on the launch of the remainder of the weapons, and how will this decision be taken if delegation has not been allowed for? On the other hand, delegation of any sort weakens central control and is more provocative and dangerous.

Secondly, the DND demands the quickest possible retaliation, which has to mean launch-on-warning of an enemy attack, or launch-under-attack, or immediate launch-after-attack. In all these modes, there is a requirement for a nuclear weapons system at a high level of operational alert and readiness, with regular training exercises for maintenance. All of these 'aggression-as-a-routine' postures are bound to be deeply expensive, provocative and destabilizing — none of them good indicators of enhanced security.

Furthermore, paragraphs 7.1 and 7.2 insist on continuous and unrestrained research and development in nuclear weapons. Once again, this indicates the shifting base of the DND's notion of 'minimum deterrence', and demonstrates that the DND is tacitly accepting the inevitability of an arms race, committing India to enthusiastic participation in that doomed exercise.

Costs Implicit in the DND

How much is the nuclear arsenal envisaged by the DND likely to cost? This is hard to answer, in part because the DND excludes nothing in principle. Triadic deployment in operational readiness is explicitly envisioned. Tactical weapons are not excluded, neither is a 'credible' second-strike capacity against large nuclear weapons states such as the USA, nor a ballistic missile defence system, nor continuous research into ever more advanced nuclear weapons, nor "space-base d assets" for early warning and damage monitoring. In fact, nothing in the DND suggests any bar to spending on the scale of the nuclear weapons programme of, say, the USA. In such a situation cost estimates can only be highly speculative, uncertain and subject to constant escalation. Even an adequate breakdown of the costs of the different components of the weapons system cannot be made. Further, the DND recognizes that there is no such thing as a 'stable minimum posture' in terms of defined quantities, estimates of which would be needed if costs are even to be guessed at. The DND also talks of flexibility and responsiveness to changing force structures of other nuclear powers and to technology advances, compounding the open-ended nature of expenditure.

However, the 'base' which this DND aims for is already so advanced (triadic rather than single-system deployment) as to impose an enormous burden. In addition, it is reasonable to assume that there will be difficulties because of supply obstacles, external restrictions, construction failures and over-runs, and costs will skyrocket. This is when only the initial development and manufacturing costs are considered. There are constantly recurring (annual) costs for maintenance and replacement-improvement which can be anything between 30% to 50% of the total costs incurred in institutionalizing a nuclear weapons system. Producing nuclear bombs takes usually around 10% of the total cost. Command, control, communications, intelligence mechanisms account for about a third, and over 50% goes towards the delivery systems. And finally, all these costs are in addition to rather than substituting for conventional defence costs (a point made depressingly clear by the Kargil confrontation in mid-1999), which themselves are likely to rise as the security environment degrades further in mutual suspicion and provocation.

Although no definitive numbers can be guessed at, what range of spending is likely to be necessary? One way is to ask the NSAB panel which produced the DND. While the DND itself is silent on the issue of costs, a member of this panel has said that costs for the proposed 'minimum deterrent' can be anything from Rs.70,000 to 700,000 crore rupees, or 15 to 150 billion dollars. A second method is extrapolation. Earlier estimates of a 'small' 100-warhead arsenal are of the order of Rs.40,000 to 50,000 crores. The arsenal envisaged by the DND which could well have 400 plus weapons is likely to cost several-fold more. A third way is to look at what other countries have spent. Its nuclear deterrent has cost the USA over 5.5 trillion (5,500 billion) dollars. The Chinese 'minimum' has so far cost well over 100 billion dollars or 450,000 crore rupees. Even if the unrealistic assumption is made that a 'modest' Indian deterrent is going to be somewhat less expensive than the Chinese arsenal, the figure of Rs.70,000 crores is a hopeless underestimate.

What Does the DND Represent? Clearly, this is not a doctrine which is any less awful than others around the world. The DND is adventurist, aggressive and destabilizing like others of its kind. It makes a mockery even of the so-called 'reasonable' notion that India should have a small 'minimum' deterrent, that there will be no competitive arms race with rivals and that the construction of a 'minimum' will be cheap. If implemented, the DND can only push India further into the nuclear abyss. The DND thus reinforces the view that the Indian government's decision to 'go nuclear' was not determined by any changes in threat perceptions, nor by any degradation of national security, but instead by the obsession with nuclear weapons as 'status symbol' and 'power currency' which needs an open-ended and highly ambitious arsenal, regardless of the cost to the nation. The DND is entirely in keeping with the self-righteous and grandiose 'nationalism' of the BJP-led government and of its ideological mentors which makes the people subservient to the 'state'.

India can either relentlessly pursue a global nuclear disarmament programme or recklessly join the nuclear arms race. It cannot move in these diametrically opposite directions at the same time. The claim of the DND that it intends to pursue both these goals simultaneously is a blatant contradiction, and its proposed espousal aims to mislead not only the people of India but of the entire world.

DRAFT NUCLEAR DOCTRINE OF INDIA: RETURN TO REALITY

With due deference to some of the best intellects comprising the National Security Advisory Board, one must admit that a reading of the draft nuclear doctrine gives the impression that it is full of generalisations generated from the cold war literature of the fifties and the sixties. Basically, a country's nuclear doctrine is closely related to its defence policies and consequent strategy. One is not aware of the details of such policies and strategies though papers on the subject have apparently been prepared by the NSAB. It is not however difficult to envisage the security threats for India in the coming century (talking of millenium is unreasonable as a country's history undergoes enormous changes in a millenium as India's own history has in the last millenium.) and hence the needed policies and strategies.

India's immediate threat to its well being as a secular democratic and prosperous country emerges from the policy of implacable hostility followed by Pakistan. After having unsuccessfully fought with India three times over Kashmir, it made another desperate attempt in its recent misadventure at Kargil which ended in its Prime Minister's journey to the prison and installation of one more despotic regime in the name of "saving the country." Predictably, Pakistan reverted to the easy and low cost method of depredations through mercenary desperados who were sought to be dignified by the epithet " mujahideens". The attack on the Military Hqrs at Badami bagh in Kashmir makes it clear that if anything, the new regime would actively and more aggressively follow the policy of low cost conflict in Kashmir. The Kargil adventure was started by Pakistan under the misplaced confidence that India would not enlarge the war for fear of escalating it to the nuclear level. Comparisons have been made between the restrained reaction of India now and in 1965 when it opened a second front to stop the Pakistanis in their track. Be that as it may, Pakistanis are emboldened enough to keep trying their hands at wresting Kashmir from India both by the so called "low intensity conflict " and occasional misadventures in the hope that one day they will succeed.

What should be India's response? Would it be forced to open a second front in the future if situation warrants and if so would it be prepared if Pakistan escalates it to the nuclear level, rejecting as they have, the policy of no first use. If such a sorry situation comes to pass what are our options since we have foregone the option of first use? No first use would mean a second strike capability ie. absorbing Pakistan's first nuclear attack and delivering "unacceptable damage" to them. This policy is predicated on Pakistani perception of "unacceptable damage" which should deter them from carrying out the first attack. The imponderables here are the extent of damage to us in the first nuclear attack by Pakistan and Pakistan's view of "unacceptable damage ". Assessing these and coming to a conclusion on what minimum capability we need is what minimum deterrence is all about as far as threat from Pakistan goes.

Next comes the so called China threat. Not withstanding the problems and trauma left behind by the inglorious war of 1962, one cannot see any immediate threat from China. Though slow and tortuous, negotiations are on between the two countries to find an equitable solution to the border disputes. China is unlikely to and in fact has no need to resort to arms to settle the issue, China's major strategic objectives in the 1962 war have been achieved. The vexing problem with China is the latter's continuos support to Pakistan in the latter's quest for nuclear and missile capability. Even here, there seems to have been considerable progress with China seemingly inclined to end its proliferation policies under American pressure. Some Indian Strategists see in a long term perspective, future conflicts between India and China over "Lebensraum". This is an intangible threat and a better way to prepare for it is by strengthening India's economic and technological potentials. Without dismissing outright security threat from China as non existent, an immediate threat from China is not apparent, given China's perception of its security problems and its anxiety to have a peaceful neighbourhood, to pursue its ambitious economic plan and reach the standards of developed countries by the middle of the next century. In any case India needs considerable time to catch up with China's weapon and missile capabilities.

The third threat justifying India's nuclear quest is what the draft nuclear doctrine calls as the absence of global nuclear disarmament requiring effective, credible, nuclear deterrence and adequate retaliatory capability in India's strategic interests, should deterrence fail. In effect this means that India should be ready to face the world with its nuclear weapons! - a controversial concept based on somewhat exaggerated view of threat to its security and the need to prepare for it.

In the light of the foregoing does India need an elaborate nuclear weapons system involving triad of bombers and land and sea based missiles? This could be examined against each of the threats discussed earlier.

Taking the nuclear threat from Pakistan, a nuclear exchange between the two countries, no matter who starts it first, would leave neither country a victor but both vanquished in the killing fields of radio active debris which does not recognise international borders. It is quite unrealistic to plan for elaborate command and control system with brief cases and buttons following the P.M. A missile from Pakistan should not take more than five to10 minutes to reach India, to be more specific New Delhi. To be somewhat light hearted on a grave issue - What happens when the P.M has a bath even for a modest 10 minutes and Pakistanis let go a nuke? Would another elaborate command and control centre be established in deep south, if - God forbid - New Delhi or its command and control centre is wiped out. As another commentator has said, it would be height of cynicism to provide only for protection of India's nuclear weapons and leave the people to their fate. With no information available on the accuracy of the missiles of either country it can only be presumed that both are planning on deterrence by city bursting capability which requires no great accuracy of the missiles. Even assuming that the second strike capability is fully established and India proceeds to punish Pakistan with " unacceptable damage" what would it be sufficient number of bombs to wipe out Islamabad and Lahore if not Karachi? How would the returning radioactive debris be taken care of from wiping out large segment of our population by cancer related deaths, not to speak of subsequent generation of maimed children. It is thus obvious that nuclear war is unthinkable between the two countries.

One hopes that such wisdom exists also among the present rulers of Pakistan though they may not be rational on other Indo - Pak issues. Fear however has been expressed that current instability in Pakistan could force it towards a fundamentalist, extremist regime which could irrationally think of using nukes. against India. Though possession of certain no. of nukes and the means to deliver them may deter nuclear attack even by the irrational Islamists building an elaborate triad of bombers, missiles and submarines at enormous cost would in no way completely eliminate this threat and would certainly not merit mention as " minimum deterrence". As a respected member of the Indian scientific establishment is reported to have once said " A bullock cart is enough to carry the bomb across the border!

The most ideal deterrence against Pakistan is to build a system of smart weapons which could be used to decapitate its nuclear capability, if it looks that a conventional war is in danger of escalating into a nuclear one. The prerequisites for such a plan is a good intelligence capability based on a robust sensor technology combined with a good chip industry (as these could be denied to us at crucial moments) to build the smart weapons. Mobile missiles may not be eliminated completely by this plan but even mobile missiles take some time to set up and fire and excellent intelligence and possession of anti missile capability are the only hopes to avert this threat. Critics might point out that it is a very expensive proposition but then you can't talk of nuclear deterrence against others without your being deterred, if you are not willing to accept the cost of being a deterring nuclear power. In the final analysis India has to accept or atleast plan for the possibility of a limited nuclear attack, having gone nuclear and having an irrational nuclear neighbour. All other nuclear powers do. Hope lies in minimum damage if complete elimination is not possible.

On the threat from China, such a threat as already indicated is not an immediate one - not in any case a threat which can escalate into a nuclear one. Both countries have declared No First Use Policy and One cannot envisage a situation where China comes under sufficient pressure from India to break its own declaration and use the nuclear weapon against India first. Today; India's nuclear and missile capabilities are far lower than that of China. China itself is in the process of modernising its nuclear and missile forces including miniaturisation of war heads for tactical weapons and MIRV capability, though the target of its modernisation may not be India. India would require a much longer time frame to achieve parity and deterrence capability against China - may be 20 years at a modest reckoning and assuming a steady increase in India's technological capability.

As for developing nuclear capability from the point of view of a global threat, India should give up any notion of preparing a plan with this perspective. A nuclear policy based on such threat perception would entail enormous cost with the system of triads (particularly nuclear armed submarines from survivability angle), acquisition of sufficient number of warheads, and missiles with MIRV capabilities to establish the deterrence of a second strike capability.Can India ignore the opportunity cost of these systems which can go into social sector like health, education and employment, especially when such systems seem to be totally unwarranted in the global context.

It is therefore reassuring to read the foreign minister's views that a triad of nuclear forces is not a prerequisite for credibility and that the idea of a hair trigger alert for Indian nuclear forces is dangerous. A sane statement that could return India to reality.

7

Nuclear Arms in India

India's defeat in war in 1962 was quickly followed by another uncomfortable military development for India, China's explosion of a nuclear device in 1964. This may have been carried out by Beijing primarily with the US and perhaps the Soviet Union in mind. However, one side effect was that India was now faced not only with a territorial foe, but also a nuclear foe, an uncomfortable power imbalance from India's point of view.

There may have been some limited moves toward reducing Sino-Indian hostilities following Rajiv Gandhi's trip to China in 1988, but relations still remained quite cool in the 1990s. Underlying perceptions of mistrust were very clear on India's side, as well as a sense of having been overtaken in the global pecking order and estimation.

China was firmly in Indian sights in the late 1990s, as someone to be strategically matched, something of an ongoing quest. At the time, 1997, Mohan felt that given "the national determination in India to liberate itself from the current second class status in world affairs ... New Delhi will find it impossible to give up its search for global status similar to that of China"; in which "New Delhi is most unlikely give up its determination to acquire a functional nuclear deterrent against Beijing ... India will remain committed to building a small but functional deterrent against China." China's installation of CSS-5s medium range missiles in Tibet, with a range of about 1,333 miles, was highlighted in the Indian media during 1997 as targeting India.

Raja Mohan's 1997 predictions were quickly met, as India moved in 1998 toward transforming its implicit 1974 nuclear capability into an explicit realized capacity. The Prime Minister Atal Bihari Vajpayee was blunt concerning China factors behind the Pokhran-II tests by India:

We have an overt nuclear weapons state [China] on our borders, a state that committed armed aggression against India in 1962. Although our relations with that country have improved in the last decade or so, an atmosphere of distrust persists, mainly due to the unresolved border problem. To add to the distrust, that country has materially helped another neighbour of ours [Pakistan] to become a covert nuclear weapons state.

Vajpayee may not have intended this letter to the US president to be publicized; but the sentiments were clear enough, objectively and subjectively. Indian commentators like General Amarjit Kalkat, who had commanded the Indian peace keeping forces in Sri Lanka in 1987, were also clear at the time where the message of India's nuclear explosions was aimed. It was not a local regional demonstration against Pakistan. Instead, Kalkat argued that:

What strikes me as being particularly significant is their effect on India-China relations.

These will be put on an even footing ... The tests are really an attempt to correct the current military and technological imbalance vis--vis China, which is already in the threshold of being a world super power ... Countries tend to respect equals and nuclear parity does help provide the level playing field needed to build such an equalitarian relationship. China has been a nuclear power for long, but India was not till it showed its capability this week.

Similar logic was apparent with India's successful testing of an Agni-II medium range (2,500-3,000 kilometers/1,550-1,860 miles) missile in 1999. Dinkar Shukla at the Government of India's Press Information Bureau asserted that "Pokhran-II and Agni-II are a symbol of a resurgent India," in which "the Pakistani threat is only a marginal factor in New Delhi's security calculus. Agni is at the heart of deterrence in the larger context of the Sino-Indian equation." Such considerations were why Chellaney argued in 2000 that "a major motivation for India's 1998 nuclear tests was the growing military asymmetry with China."

IR theory enters the picture with regard to China's differing responses in 1962 and 1998. Whereas China took military action against India in 1962, it initially responded fairly mildly to India's nuclear explosion in 1998. Lei Guang argues that different perceptions were in play. In 1962, China could feel that its identity was at stake through India refusing to negotiate over what China considered was an unequal treaty imposed on it in earlier times of weakness. Guang argues that "given the centrality of territory to the Chinese national identity, what constituted the border between China and its neighbour was no longer simply a matter of administrative marking." Instead, there was a threefold challenge to China, to its perceived territory, sovereignty and legitimacy. Consequently, this "triple assault on China's fundamental identity as a nation-state contributed to its final decision to resort to violence in 1962." Such consideration are rightly seen by Guang as an example of IR constructivism.

Conversely, China took a more subdued and restrained approach to India's nuclear testing in 1998. Guang explains this difference by arguing that China's core identity was not particularly threatened by this event; India's nuclear explosion "did not constitute a frontal attack on the PRC's identity in 1998. On the contrary, it testified to China's nuclear power and affirmed its position as a major power in the region." This did not mean that China was not concerned about India's nuclear explosion. What it did mean was that China responded in different ways and at a different pitch than in 1962. As Guang argues, "a main thrust of the Chinese reaction to India's nuclear tests in 1998 was geopolitical in nature. Unlike in 1962, what was at stake for China in 1998 was its national security, not its fundamental identity as a modern nation-state." Its power advantages enabled a cooler calculated restraint in 1998.

Nuclear rivalry continues to affect Sino-Indian relations. A nuclear arms race, and its "nuclear security dilemma" dynamics, adds a competitive spiral element to their relationship. Even as the dust from India's Pokhran-II tests was settling, further deployment of Chinese missiles was causing alarm in India, Chellaney pointing out in 2000 that "India's largest neighbor [China] is conducting the biggest expansion of missile capabilities anywhere in the world. The first of these new missiles, the Dongfeng (DF) 31, last tested in July 1999, can reach every corner of India but little of U.S. territory."

Chellaney's own sense of the political context of China's nuclear program was stark, "India's existing modest deterrent capabilities will be gravely undermined as China builds up its nuclear and missile armories.

The Sino-Indian asymmetry will increase ... India will have every incentive to acquire similar assets that play a primary role in power-projection strategies." An offensive weapons spiral was in the offing from both sides. Whilst welcoming US attempts to develop a AMD (Anti-Missile Defence) system, Chellaney acknowledged and concluded that "nevertheless, the likely response of those states whose security will be directly affected, particularly China, will significantly affect India's interests.

This is what India has to worry about"; even though "in due course, the action-reaction cycle triggered by missile defences could drive India closer to the United States." Strategic alignment between India and the US is Beijing's nightmare.

In terms of power projection, China's control of Tibet has seen its installation of various medium and intermediate range missile systems. These missile systems are irrelevant to curbing domestic discontent inside Tibet, but do literally and strategically point outside Tibet toward India, its capital Delhi and other major Indian cities. Indian analysts are acutely aware of these implications.

For Mahapatra, this military buildup in Tibet is "not only aimed at overwhelming India militarily, but to enable Chinese coercive diplomacy in respect of the border dispute." Asymmetrics is in play. Installation of intermediate and medium range ballistic missiles enables China to immediately and easily threaten India; whereas the main centers of China, Beijing, Shanghai, Guangzhou remained far away from India. Back in 1999, Kanwal was lamenting that "realistic deterrence against China can only be achieved by developing a demonstrated capability to target major Chinese cities such as Beijing and Shanghai with nuclear weapons." However, India's successful testing of the Agni-III intermediate range ballistic missile in 2007 and 2008, with a range of 3,500 kilometres (2,170 miles), for the first time brings many of China's main cities within range of India's nuclear strike capability. The Agni-I short range ballistic missile is clearly oriented towards Pakistan, Agni-III is equally clearly oriented towards China, "China-specific" in Pandit's eyes. India's nuclear mobility is strengthened by the submarine based Sagarika ballistic missile launches carried out in 2008. India is set to test its augmented Agni-III+/IV missile system, with a range of 5,000 kilometres (3,110 miles) in early 2009, enabling India to target all of China for the first time. From China's point of view, this increases its nuclear encirclement, in part from India, in part from India in conjunction with the United States.

Of course, India's and China's modernization and expansion of their nuclear and missile capability is not necessarily just aimed at each other. India has its ongoing concerns with Pakistan, China has its own set of concerns with the United States. Nevertheless, India and China also feed off each other's nuclear programs. The final twist in the nuclear relationship is India's drive to establish an effective anti-ballistic MDS (Missile Defence System), in part through collaboration with the United States, but in part under its own efforts. Following successful interceptor missile tests in 2006 and 2007, India claims to have developed an ABM (Anti-Ballistic Missile) capacity, with operational deployment scheduled by 2011. Classic security dilemma dynamics operate here. As admitted by Mohanty, "China would watch India's growing missile defence capability very carefully ... there is hardly any doubt that both China and Pakistan would most likely try to strengthen their missile strike capabilities to maintain the strategic deterrence." From India's point of view, China's close nuclear links with Pakistan remains a further exacerbating and exasperating factor in Sino-Indian relations, and is part of their respective encirclement and alignment scenarios to which we now turn.

INDIA - NUCLEAR NEIGHBOURHOOD: CHALLENGES FOR INDIA

An excellent civilian perspective on the aspect of Limited wars against a Nuclear backdrop. India is perhaps the only country that faces the challenges arising from having two nuclear neighbours, who closely cooperate with each others' nuclear programmes and who maintain adversarial relations with her. A nuclear-weapon enabled terrorist threat is supported by strong and consistent denials of culpability for any such 'non-state' attack and a reliance on its 'protector' and mentor, China, to handle the inevitable diplomatic furore that is bound to rise if the taboo on nuclear weapons is broken with however limited an application.

It would appear that Pakistan has adopted a policy of battlefield use of its nuclear weapons, a likely escalation of a conventional confrontation to a nuclear level, arrangements for rapid deployment which could entail pre-delegation to unit commanders in the event of a loss of communications, (which is what apparently happened at Salala recently when 24 Pakistani soldiers were killed in an ISAF air attack on two border posts). She asserts that there is a need to slightly tweak our nuclear doctrine; the objective would be not to change our No First Use policy, but to revert to the language of the Draft doctrine on the question of retaliatory strikes - these should be 'punitive' rather than 'massive' as now exists.

Lastly, she makes the very bold assertion that in order to disillusion the adversary of our intent to retaliate, the control of the weapons should be placed squarely with the Strategic Forces Command. Recent developments in India's neighbourhood have led to an increase in the instability in the region with particular implications for India's security. Pakistan's foolhardiness - or as the Pakistanis view it, their boldness - in challenging the international community by deciding to not attend - and to not allow its surrogates, the Taliban - to attend the just concluded Bonn Conference on Afghanistan, in taking actions which could see a military confrontation with the US and the ISAF forces on its western border and when it is such a parlous situation at home, can only arise from their assurance that at least politically and diplomatically, if not militarily, they can depend on the support of China.

Despite India's own efforts to manage her prickly relations with China, such unqualified support of Pakistan, particularly in the military and nuclear areas, must inevitably raise concerns in India. India is perhaps the only country that faces - or has ever faced - the challenges arising from having two nuclear neighbours, who closely cooperate with each others' nuclear programmes and who maintain adversarial relations with her.

To be sure, during the Cold War, the Soviet Union faced several hostile nuclear neighbours, which were bound together in an alliance and from 1971, another nuclear neighbour that formed a formidable challenge to its security. China, too, till 1971 and for about a decade before that, faced both the United States and the Soviet Union in adversarial positions. It was in the context of the Cold War that theories of limited conventional wars under a nuclear overhang - usually on different continents - has been developed by scholars, mainly in the West. Whether such theories are applicable to the dual challenge facing India is a question that needs to be carefully considered.

Unique Scenario

The situation that India faces today is unique; firstly, it shares common and disputed borders with both hostile neighbours; China has, according to several knowledgeable commentators and intelligence sources (of the West) built-up Pakistan's nuclear arsenal almost from scratch - providing designs, material, including fissile material, technology, delivery vehicles (either directly or through North Korea) and even conducted a weapons test in 1990 on its Lop Nor Test site, for Pakistan. Today it is supplying reactors, which it claims will be under IAEA safeguards; but given the short shrift it has given the Nuclear Suppliers' Group, not to mention its obligations under the NPT in arriving at the agreement to do so, it is unlikely that the material from these reactors will remain for civilian purposes only.

Thirdly and most dangerously, Pakistan has been using its growing nuclear arsenal as an umbrella under which it appears to feel that it can use sub-conventional attacks against India with little or no danger of (conventional) retaliation. None of the above has been seriously disputed by either party; nor has the vague but ominous 'red lines' that Pakistan seems to have evolved regarding its stated doctrine of first use of nuclear weapons. It appears to have in mind the escalation of any conventional response from India to even an armed attack on Indian soil by its nationals, to a nuclear counter-response.

The theories of deterrence would seem to not be applicable in a situation if there is a 'failure of rationality' on one side. Of course, it could very well be that the intention is to indeed give an impression of irrationality, to act as a deterrent to any action on India's part for fear that Pakistan would react 'irrationally'. This stand, of what has been termed 'a nuclear-weapon enabled terrorist threat' is supported by strong and consistent denials of culpability for any such 'non-state' attack and a reliance on its 'protector' and mentor, China, to handle the inevitable diplomatic furore that is bound to rise if the taboo on nuclear weapons is broken with however limited an application. India's doctrine calls for 'massive retaliation' in the event of a nuclear first strike; that would entail attacking counter-value targets, which could include cities and other population centres.

There would inevitably be calls for restraint on India's part, despite the enormity of the action by Pakistan and there is also likely to be some domestic resistance to attacks on cities or towns. In this, perhaps, worst-case but not improbable, scenario, what are India's options?

There are some facts which are needed to be factored in to any consideration of the issue

Difference between a 'declaratory' doctrine and an operational one; the latter can only be deduced from the information available on acquisitions and capabilities, statements of policy by albeit retired senior military men from Pakistan and such Western sources, presumably from intelligence inputs. On the basis of these, it would appear that Pakistan has adopted a policy of battlefield use of its nuclear weapons, a likely escalation of a conventional confrontation to a nuclear level, arrangements for rapid deployment which could entail predelegation to unit commanders in the event of a loss of communications, (which is what apparently happened at Salala recently when 24 Pakistani soldiers were killed in an ISAF air attack on two border posts)

Sino-Pak Nexus

Firstly, we need to take China's support of Pakistan for granted, even the use by the latter of non-state groups as a part of their foreign and security policy. This has been demonstrated repeatedly and not only in the UN Security Council, where China has blocked any forward movement on the naming of specific Pakistani nationals and sponsored groups as terrorists. Secondly, while the state of the internal instability in Pakistan is probably exaggerated in the media, Indian, Pakistani and the Western, there is no doubt that there is a considerable rise in religiosity with strong sectarian and intolerant strains in Pakistani society in general; this would have an inevitable impact on all state institutions, including the military. At the same time, the military has not yet abjured its support for specific non-state groups as 'assets' in the furtherance of its foreign policy objectives.

Some of the groups may well be out of control of the military, though there is little apparent effort to control them in any effective way, though some other groups, targeting the Pakistani state, are being attacked or negotiated with, according to press reports. Thirdly, while like many other developing countries, Pakistan's economy is currently in a very fragile condition, the worsening of relations with the US may adversely affect the budgetary support that Pakistan has been used to receive - China usually restricts itself only to project and commodity aid and does not give budgetary support to any of its allies, however close.

Notwithstanding these developments, the ambitions of Pakistan's military remain vaulting. Given these facts, it is clear that the situation is such that in the event of any crisis, or with the intention of creating one, India could face nuclear threats at multiple levels from Pakistan - it is not unlikely that these would be supported by China, which, however, will ensure that it is not directly involved.

The Pakistani nuclear doctrine, at least our knowledge of it, is today based on an interview given by Lt General Khalid Kidwai (retd), Director General of Pakistan's Strategic Plans Division to Paolo Cotta-Rassmussen and Maurizio Martinelli published by Pugwash International in 2002. There is, however, as has been noted elsewhere, a difference between a 'declaratory' doctrine and an operational one; the latter can only be deduced from the information available on acquisitions and capabilities, statements of policy by albeit retired senior military men from Pakistan and such Western sources, presumably from intelligence inputs.

On the basis of these, it would appear that Pakistan has adopted a policy of battlefield use of its nuclear weapons, a likely escalation of a conventional confrontation to a nuclear level, arrangements for rapid deployment which could entail predelegation to unit commanders in the event of a loss of communications, (which is what apparently happened at Salala recently when 24 Pakistani soldiers were killed in an ISAF air attack on two border posts) and increasing risks of inadvertent or accidental launch. Ashley Tellis in his 2000 book on India's Emerging Nuclear Posture has written of the 'uncertainties' which arise from "The severe motivational and cognitive biases that have historically afflicted Pakistan's higher decision making institutions on matters of war and peace (which) raise fears about the prospect of extreme responses that might be precipitated in a crisis ... These failures of rationality ... could be compounded by exigencies of domestic politics, civil-military discord and biased and unreliable intelligence ... "This posture is one which appears to be based on the assumption that India will not permit the situation to escalate, by considering a limited and targeted use of, for example, air strikes.

Non-state Actors

At another level, non-state groups could be used either to provoke a military response from India, or, more dangerously, nuclear material could become available to these groups through theft or through insider linkages. The attack on Pakistan's Mehran naval base was apparently enabled by insider collusion. At the same time the already friable situation could be exacerbated to intolerable levels if the state itself, following the trends within Pakistani society, becomes a theocratic intolerant state, bent on the establishment of a Caliphate in the region. The military and non-state groups are certain to have been emboldened by India having been 'deterred' in 1999, following the Kargil attack, in 2001 after the attack on Parliament and Operation Parakram and more so, after 2008, after the attack on Mumbai.

Would India react differently in the event of another Mumbai-type attack? *There is a need to slightly tweak our nuclear doctrine; the objective would be not to change our No First Use policy, but to revert to the language of the Draft doctrine on the question of retaliatory strikes - these should be 'punitive' rather than 'massive' as now exists. Massive retaliation would imply counter-value strikes and would lead to incorrect assumptions on the part of the adversary, whereas a punitive strike would retain the flexibility of options. In addition, in order to disillusion the adversary of our intent to retaliate, the control of the weapons should be placed squarely with the Strategic Forces Command* There is no doubt that the current dialogue with Pakistan helps us to buy some time, though given the political instability in Pakistan and the split polity in India, the chances of it being sustainable or effective remain slight unless other signals are sent.

There is a need to use this time to formulate other tools to reinforce the message behind the talks; a need for example, to start serious discussions with Pakistan on nuclear doctrines. It will be more difficult to get this accepted by the Pakistanis, particularly as the Pakistani military is at the moment more preoccupied with consolidating its somewhat frayed image within the country and dealing with the immediate challenges of dealing with the US and Pakistan's ambitions in Afghanistan. Nonetheless this objective has to be followed with persistence and patience, with as much importance given to this objective as to our overall military preparedness. So far, there have been some discussions on nuclear CBMs with Pakistan, mainly at the Track II level, but they have been over-modest efforts and at the official level, the steps have been faltering and weak. Pakistan sees its nuclear weapons not only as essential to their security but as their 'crown jewels' almost as a symbol of their nationhood.

Without disputing their possession of these weapons, however, an increase in efforts to prevent any nuclear misadventure is urgent. At the same time, discussions on nuclear issues with China too, need to be started and again it will be a difficult task. The discussions need to be at high political levels or even with trusted back channels. Some Track II discussions have indeed taken place with China, but they remain sporadic and with little substance or follow-up.

Retribution

Within our own establishment, there is a need to slightly tweak our nuclear doctrine; the objective would be not to change our No First Use policy, but to revert to the language of the Draft doctrine on the question of retaliatory strikes - these should be 'punitive' rather than 'massive' as now exists. Massive retaliation would imply counter-value strikes and would lead to incorrect assumptions on the part of the adversary, whereas a punitive strike would retain the flexibility of options. In addition, in order to disillusion the adversary of our intent to retaliate, the control of the weapons should be placed squarely with the Strategic Forces Command.

The Pakistani and Chinese militaries have the 'advantage' of greater coherence and congruence in their weapons policies, as the military is in full control of the nuclear weapons programme, whereas our weapons remain under civil control even while the delivery vehicles may be with the military. *India is perhaps the only country that faces - or has ever faced - the challenges arising from having two nuclear neighbours, who closely cooperate with each others' nuclear programmes and who maintain adversarial relations with her.* To emphasise, these are signals to the adversary in this interim period, without any other change in our nuclear posture. There are bound to be many who will see this as too hawkish and too dangerous; they should then propose less dangerous methods of signalling. Others might see it as too little in terms of preparedness for retaliation, but the hope is to try and avoid the necessity of nuclear retaliation.

The ultimate objective must always be to ensure that the chances of adversarial nuclear incidents are minimised and that nuclear weapons are never actually used in a war. *The already friable situation could be exacerbated to intolerable levels if the state itself, following the trends within Pakistani society, becomes a theocratic intolerant state, bent on the establishment of a Caliphate in the region. The military and non-state groups are certain to have been emboldened by India having been 'deterred' in 1999, following the Kargil attack, in 2001 after the attack on Parliament and Operation Parakram and more so, after 2008, after the attack on Mumbai. Would India react differently in the event of another Mumbai-type attack?*

AGNI MISSILE TESTING IN INDIA

On 19 February 1994 Agni took its third test flight at the Indian missile test range at Balasore, this time successfully with its range extended to 1200 km. The third flight marked the end of the first phase of Agni development program. The program went into a period of dormancy while the new Agni II began development, a longer range version that replaced the liquid fuel upper stage with a solid fuel version to make an all solid fuel missile India became a nuclear weapon state in reality in May 1994, though most observers thought that this milestone had been passed years before. It was then that India completed its development of a fully combat ready system for delivering nuclear weapons by successfully conducting acceptance tests. The ARDE developed bomb case, and the TBRL developed implosion system were mated with a modified Mirage 2000 and successfully test dropped at Balasore. The bomb, complete except for its plutonium core, was fuzed for an airburst and released over the ocean. If it been required due to national crisis, no doubt the system could have been pushed into service at an earlier date as a stop gap, but in May the fully mature reliable and safe system entered service. India now had an arsenal of at least a couple of dozen operational nuclear bombs.

The years 1995-1996 proved to be watershed in the history of South Asia, and in nuclear proliferation efforts world-wide. The Non-Proliferation Treaty (NPT) came up for review and extension in 1995. Since its original drafting in 1968 the NPT had steadily gained adherents until by the mid-90s the vast majority of states in the world had signed it (by 2000 only 4 states out of 191 had not signed it - with India and Pakistan being half of the four). India had endorsed the NPT in principle, but had refrained from signing because it objected to the establishment of "legitimate" nuclear weapon states limited to the 5 nuclear armed nations then in existence. The NPT committed these nuclear states to good faith efforts at eliminating their arsenals but in the nearly 30 years since no effort in that direction could be discerned. India refused to sign the NPT unless the nuclear states committed themselves to a specific timetable to accomplish disarmament, an approach they unanimously refused to consider. As the NPT extension date approached the nuclear states began pressing for making the NPT permanent so that it would never expire again, while the non-nuclear signatories to the treaty began insisting on a firmer commitment to arms limitation from the nuclear powers in return. In lieu of an actual disarmament commitment, the nuclear powers pushed two treaties that provided for restrictions on specific proliferation activities - the Comprehensive Test Ban Treaty (CTBT) to prohibit all nuclear tests, and a treaty to cut-off the production of fissile materials for weapons. Neither of these treaties would seriously inconvenience the states already possessing extensive stockpiles of tested weapons, but they would have serious effects on states with less well developed arsenals - like India.

This situation presented India with the worst of all worlds. They found themselves under intense pressure, particularly from the U.S., to assent to these treaties which would lock them in to a permanent status of a "second tier state", sharply constrain or wholly foreclose their nuclear capabilities developed at great expense and now at a stage of advanced development, while exacting a negligible price from the nuclear weapon states. To add further insult, two of the nuclear states - China and France - embarked on a new round of nuclear tests to add still more sophisticated designs to their arsenals before the CTBT shut down all testing. The dilemma was strongly reminiscent of the 1980s when developing international restrictions on ballistic missile technology induced India to push ahead with its missile program before the door could be shut on them. The new international push for limiting the spread of nuclear weapons (but not reducing those already held by the major powers) created pressure in India to breakout of its closet status, test its new weapons, and openly deploy them.

The linkage between U.S. pressure on the NPT and India's decision to move ahead aggressively on its strategic programs seems to have been quite direct. The full court press for the NPT began in January 1995, PM Rao responded by meeting with Chidambaram and authorized him to prepare to conduct a series of tests, including a hydrogen bomb test device and sub-kiloton devices to provide data for post-CTBT weapon simulations. Rao even specified that the scientists should be ready to conduct a test on 10 days notice, after the Prime Minister's decision to do so. Later, on 13 April 1995, Rao authorized 6 billion rupees for the development of the Agni II. Kalam was directed to intensify work on setting up a sophisticated command and control system for India's nuclear weapons, and to build additional weapon storage sites around the country (up to that point they nuclear components for weapons were all stored at BARC in Trombay).

It was after Rao's meeting with him that Chidambaram authorized Satinder Kumar Sikka at BARC to begin the development and preparation of a thermonuclear test device - a hydrogen bomb. BARC had developed some designs for thermonuclear weapons in the 80s, but these had languished without any serious effort to move forward with device fabrication although important work in the basic physics and in producing many of the essential materials like enriched lithium-6 and tritium provided a sound foundation. Sikka began developing a new design — a sophisticated one intended for deployment on ballistic missiles (with a weight thus limited to 1000 kg) and using a boosted fission bomb primary.

The NPT extension passed overwhelmingly on 11 May, four days later on 15 May China conducted another nuclear test, and the next day PM Rao announced that India was considering deploying the Prithvi missile in the near future. In August K. Santhanam, DRDO's chief technical adviser, was appointed mission director for the planned test series. That month U.S. intelligence satellites observed water being pumped out of the test shafts at Pokhran, which had become flooded in the intervening years. Construction also began on a new shallower test shaft.

In October 1995, 20 pre-production models of the initial Prithvi SS-150 (with a 150 km range) were secretly delivered to the Army to form the 333rd Missile Regiment based in Secunderabad. At this time the Prithvi was not yet equipped with a nuclear warhead. Rao had never actually authorized tests though, simply preparations for them to keep his options open. Unlike in 1974, PM Rao conducted an extensive series of reviews to determine involving political, foreign policy, and economic advisers (but, in keeping with long-standing Indian practice, not the military) in addition to the nuclear scientists and engineers to determine whether tests should be conducted. Although the nuclear scientists, and members of the "strategic enclave" (like Sundarji and Subrahmanyam) strongly advocated tests, the net result of the reviews were negative, by the fall Rao had decided not to conduct tests. The principle reason for not testing were again economic, Rao recognized the principle source of China's international clout was its economic strength and that India needed to focus its energies on its economy to compete. Thus when the news that the U.S. had detected test preparations broke in the press in December, actual tests were no longer under consideration and test devices had never been transported to Pokhran. The shift of Indian public opinion towards favoring tests is illustrated by an *India Today* survey of 2000 adults on 5 December 1995 showing that 62 percent of the respondents would approve if India exploded an atom bomb to develop its nuclear weapons capability.

The disclosure created a storm of controversy booth inside and outside of India. Pres. Clinton called PM Rao soon after the disclosure to ask him not to test. Rao responded that India would not act "irresponsibly" but gave no other assurances. On 18 December the government declared that it would not succumb to external pressure, but the next day Foreign Minister Pranab Mukherjee denied that tests were planned.

But Rao's term in office was drawing to a close. Elections were held in April-May 1996, and the Congress Party was voted out of office. The balance of power in the Lok Sabha was indecisive - the BJP won the largest seats with 186. Congress and its allies won only 138 seats, and the National Front took 113 and remaining 95 split among smaller parties. A governing coalition required 273 seats and it was not clear what part could assemble a sufficiently large coalition. Since the BJP had gained the largest share of seats President Shankar Sharma asked the BJP led by Atal Behari Vajpayee to form a government on 15 May. Vajpayee was faced with the challenge of marshalling at least another 75 votes within 15 days to win a vote of confidence and remain in power.

Vajpayee had supported open nuclearization of India for 30 years, since the first Chinese nuclear test, as had the BJP for its entire existence, and as had its predecessor, the Jana Sangh before that. One of the planks in the campaign platform for the BJP had been "to exercise the option to induct nuclear weapons". So it should have been to no one's surprise that one of the first actions taken by Vajpayee upon taking office would be to set in motion the test operations that Rao had ordered to be made ready. That it appears to have actually been *the* very first issue acted upon by Vajpayee though is notable.

According to Chengappa, Vajpayee's attempt to order nuclear tests was delayed until the day after his inauguration due to problems in contacting Abdul Kalam to receive the order. Three test devices were brought to Pokhran and emplaced in the test shafts:

- a lightweight pure fission bomb (12 kt);
- a boosted fission bomb; and
- a sub-kiloton experimental test device.

The site preparations at Pokhran came within about a day of being completed, when it became apparent that Vajpayee's government was not going to be able to win the upcoming vote of confidence. Although he had the authority to order the test, Vajpayee recognized that it would be improper to saddle a successor government with dealing with the consequences of a test with which it had no involvement. So Vajpayee rescinded his authorization until after the vote was held. On 28 May the BJP lost the vote of confidence and Vajpayee's government was dissolved.

Vajpayee's aides felt that without the one day delay in locating Kalam the tests would have been conducted in 1996. Within several months information about Vajpayee's initial authorization of nuclear tests leaked out, and although it did not become widely known this was undoubtedly picked up by U.S. intelligence - making the later admission of "surprise" by the U.S. when Vajpayee took office in 1998 and conducted tests soon after difficult to justify. The delay in testing brought about the hesitance of Rao and Vajpayee was actually a boon to the weapons scientists. The thermonuclear device was not ready yet, and the delay gave them time to prepare additional devices - two sub-kiloton experiments, and a boosted fission device using reactor-grade plutonium to enable India to draw upon its very large inventory of power reactor produced material if desired.

INDIA'S UNENDING DEFENCE EXPENDITURE

Despite criticism from various circles that India is not investing more to tackle development issues as millions remain mired in poverty; the Indian government's ambitious modernisation plan for its military is in full swing. In February this year, Indian military procurement units descended on the DefExpo 2010 trade fair in New Delhi. Inaugurating the Indian Defence Exhibition, Defence Minister A.K. Antony said that India's defence expenditure, which is 2.5 percent of its gross domestic product (GDP), is going to increase. He pointed out, "our defence industry is open up to 100 percent for Indian private sector, while foreign direct investment is allowed up to 26 percent." Antony further indicated that our government is committed to rapid modernisation of armed forces. Over the next 12 years, India is set to spend a whopping US$200 billion on defence acquisitions to replace its outdated inventory. In this regard, on February 15, 2010, a report of the Indian strategic defence magazine (India Strategic's DefExpo) revealed that 70 per cent of the inventory of the Indian armed forces is 20-plus years old, and needs to be replaced with the modern technology.

It explained that nearly half of this funding ($100b) will go to the Indian Air Force (IAF), which would need to replace more than half of its combat jet fleet as well as the entire transport aircraft and helicopter fleet.

The army needs new guns, tanks, rocket launchers, multi-terrain vehicles, while the navy needs ships, aircraft carriers and new range of nuclear submarines.

In three from 1994 to 1997 India's defence budget was increased from 20 percent to 24.4 percent. For the financial year 2001-2002 defence has been allocated Rs 620,000.00 million. This amount shows an increase of Rs 75,000 million as compared to previous year's revised estimates of Rs 544,610 million. In 2009, India increased its defence budget by a whopping 28.2 percent or Rs 130,000.00 million. Some experts estimate that military spending will increase further, totalling as much as 200 billion dollars over the period to 2022.

India's military has planned a massive upgrade of its mainly 1990s-era weapons systems which is mostly from the former Russia. The plans include the purchase of 126 new combat aircraft to replace an ageing fleet of MiG-21s..The US has emerged as a potential military supplier to India since the two countries signed a deal of civil energy technology in 2008, which lifted sanctions on New Delhi in order to import nuclear technology. India is likely to become a major customer for the US military-industrial complex over the next few years. During the recent visit of the US Secretary of State Robert Gates to New Delhi, American Defence officials, however, have said that US weapons sales to India would not be a focus of the trip. Regardless of such denials, the key reason for the Gates' visit can be found in the fact that India is planning to raise its military budget by 50% to almost $40 billion, making military expenditure 3% of the annual GDP. In contrast to India's planned defence expenditures, Pakistan's entire 2009-10 budget amounts to little over $30 billion.

India, the largest arms buyer among emerging nations, accounted for 7.5 per cent of all international arms sales between 2000 and 2007. It has spent billions of dollars in the past few years on purchases of planes, radars and ships from Britain, France, Germany and Russia and Israel. In recent years, India has bought reconnaissance aircraft from US aerospace major Boeing worth 2.1

billion-dollars, medium range missiles for 1.4 billion dollars from Israeli Aerospace Industries, and signed an upgrade service contract with the Russian Aircraft Corporation to upgrade its MiG 29 squadrons for 965 million dollars. Several deals are planned for the near future including one of the largest arms contracts of recent times—a 11-billion-dollar project to acquire 126 multi-role combat aircraft.

It is mentionable that after 9/11, both India and Israel which had openly jumped on Bush's anti-terrorism enterprise are acting upon a secret diplomacy, targeting Pakistan China, Iran and Syria. In this context, Indo-Israeli secret diplomacy could be assessed from the interview of Israel's ambassador to India, Mark Sofer published in the Indian weekly Outlook on February 18, 2008. Regarding India's defence arrangements with Tel Aviv, Sofer had surprisingly disclosed "We do have a defence relationship with India, which is no secret" and "with all due respect, the secret part will remain a secret." As regards joint exercises, Sofer replied, "Certain issues need to remain under wraps for whatever reason."

Notably, India's 'The Tribune' wrote on September 10, 2003, "India and Israel took giant leaps forward in bolstering the existing strategic ties", and Tel Aviv has "agreed to share its expertise with India in various fields such as anti-fidayeen operations, surveillance satellites, intelligence sharing and space exploration." With the support of Israel, New Delhi has been acquiring an element of strategic depth by setting up logistical bases in the Indian Ocean for its navy. In fact, India wants to become a mini-superpower of the region and hence it uses the pretext of deterrence against Pakistan and China. In this context, New Delhi with the support of US and Israel has presumed peace-loving Pakistan and China as their arch enemies, but it does not admit officially.

In May, 1998, when India detonated five nuclear tests, Islamabad was compelled to follow the suit through its own atomic experiments. But Pakistan which so far relied upon the minimum nuclear deterrence has again been forced by India's unending spending on arms purchases to counterbalance the former. In this regard, Pakistan has signed a number of agreements with China. Nevertheless, currently, more than half of India's budget is allocated for military, paramilitary, various security forces and debt servicing. That leaves less than half for everything else including infrastructure development projects, education, healthcare, poverty alleviation, and various human services. New Delhi' s latest arms buildup will leave even less for what India needs most to lift hundreds of millions of its citizens from abject poverty, hunger illiteracy and disease.

Indian civil society organisations, while complaining of excessive defence spending indicated that the government spends 2.35 per cent of GDP on defence, but only 1.72 per cent on the social sector. The defence budget for 2009-2010 is 29 billion dollars, up 34 percent over the previous one. Indian defence analyst Ravinder Pal Singh, while calling New Delhi's unending defence spending at the cost of poverty-alleviation—with security requirements competing with socioeconomic concerns for money calls it guns-versus-butter question.

Even some of Indian officials are surprised in relation to Indian defence expenditure which has no bounds. For example, an official of the country's finance ministry remarked, "There is a dilemma...poverty needs to be eradicated to prevent men from taking to the guns...but more funds for security means less money for poverty alleviation." Meanwhile, a report of United Nations pointed out that India ranks 134th of 182 countries on the United Nations Development Programme's Human Development Index. It estimated that 50 per cent of the world's undernourished population lives in India. Nearly 31 per cent of the billion-plus Indians earn less than a dollar a day.

Secretary General of the Control Arms Foundation of India Binalakshmi Nepram said, "When people are dying of poverty and bad sanitation, what protection will arms provide them?" On the one hand, international community has been making strenuous efforts for world peace in wake of global financial crisis and war against terrorism, on the other, India has initiated deadly nuclear arms in South Asia where people are already facing multiple problems of grave nature. Majority of South Asian people are living below the poverty level, lacking basic facilities like fresh food and clean water. While yielding to acute poverty, every day, some persons commit suicide in India, Pakistan, Sri Lanka etc. Setting aside regional problems, and resolution of Indo-Pak issues-especially thorny dispute of Kashmir, Indian rulers state that they don't have any aggressive designs. But it becomes a big joke of the 21st century, reminding a maxim, "armed to the teeth, but no enemy", if we take cognisance of India's unending defence expenditure.

DOMESTIC PRODUCTION AND IMPORTS THE FUTURE BALANCE

Ever since it gained independence from the United Kingdom in 1947 India has aspired to economic self-sufficiency in economic power and to be accorded the international status commensurate with its size and history. Increasingly, it has viewed the possession of a capable military supported a by a home grown and state controlled defence industry and more recently a research and development capability as central to this strategy. India now has one of the largest and most significant defence production capabilities in the developing world.

It has nevertheless been spectacularly unsuccessful in growing its defence R&D capability. Indeed, having claimed in the mid-1990s, that it would significantly reduce its dependence on foreign suppliers for high-technology defence equipment by the middle of this decade, the country has therefore had to turn once again to the outside world to help it meet its defence needs. Many within the Indian military establishment and the government have also started to re-assess the viability of India's established approach to defence development. Thus far, attention has been largely focused on allowing private sector and foreign participation in defence production and R&D. Still, if the general experience of economic reform in India is anything to go by this will take time, and India will have to rely on imports in the interim.

Furthermore, the ability of India's defence industrial base to meet the country's high-end defence requirements in areas such as aerospace will probably remain limited, not least because the expense of designing and producing such systems is increasingly rapidly.

INDIA'S CURRENT DEFENCE PRODUCTION CAPABILITY

The foundations for India's defence industry are widely believed to have been laid in 1801 with the establishment of the Gun Carriage Agency in Calcutta by the East India Company. Although historically true, the birth of India's current defence industrial really came during the Second World War, when the decision was taken to establish a limited defence production capability in the country, to support the British war effort in Asia and the Middle East. Before then, the British had decided against establishing a significant defence equipment manufacturing capability in India, for fear of 'giving the natives access to modern military industry'.

Ordnance Factories and Public Sector Undertakings

At the end of the WW2 India's defence industrial capacity amounted to 16 ordnance factories, a clothing establishment, and an aircraft production plant; and the new government subsequently inherited this capability. No new factories were built in the first years after independence.

From 1958 onwards, however, the ordnance factories were steadily expanded. The war against China in 1962 (described by some as India's 'Pearl Harbour') prompted a further expansion in India's ordnance capability. By 1970, the number of ordnance factories had risen to 31 and by the 1980s the number had reached 35. Today the country has 39 ordnance factories.

The Indian Ordnance Factories Organisation (OFO) is currently the largest departmentally run industrial undertaking in the country. In addition to its ordinance factors, India has eight defence focused public sector undertakings (PSUs).

These are Bharat Electronics; Bharat Earth Movers; Mazagon Dockyards; Garden Reach Shipbuilders and Engineers; Goa Shipyard; Bharat Dynamics; Mishra Dhatu Nigam (Midhani); and Hindustan Aeronautics. The PSUs produce a range of defence equipment including helicopters, state of the art electronics, heavy trucks and tank transportation trailers, submarines, missile boats destroyers, frigates, corvettes, fast attack craft, guided missiles, and aeronautics. They also provide overhaul and maintenance facilities.

DEFENCE RESEARCH AND DEVELOPMENT

India also has a defence research and development capability: the Defence Research and Development Organisation (DRDO). The DRDO has its roots in the Technical Development Establishments (TDES) formed during the Second World War. These were amalgamated in 1959 to form the Defence Science Organisation (DSO). This, in turn, was amalgamated with the Defence Science Services in 1958, to form the DRDO. The organisation employs in the region of 25000 people (about 6000 of which are scientists and engineers and 10000 technicians). The DRDO draws on the work of 51 laboratories/establishments across the country, and (in theory at least) has close links with the eight PSUs. It also co-operates with 70 academic research institutions, 50 national science and technology centres, and some companies in the private sector. The organisation really came into its own in the 1980s, under the leadership of Dr A.J.P Abdul Kalam, when a number of major programmes were launched. These were the: Integrated Guided Missile Development Project (1983); the Light Combat Aircraft (1983); the Advanced Light Helicopter; the Arjun Tank (first conceived in 1974); and a number of smaller projects, such as the Pinaka, a multiple barrel rocket launcher (MBRL).

Major Government Actors

India's defence planning system is centred on the Ministry of Defence (MOD), which uniquely, is manned only by civilians. In simple organisation terms, the Ministry of Defence (MOD) is the major coordinating body for defence production and R&D. It consists of three main departments: the Department of Defence; the Department of Defence Production and Supplies; and the Department of Defence R&D. In addition to this, there is the MOD Finance Division, which exists at the same level. The Department of Defence (DOD) is headed by the Secretary of State for Defence. He co-ordinates the activities of the other MOD Departments and the three armed services.

The Department of Defence Production was established in 1962 after the war with China in order to create an indigenous defence production base, while the Department for Defence supplies was established in 1965, with a view to forging links between the civil industries and defence production units. The two departments were eventually merged into one 1984. The Department of Defence Research and Development, meanwhile, is headed by a secretary who is also Scientific Adviser to the Defence Minister.

Its main responsibilities are R&D planning and advising the Defence Minister on scientific aspects of military equipment. Several committees are also involved in the defence planning process: The Defence Minister's Committee (now replaced by the Defence Minster's weekly morning meeting); the MOD production and supply committee, which deals with matters relating to import substitution, domestic arms production, and the operation of the ordnance factories; and the Defence R&D Council, which formulates and reviews R&D defence programmes, and brings together the Defence Minister and the Directors General of the Council for Scientific and Industrial Research. The Chiefs of Staff Committee, which comprises of the three Chiefs of the Armed Forces, provides a channel for providing military advice to the Prime Minister. A defence-planning cell, which was established in 1965 with a view to improving liaison between the National Planning Commission and other relevant Ministries to ensure that overall defence planning is integrated with overall economic planning, is rumoured not to have functioned as intended.

APPROACH TO DEFENCE PROCUREMENT AND INDUSTRIALISATION

The approach that India has adopted in defence procurement and defence industrial development is similar to that that followed other less developed countries (LDCs). Within this general model, however, the country's experience can be divided into three stages. The first was from independence in 1947 until the early to mid-1960s. The second went from the period following the Sino-India war (1962) and second Indo-Pakistan (1965) conflict until the mid-

1980s. And the third went from the mid-1980s until the present day.

In the first period, India only possessed the ability to make things such as shells and other ammunition, small arms, guns and explosives; it also had a limited aircraft and ship maintenance capabilities based in Bangalore and Calcutta. Thus, it had to look abroad to foreign defence equipment suppliers, such as the United Kingdom and France to meet its needs. During the second stage, efforts were made to build up domestic production, mostly through assembly under license from the Soviet Union and the United Kingdom. (This programme was centred on the PSUs). During this period, the range of activities undertaken by defence sector was also deliberately widened to include previously peripheral items such as clothing. The third period started with large purchases from the Soviet Union by the former Prime Minster Rajiv Ghandi's government (1984-1989). During this period, India consistently spent over 3.3 per cent of Gross Domestic Product (GDP) on building up its armed forces. By the end of the decade, India had the fourth largest armed forces in the world, the fifth biggest airforce, and the sixth biggest navy. Likewise, India became the world's largest importer of conventional weapons, spending $US12.2 billion in the period, of which Russia was the largest supplier. By the end of the 1980s India was assessed as being able to assemble Complete Knock Down (CKD) and Semi-Knock Down (SKDs) purchased from foreign companies and production under license.

Furthermore, gradual improvements were also made in and greater attention paid to the country's defence research and development capability, as well as systems integration for the in-country assembly of weapons. Between the financial year 1991-1992 and the FY 1994-1995, for example, funding for military R&D increased by 36 per cent to UD$430/454 million. And in 1995 India announced its intention to double the share of the defence budget allocated to defence R&D to ten per cent of the total defence budget with a view to reducing the imported content of defence goods to 30 per cent by 2005. Broadly speaking the decision to allocate increased funds to defence R&D came at the expense of funding for more traditional procurement programmes. The move towards defence indigenisation and the tensions associated with it in the 1990s did not occur in a vacuum; indeed it arguably happened earlier than India either predicted or was ready for. For example, the 1991 economic crisis that best the economy forced India to reduce defence spending as a percentage of GDP, from four per cent in the late 1980s to below three per cent in 1994, while the amount of funding allocated to procurement was slashed. The end of the Cold War and the collapse of the Soviet Union, meanwhile, led to the end of the supply of cheap and subsidised weaponry from Moscow. As the previously centralised Soviet arms industry was now spread across the new Republics, India also found it increasingly difficult to acquire spare parts for much of this equipment. Against this backdrop, indigenous R&D was apparently seen (*or at least presented as*) a way around the problem.

India's approach to defence industrial development from Independence onwards is also closely related to its approach to economic development generally. Crucially, a significant proportion of India's defence production and R&D base is entirely under state control. This is the result of the Industrial Policy Resolutions of 1948 and 1956. These placed the development of all key sectors of the economy, such as machine tools, railways, iron and steel and defence production, under state control. The large-scale participation of private sector companies in defence production, in the meantime, is limited to providing components to the PSUs. Even though the manufacture of components, assemblies and sub-assemblies was opened up to the private sector in 1991, the Indian armed forces procure 250 per cent more from the public than the private sector. A survey of 500 top companies in Indian in the same year also reported that only 30 of them had (or are currently) involved in defence contracts.

INDIA'S CURRENT DEFENCE PRODUCTION AND RESEARCH AND DEVELOPMENT CAPABILITY

India's experience of developing its defence industry and research and development capability over the past decade has been mixed.

Ordnance Factories and PSUs

Outwardly, both the ordnance factories and the PSUs can be considered successful enterprises. The country's ordnance factories are capable of providing the Indian military with a significant proportion of their ammunition and low level material needs. In the period 1992/93-1997/98, for example, India only imported 11 per cent of its total ammunition needs. India is also planning to open a 40th Ordnance factory in the near future. Furthermore, speaking in the Indian Parliament, the *Lok Sabha*, on 4 July 2000, George Fernandes, the Indian Defence Minister, stated that the country's ordnance factories recorded a surplus of Rs 780 crores (a crore is ten million rupees) during the period 1999-2000. In addition to this, Fennandes stated that due to last year's Kargil conflict, output increased from 33 per cent to 900 per cent for ammunition items; 20 per cent to 108 per cent for clothing items; and 76 to 233 per cent for cables. More generally, an overall increase in output value of 34.6 per cent in 1999-2000, as compared to the value of issue in 1998/99. The picture for the PSUs is similar. Output in the sector has been rising rapidly since the 1980s, and all the companies have started to move into profitability. According to the latest MOD, moreover, the value of production in 1998-1999 (Rs 7205.55 crore) registered growth of 15.57 per cent over that in 1997-1998 (Rs 6234.75 crore). In addition to this all the defence PSUs reportedly earned a profit in 1998-1999.

Set against that is the fact that these two elements of India's defence industrial base continue to receive large amounts of money from the government in the form of government loans. Between them they also employ in the region of 300000 people. The picture is further complicated by the fact that almost half the production of the PSUs goes to the civil sector; a small proportion of the Ordnance factory production also goes this way. (Put another way if is arguable that, certainly in the case of the PSUs, it is the production of equipment for civil use rather than for military use that is actually making money). Against this backdrop, questions have been raised about their efficiency and ability to meet production targets, as underscored by the fact that it has taken Garden Reach Shipbuilders 12 years to build the Indian Naval

Ship (INS) Brhamaputra; three times longer than it would take Russia's cash strapped shipbuilders to do. Traditionally, the price of purchasing systems and platforms from the PSUs has also worked out more expensive than purchasing them from abroad. For example, back in 1956 it was estimated that the cost of independently producing under license the HS-78 plane would be in the region of US$320000; come the end of the 1970s it stood at $1.5 million per unit.

Indigenous R&D

The success of India's indigenous R&D efforts is even more questionable: despite considerable investment through the 1990s nearly all major programmes implemented in the 1980s are experiencing time and cost over-runs.

The IGMDP: Covering the Prithvi and Agni short and medium/ long range ballistic missiles, the Nag anti tank missile, and the Akash and Trishul surface to air missile, this programme has scored a number of notable and high profile successes. For example, the Prithvi has been tested regularly since 1988 and three versions of the missile (150km, 250km, and 350km ranges) are now believed to be in (or close to) production. The Agni was first tested in 1994 and in a 1998 missile test the missile flew close to 2500km. According to some reports, moreover, the missile is now operational. The Aksah, Nag and Trishul, meanwhile, are expected to enter service soon. However, none of these missiles are entirely indigenous. Some reports suggest, for instance, that five to ten per cent of the technologies used in the Prithvi are imported from abroad.

The Arjun: India's experience of designing an indigenous tank has been less successful. Take the example of the Arjun tank. Originally, expected to be in operation service by 1985 the tank has suffered from continued problems, such as problems with the engine overheating. Limited production of the tank has now started; however the Indian Army has cut back on the number of tanks that it is ordering. *The LCA* The story of the LCA is almost identical to that of the Arjun tank. The programme has experienced delays since its inception in 1983 for a variety of reasons. And the first flight-test, originally scheduled for 1996, is now not expected to take place until some time in 2002. The cost of the programme, in the meantime, has increased from Rs 560 crores. This increased to Rs 2188 crores in 1993, when approval was given to enter the Full Scale Engineering Development Phase-1.

Other Programmes: The picture is much the same for a number of other less high profile programmes, such as the Pinaka, MBRL. This was initiated in 1986 with a budget of Rs 25.6 crores. This was subsequently increased to 49 crores. The system underwent troop trials in October 1999, moreover, but is still waiting for acceptance by the Army before entering full production. A similar story emerges for products such as the Indian Small Arms System (ISAS). The only product deemed to have been a complete success is arguably the ALH. The failure of many of India's R&D programmes and its reliance on the outside world for key technologies is confirmed by a number of by external assessments, such as the United States government Military Critical Technologies List (MCTL). For example, India's capability to manufacture, gas turbine engines, and human crew systems (aeronautic systems technology) is not even considered worthy of a mention in the MCTL. Likewise, its ability to manufacture the systems necessary to ensure that a combat vehicle is superior to the technology that it is confronting. India scores a little better in the area of Marine Systems Technology, where it is rated to have limited Sub-surface and Deep Submergence Vehicle Capability. One area where India is deemed to have been successful is in the area of Means of Delivery Technology for nuclear and other non-conventional weapons, where it is rated as having a sufficient Theatre Ballistic Missile Capability (TBMC), some ICBM capability; and a sufficient Cruise Missile capability. By way of a comparison, outside the core-areas of competency that it has developed, India's defence production and R&D capabilities do not compare that favourably with other developing countries such as China, which has managed to develop its defence industry across a broader spectrum.

Consequences and Responses

India's inability to meet its top end defence needs have been compounded by the approaching obsolescence of a number of platform and systems; a problem that has been made even worse by the fact that Indian has not made any major defence purchases for the past ten years. Last year's crisis in Kargil has also impressed the need to introduce new equipment on the armed forces-according to the reports, for example, the Indian military assessed Pakistan's Ukranian T-80s as being 'almost a generation ahead of what we had'. In response, as far as major systems and high-technology products are concerned, the government has reversed the pattern of the 1990s and shifted the balance of procurement funding away from its home grown programmes and back towards external procurement. This re-evaluation started in the late 1990s and has progressed since there. Thus in 1996-97 and 1997-98 the DRDO's share of the defence budget decreased in real terms for the first time in that decade. At the same time, India announced its decision to purchase 40 SU-30MK fighter/bombers from Russia in India's largest ever defence deal. Likewise, even though India announced that it would increase its defence budget by 28 per cent to $13.94 billion (2.5 per cent of GDP) in 2000-2001 this March, funding for domestic R&D was only raised by 5.2 per cent; the percentage of the defence budget allocated to defence R&D has also slipped to 4.4 per cent of the total budget. At the same time, while this year's defence budget has seen the amount of money for R&D fall in relative terms, the funds for the purchase of defence equipment from abroad have been steadily increased since 1998.

Reviving the Russian Link

Despite the challenge to their defence relationship that occurred following the end of the Cold War and the economic crisis in India, Russia and India still managed to maintain close defence ties throughout the latter part of the 1990s. For example, the two countries signed a long-term defence co-operation programme in 1994; a number of agreements for the upgradation of Indian defence equipment were initialled; India also agreed to buy 40 SU-30MKs in 1997; and according to the Russian Vice Premier Liya Klebarov, defence sales to India account for between 20 and 25 per cent of the annual total export of Russian military goods, making it India's largest arms supplier. It comes as little surprise to find, therefore, that much of the money allocated for procurement will be spent in Russia.

Although many of the deals have been under negotiation for some time, the October visit of the Russian president, Vladimir Putin, appears to have broken the logjam. Thus, although the details still have to be finalised, India and Russia officially agreed to extend their defence co-operation programme until 2010. Furthermore, India announced its intention to buy Russian arms worth more than $2 billion. Intended purchases include, additional Su-30 long range fighter bombers, a number of which will be made under license in India, more than 300 T-90 Main Battle Tanks (MBTS), one third of which will also be made in India, the ageing Soviet-era aircraft carrier, the Admiral Gorshkov, which will be provided for free but would cost $500 million to refurbish; an, as yet, unspecified number of MiG-29s for the ship; and a number of Smersh MRBLs.

European and Other Suppliers

India has also looked to solidify its links with European suppliers. For example, although the details of the deal have yet to be finalised the British based company BAE SYTEMS is also believed to have secured the deal to provide India with the Hawk advanced jet trainer aircraft. (India has been negotiating this purchase for over a decade). France has also been particularly successful, recently concluding an agreement to sell India additional Mirage 2000 fighters. Outside Europe, India has established a close defence procurement relationship with Israel, which is thought to have provided it, among other things, with equipment suitable for border surveillance. Furthermore, reliable sources have suggested that the Phalcon early warning plane (AEW) that Israel was building for China but recently agreed not to sell to Beijing after pressure from the United States will be delivered to India. South African arms exports have also managed to carve out a small niche for themselves in the country. A number of Eastern European nations are also looking to provide India with new equipment and to help it upgrade its existing inventory. Quite simply, these purchases will fill those gaps that have appeared in India's armed forces in recent years.

The Fourth Phase-All Change in Indian Defence

In hindsight it appears that India, along with other LDCs, has learnt the lesson that while it is one thing to produce equipment such as ammunition and manufacture other people's platforms under license, it is another all-together to be able to locally design and build high-technology weapons systems, particularly in an environment in which the R&D programmes of the developing countries are producing increasingly sophisticated and indeed expensive weapons systems. At this stage, however, nobody is talking about getting rid of defence production and R&D-India is still officially committed to purchasing 70 per cent of its defence needs from indigenous sources by 2010. Rather, a growing number of military officials and businessmen are now calling for a radical shake up in the way in which India approaches defence procurement and indigenisation, largely by allowing greater private sector and possibly foreign participation.

Promoting Privatisation

Of course, interest in promoting greater private sector participation in defence is not new: as stated earlier the law was changed in 1991 to allow the private sector to provide components as well as assembly and sub-assembly to the military. Likewise, in 1994 the country's former Prime Minster Narashima Rao gave a speech in which he noted that 'the domestic arms industry must be opened up to private investment and competition'.

However, in a sign of growing convergence between the government and the private sector on the need for change the Confederation of Indian Industry (CII) and the Ministry of Defence (MOD) agreed in 1998 to establish six task forces to look at the subject. They recommended 1) reviewing the existing partnership between the MOD, industry and the military; 2) evolving strategies for long-term partnerships between these group; 3) studying the existing capacity of the defence PSUs and ordnance factories; 4) exploring the possibility of joint ventures; 5) developing joint marketing arms for exports; and 6) leveraging India's strengths in information technology in the defence sector. Both the government and the military appear to be embracing these suggestions. For example, in July this year the Defence Minister, George Fernandes, called for greater co-operation and interaction between the Ordnance factories, the PSUs, and the DRDO. Speaking at a September conference organised by the Confederation of Indian Industries (CII) and the Indian Airforce (IAF), meanwhile, the Chief of the Airforce, Air Marshal A.Y. Tipinis, called for much greater participation from private manufacturers in the production of aircraft and weapons support systems. At the same conference, Vijay Kapur, Chairman of the CII National Committee on Communications, stated that: 1) the private sector should be allowed to manufacture arms and armaments and that the government should review its industrial policy accordingly; 2) that foreign collaboration should be allowed; 3) that arms and armaments currently in the 'reserved' category should be moved to the licensed category; 4) that industry should come forward as a partner with the services and not as contractors; and 5) that the government should fund private sector R&D. He concluded that if these steps were followed India would be able to soon meet its defence requirements indigenously. In an interesting development, at an earlier CII conference, George Fernandes, also welcomed the suggestion that the private sector be allowed to play a larger role in defence research and development (R&D) by calling on the private sector to compliment the role of the DRDO. The main advantage of private sector participation in defence R&D and/or increased government funding for private companies engaged in defence R&D is that the government can tap into the private sector's recent success at IT R&D. Private sector involvement should also serve to reduce costs as these firms operate on free-market principles.

Drivers of Change

Interestingly, this willingness to consider a change of direction is not only the result of the failure of India's ambitious R&D programme, but also due to a number of domestic and international factors. *The End of the Cold War:* In addition to the defence production issues and problems with Russia, the end of the Cold War has had a number of often contradictory impacts for Indian defence planners. On the one hand, India, like China was shocked by the quick success that the Allies scored over the Iraqis during the Gulf War. Particularly, the sight of a large army equipped with much Soviet equipment struggling to compete with European and North American technology was not lost on the Indians, convincing the country's senior military officials of the needs to introduce high-technology equipment. Likewise, India was disturbed by NATO intervention in Kosovo on the basis of support for human rights. America's desire to deploy a National Missile Defence (NMD) system has also been opposed in India. (Its opposition is partly related to the fear that advances in technology in this area will undermine the limited advances that India has made in its own nuclear and missile capabilities). On the other hand, thanks to its emergence as a major IT power, India's decision to fly in the face of international convention and conduct nuclear tests in May 1998 has been largely forgotten by the international community and particularly the United States. The crumbling of the traditionally strong bonds between Pakistan and America in the wake of Pakistan's decision to test nuclear weapons shortly after India; the Kargil crisis and the October military coup have helped this process of rapprochement. In response, India has attempted to maintain and build on its existing relationship with Russia, particularly in the area of defence sales, while establishing new ties with the United States in both the economic and diplomatic spheres.

Global Defence Industry Restructuring: Since the end of the Cold War global defence spending has decreased by 28.6 per cent between 1990 and 1999. Over the same period there has been a rash of consolidation among major arms producing companies in the United States and Europe. The decreasing size of the major producers' home markets has encouraged them to look abroad to new markets, in which defence spending is still growing. The impact of this process on India has been two-fold. Firstly, as the process of globalisation continues there is growing scope for partnerships to be established between Indian defence producers looking for access to new technology, and foreign defence manufacturers keen to tap the sales potential in the Indian market and also its strengths in areas such as IT. They may also wish to use the country as a platform from which to launch its products into other markets. Domestically, meanwhile, those civil servants and bureaucrats at the heart of the Indian government are unlikely to have missed the fact that process of privatisation and consolidation in defence was a reaction to declining defence budgets after the Cold War. And that these new companies are often leaner and more competitive than their predecessors; while strategic alliances and joint ventures are now the rule rather than the exception in the sector due to the rising costs of designing and producing the next generation of defence equipment.

The Election of the Bharatiya Janta Party (BJP). The BJP led coalition government is more committed to tackling defence issues than its predecessors. Examples abound: in May 1988, shortly after first coming to power, it presided over India's first nuclear tests since 1974; while March 2000 saw the government reverse the downward trend in defence spending established in the 1990s. From the start the BJP government has also made an effort to articulate what the country's defence and security policy was, in opposition to the previous government, which according to the BJP was merely to assure Indians and indeed the world that India actually had such a policy.

Economic Reform. India's economic reform programme has gained momentum since it was introduced in 1991. Crucially, it now has support from across the political spectrum. As the government slowly retreats from the 'commanding heights' of the economy, moreover, greater attention is starting to be focused on the benefits to be gained from allowing greater private participation in defence, which to a large degree explains the involvement of the CII. India's moves towards privatisation, however, have not been plain sailing. Despite moving away from its policy of 'Swadeshi' or self-reliance, there remain elements of the BJP who still oppose the process; the same is true of many of the country's citizens. Efforts to dismantle the so-called 'Permit Raj' through a process of 'dis-investment' have also progressed more slowly than many had hoped, due largely to bureaucratic opposition and inertia.

Information Technology: India is quickly becoming a major player in the field of information technology (IT). For example, there are currently 340000 software professionals employed in the country-in 1996 there were only 180000-while India's technology schools are producing 100000 software professionals a year. The country has also developed its own super-computing capability, the Paran, which it has exported to Russia. India's strength in IT having a major impact on India's economy: total exports of IT related products amounted to about $9 billion in 1999. This sector of the economy has also managed to attract significant amounts of foreign investment, much of it into the cities of Bangalore and Hyderebad. The emergence of India as a major IT power is interesting for a number of reasons. For instance, although the principle of IT development was supported by the late Prime Minister Rajiv Ghandi in the 1980s, the sector has grown up outside the normal regulation and red tape associated with the Indian economy. Dominated as it is by private sector companies it has also proved to be rather more innovative and flexible than other industries. Additionally, information technology has been India's bridge with outside world: its technicians and programmers are at the forefront of the IT revolution in the United States and are being courted by Japan, Germany and the United States. Attracted by the loosening of government control over the economy, moreover, many of these people are now returning to India, thereby breathing new energy into the economy.

ASSESSMENT OF MOVES TOWARDS PRIVATISATION

As a result of the above, increase private sector participation in defence production is increasingly being pursued: according to the latest reports more than 300 companies have already registered their interest in participating in the defence sector. Thus far, the following areas appear to have borne the greatest fruit.

IT and Communications. According to the MTCL India's capabilities in areas such as super-computing and software development are very strong indeed. With this in mind, it is understandable that a number of senior military figures have recently made clear their desire to upgrade the Armed Force's communication and IT capabilities through private sector involvement. Speaking during an August 2000 CII seminar, for instance, General V.P Malik observed that: "the private sector, which had not previously participated in defence production, had expanded in size and reach and now has the capability to produce non-lethal items such as communications and IT related' products He also stated that: 'the army would be requiring radios of all types, ATM switches, optical fibre cable, satellite systems, power sources of all types and micro and macro cellular systems' and that the Army was looking at buying these technologies off the shelf from private companies.

Service Contracts and Outsourcing: There is a growing interest in outsourcing to the private sector within the military The IAF, for example, is exploring the possibility of privatising its base-repair depots, accounts, and areas of administrative work. According to the Chief of the Air Staff, Air Chief Marshall A.Y. Tipinis, there is also scope to involve the private sector in the maintenance and operation of fighter aircraft, air-launched guided missiles and ground to air missiles as well as support equipment such as radars, communications networks, and specialist vehicles. Outsourcing is also an option for the PSUs; indeed they are increasingly shedding the production of low technology items to the private sector. For example, both Bharat Electronics and Garden Reach Shipbuilders have developed a network of small-scale industries and ancillary units around them. Likewise, the ordnance factories have been sourcing various raw materials and small parts from a range of indigenous industries. Some effort has also been made to involve the private sector in the production of middle level technologies: for example, at one stage Kirloskars was involved in the development of an indigenous engine for the Arjun tank.

Foreign Participation. There is mounting evidence to suggest that the country's eight PSU's will be allowed to enter into 'strategic alliances' and partnerships with foreign defence manufacturers. On 12 October, for example, George Fernandes, stated that 'India provides an excellent opportunity for the developed and developing world to source cost-effective goods and services from our defence production industry' He also talked of the 'opportunities that India offers for joint-ventures, technology transfers, and co-production facilities for export to other markets'.

Currently the amount of foreign investment in the Indian defence sector is small. But a number of foreign manufacturers have already taken him up on the offer. During the visit of the Russian President Vladimir Putin to India this October, for example, the two sides signed a new military and technical co-operation agreement to establish joint ventures for the production of a variety of armaments and military hardware and establishing joint sales and marketing structures for the products. The Russian government is also thought to be considering investing a share of proceeds of its recent sales to India for creating after-care and upgrading facilities in the country. Looking to the future it is possible that Russian companies will invite their Indian (and Chinese) counterparts to participate in the development of next generation weapons systems. Russia is not the only country assessing this option. Somewhere in the region of 20 partnership agreements covering a range of cooperative arrangements, including co-production of aircraft equipment, joint development of communications equipment, and co-operation in software and electronic design, are believed to have been signed between British companies and the eight PSUs. Similar discussion have also been held with France, Poland and others. Every effort is also being made to ensure that these partnerships are not limited to the public sector.

Research and Development: There is some reason to believe that private companies will be encouraged to participate in defence R&D. Participation in this area received a significant boost following the May 1998 nuclear tests, when the imposition of sanctions on India prompted the Defence Research and Development Agency (DRDO) to open up eight labs in non-strategic areas to private participation. In addition to this, the DRDO now claims to have 'various levels of partnership' with 250 industries.

Defence Exports: In a related development, the government is now actively assessing the possibility of increasing exports of defence related equipment. Traditionally, modern India has eschewed the option of selling arms abroad, and relatively speaking its defence exports are minimal, although a defence exports cell was established in 1973. In recent years, however, the country has held a number of defence export shows in co-operation with the

CII, while Indian PSUs have participated in defence shows abroad. Currently, the main products exported are from the country's ordnance factories and include small arms ammunition, explosives, rockets, spares for rifles and guns, clothing items, parachutes, aeronautical stores, communications equipment, and components and sub-systems. India's main export markets are Asia and Africa although some equipment has gone to Europe. Old export markets are also being expanded and new ones being sought out: following a visit to Vietnam in March 2000 by George Fernandes, for example, both countries, who signed a Protocol on Defence Co-operation in 1994, initialled a new agreement to enhance defence cooperation in areas of training. Algeria is also considering buying defence equipment from India, including spares for its MiG combat aircraft, and helicopters, vehicles, night vision devices and communications equipment. India's hope is probably that it will be able to use the revenue from sales to reduce its own unit purchase costs as well as provide an extra flow of money into defence R&D.

Future Prospects

Despite these positive signs, at this stage there are still a number of factors inhibiting increased private sector (and possibly even foreign) involvement in defence production.

The main stumbling block is that in order to increase private sector involvement the Indian government would have to scrap the 1948 and 1956 Industrial Policy Resolutions. This is unlikely at this stage because many of the country's bureaucrats and politicians fear that such a decision will lead to mass lay-offs and possibly social turbulence. (Incidentally, these same individuals are also against the privatisation of India's other PSUs). As is traditionally the case, pressure against change is also likely to come from both the management and the workforce from within the sector. In short, the momentum and support for the economic reform programme in India has yet to gather the momentum necessary to allow fully fledged private participation and competition in defence production. Private participation in the sensitive areas of defence R&D is likely to be limited due to concerns about security. Substantial foreign participation in the form of joint ventures particularly with Western companies, meanwhile, is likely to be limited by concerns about security and the reliability of Western suppliers in meeting their obligations. (By way of an example, the fact that a number of Indian Navy SeaKing helicopters have been stranded in Britain because they contain American parts, which the country is restricted from selling to India as part of the sanctions imposed following the May 1998 nuclear tests, is believed to one of the reasons why the deal to sell the BAE SYSTEMS Hawk has been further delayed) Organisational problems within the MOD are also likely to hinder any advantages to be gained by through the greater involvement of the private sector. The isolation of defence production from defence R&D, for example, is seen by many in India as inhibiting sensible planning and management of India's defence programmes.

Conclusion

Despite all the problems and challenges of the past decade India is unlikely to abandon the dream of establishing its own defence industry. Paradoxically, however, it is becoming increasingly apparent to all concerned that the only way that the country will be able to fulfil (even partly) its ambition of designing and manufacturing its own top-end defence equipment will be to dismantle the system of public ownership on which it is based. As the process of globalisation and consolidation in the defence industry continues to gather pace and the price of designing, developing and producing modern defence equipment increases rapidly, India's aspirations would also be greatly helped if it could rapidly involve foreign companies in the process of defence production.

Five to Ten Year Forecast

In the near term (5-10 years) the evidence collected in the paper suggests that this is unlikely to happen. Rather, the development of a hybrid model in which the core of PSUs and the DRDO will be maintained, while private sector participation will be sought in non-sensitive/peripheral areas such as IT and communications will probably dominate. This process will be complemented by an increased effort both to seek partnerships with largely Russian put possibly some European defence companies. However, if past efforts to establish joint ventures with Indian companies in both the civil and defence sector are anything to go by the scope of these will be limited. India's attempts to increase its defence exports profile partly as a way to fund its indigenous R&D programme will also be limited to the sale of low and middle level technologies to cash-strapped and politically isolated regimes, such as Algeria and Vietnam. The perceived need to modernise its armed forces quickly, which has taken root in the wake of the Kargil crisis and the impending obsolescence of many of its existing platform, however, means that India will continue to look abroad to full-fill the majority of its top-end defence needs. This will be reflected in the division of resources within the defence budget, which is also likely to continue to grow over this period.

Ten to Twenty Year Forecast

Potentially, India's long term prospects (10-20) years are better. There is a good chance, for example, that by 2010 the Indian government will have made real advances down the path of economic reform and that the climate for private sector participation and perhaps even the privatisation of the PSUs will be more favourable. Crucial to India's success, however, will be its ability to bring together its civil and military R&D capabilities, not only in non-military/dual use areas, but across a broad spectrum. India could also use its strength in IT to strengthen its partnerships with foreign defence manufacturers and secure maintenance, upgrading and possibly production facilities in return. Parallel to this, and bearing in mind the fact that future defence platforms, such as the JSF, are unlikely to be single country ventures, there are also added advantages to be gained from India linking itself into those foreign companies associated closely with this process; indeed it may even be able to contribute in certain key areas. If this happens, although it is unlikely that India will be able to produce 70 per cent of its requirements domestically, it will certainly be able to source more from domestic producers, and more crucially will benefit from its access to technology, and participation in R&D programmes. (It is possible that India will be able to reduce its total reliance on imports to 50 per cent, although it is still unlikely to be able to produce whole systems indigenously).

Final Assessment

Naturally, this rather rosy outlook depends on India's willingness to accept not only the advantages of privatisation, but more importantly the direction in which defence industries today are going.

Arguably, the room for companies focused solely on their home markets and expecting to provide their militaries with state of the art defence equipment, not only in the developed world but also in the West, is shrinking rapidly, due to the rising cost and sophistication of the systems involved.

Put another way, participation in regional or global defence programmes will become the norm. India, with its growing strength in the new economy, has the chance this time not to miss the boat, although there is always a danger that misplaced nationalism and an unclear understanding of developments will prevent it from making the most of the opportunity.

DEFENCE INDUSTRY

It is almost seven years since the first set of major policy changes were promulgated by the Government to give a fillip to our stagnating and moribund defence industry. The fundamental underpinnings to the policy changes were two: firstly, bring in the private sector; and secondly, opening the door for foreign companies by permitting up to 26 percent investment, so that technology inflows are facilitated. It was perhaps rightly believed that these were the two principle measures that were required to catalyse our ailing military industrial capabilities.

While most observers welcomed the policy announcements, there was considerable scepticism over the Governments' resolve to implement them. Could a system that was wedded to the philosophy of state led industrialisation for almost fifty years, change course that easily? Unlikely! Then there was the problem of our establishments' recognised and reputed talent for conceptualising great ideas, but seldom demonstrating the capacity to execute them. However, after having out-of-habit taken recourse to castigating the Government, it would be prudent to also try and understand its compulsions and concerns. The first is that given the nature of the UPA Government, no reforms can be implemented without the Left's concurrence.

The Left's dogma is to stonewall any measure that appears to threaten the interests of the PSUs and the Ordnance Factory Board (OFB). Thus the Left would not be inclined to acquiesce to proposals that contemplate the relaxation of state control over most core industrial sectors. Similarly, the defence PSUs and the OFB, would also not be willing to dilute their monopoly of their defence market.

Then there is the problem of the huge investments and the capacities created in all our Government owned defence industrial under-takings. Logically, it cannot be any one's case, that these assets are permitted to decay instead of putting them to optimal use. With the private sectors' case for a level playing field, the fear that over time, the Government owned defence industrial establishments would be progressively edged out of business, is genuine.

The third concern, and not easy to counter, pertains to the argument of national security. Since the private sector is not under Government control, in times of a crisis it may not respond to national requirements in the same manner that a Government owned unit would do. It is a combination of the preceding concerns that explain the Government's hesitation in letting go the control that we have witnessed since the policy changes were promulgated in May 2001.

Having acknowledged the issues, it must be conceded that these are not new or unique to us. All nations have had to grapple with the same set of dilemmas, and since we are in the catch-up game, our problems ought to be easier to solve, for we have the experience of other countries to learn and benefit from.

So, while the Government at one level remained wedded to the policy of reforms, in its implementation, it dragged its feet. Consequently, the practice of doing business only with the Government owned industries did continue unchanged for three to four years, much to the frustration of the private sector. This ambivalence of the Government impacted negatively on the private sectors' attempts at collaboration with foreign companies. It should therefore be accepted that foreign partnership was, and is, vital for our industry to take off.

Indigenously we do not have the technology, nor the know-how, for state-of-the-art systems that the defence services aspire for. Since foreign defence companies were unclear of the Governments' intent, they were not prepared to enter into collaborative arrangements with the private sector. For quite a while they remained cautious, indulged in fence sitting-hedging their bets.

The air was finally cleared with the Government's announcement of the Defence Procurement Policy of 2006. The most significant features of this policy were its 'offset clauses' and the concept of RURs (Raksha Utpadan Ratnas). Of the two, it is the offset policy that has the potential to yield spectacular results in energising our defence industry.

The billions of dollars of business that this policy will bring to the Indian industry has generated unprecedented excitement among our domestic players. In excitement lies the challenge. They will have to be prepared to absorb complex technologies and engineering skills, and then manufacture components, assemble sub-systems, and systems, at a cost that is competitive and sufficiently profitable.

Ever since the idea of the offset policy was mooted, all foreign multi-nationals have been lobbying intensely to sabotage it. Arguments-that the policy would push up prices, that the Indian industry is incapable of absorbing high technology 'direct offsets', that monitoring mechanisms cannot be effective etc-have been in the air for a while.

A few days back, it was reported, that the Government is considering some relaxation in the policy. The areas mentioned were the adjustment of the cost of technology transfer against offsets, banking of offsets and the acceptance of indirect offsets. Though these issues may merit consideration, it would be somewhat premature to accept policy changes even before we have begun. The pressure on foreign vendors to fulfil their offset obligations must remain undiluted. Concurrently, we must concentrate on finding satisfactory solutions to the issues being raised. Having dwelt somewhat cursorily on policy issues, an objective assessment of our present industrial capability and its growth potential would now be in order. The Defence industry cannot be viewed in isolation. It has to be a manifestation of the nation's overall industrial and technological capabilities. Often we tend to ignore this fundamental.

The first place to begin this survey would be to look at the captains of our industry. There is a growing realisation that they have arrived. Globally, they are winning admiration and recognition. In the early nineties, when the first steps of liberalisation were initiated, they nurtured apprehensions about their survival.

Having successfully negotiated that phase of transition in our economy, they have at the beginning of the twenty first century emerged with renewed strategic sense that has a global sweep. Witness the takeovers and the expansion plans of quite a few of our companies. Just a decade ago, who could have imagined, that the Jaguar brand car would be owned by an Indian Company? They have in the recent past displayed vision, and matched that vision with the capacity to implement.

The next requirement is of the work force. It is abundantly available in all categories; managerial, technical and in terms of working hands-our biggest asset being the young age profile of our people. Some intervention can be expected from the government in its labour policies. But being a politically sensitive issue, the Industry will have to live with this problem, till a change becomes environmentally possible.

In terms of spheres in which we have advanced to global standards our range has remained somewhat limited to the automobile sector, pharmaceuticals and a few other disciplines. We have hardly any capabilities in electronics, communications, optics and in the field of aviation. Our industrial policies should focus on these voids. To become a meaningful player in the defence sector, these technologies are vital.

Our biggest strength is software services. Infosys, Wipro and TCS are globally among the best. In addition, there are a host of second tier companies, clocking rapid growth, while doing both domestic and international business. Unfortunately, this strength has not been effectively harnessed to give the requisite impetus to our defence industry. Particularly, because the new generation of weapon systems and related support systems, are all heavily dependent on extremely sophisticated software, the cost of which may be as high as 30-40 percent of the total value of the platform. Electronics we know takes up another 30-40 percent.

The Left and a few other groups have consistently opposed the opening up of the defence industry to the private sector. They have repeatedly been claiming that the public sector units can produce all that our armed forces need. A brief look at their track record will establish that such confidence in the state owned establishments is quite misplaced.

We have 39 Ordnance Factories, 8 Defence PSUs and 50 Defence Research Laboratories, ie. close to 100 establishments, all well equipped, extravagantly staffed, with some excellent scientists and managers, and yet no creditworthy achievements to show. And what equipment do they produce which is to the satisfaction of our Armed Forces?

It would be difficult to list any, other than the ALH from HAL, which has the potential to be a good product. The DRDO might want to take credit for the Agni (1 and 2) and the Prithvi. These are good systems but lose a fair amount of their sheen since they come twenty to thirty years after similar systems were inducted in China.

Our process of reforms in the management of the Government controlled defence research and production establishments, have regrettably floundered. Many studies have been done, yet-to all intent and purposes-the drift continues. Over the last three to four years the Government has been pushing for public private partnership. The idea being that such association would bring about the desired efficiencies in the public sector. But the problem is that such forced marriages do not really work. Driven by expediency, some private companies, may consider coming to an under-standing with PSUs for the short term, but such arrangements are not likely to be conducive to the real growth of the defence industry.

The policy of opening up of the defence industry to the private sector was successful in attracting quite a few industrial houses-large, medium and small, to enter the fray. Even prior to the formal opening of the defence sector, some had indirectly been in the business by manufacturing components, sub-systems and systems-for integration by the defence PSUs.

Besides, our nuclear and space programmes had involved the private industry. Such companies have executed sophisticated design and engineering jobs that include special metals and alloys, and therefore have acquired the confidence to take on the development and manufacture of defence systems.

L&T, Tatas, Mahindras, Godrej Boyce, Bharat Forge and more recently Punj Lloyd, are some of the major industrial houses that have staked their claim for defence contracts. Following them, are a large number of second and third tier companies covering a wide range of technologies.

The basic handicap of all these companies at the time the policy change was announced in 2001 was their lack of domain knowledge. They did not know weapon systems, or what force multipliers were, or how the procurement procedures worked. They also did not know how the global arms market operated. They were equally unaware of the equipment profile of our armed forces and their future requirement.

Even though these companies inducted service officers whose advice was available, lack of personal knowledge of the business inhibited executives from pursuing projects that entailed taking investment decisions. Increased involvement in the defence sector; and interaction with the defence services, the procurement arm of the Ministry of Defence, and the big multi-national defence companies, over the last five to six years; has impacted positively on the confidence levels of company executives.

The role of defence service officers in galvanising the industry merits special attention. Other than these officers, not many in

India, have any idea of modern warfare, military organisations, weapon systems, munitions and the support systems. Such domain knowledge within the industry is imperative. All over the world companies engaged in the business of military hardware extensively employ service officers to develop products and promote business. Not only this, even governments in order to support domestic industries, lend serving officers and men to participate in trials or make presentations. We may recall some of the service-industry seminars held in Delhi in the recent past which had serving officers endorsing products.

Unfortunately, the environment that we have nurtured in India discourages our retired/retiring officers from being employed. If employed they cannot be optimally used because of the establishments' attitude towards them. Who benefits? Only the foreign companies and maybe our adversaries!

This must change. By encouraging the absorption of service officers by the defence industry, the nation will reap multiple benefits. Firstly, the users would have access to informed inputs on developments, which would contribute to better decisions on choice of systems and the formulation of specifications. Rather the industry would gain from the expertise of these officers in an area which they have much to learn about. Secondly, to some extent, the problem of rehabilitation of officers who retire at relatively younger ages would get addressed. It is important that the Government revisits this issue.

The central issue facing the defence industry is access to contemporary technology, its absorption and assimilation, and then the use of domestic research and development to graduate to next generation systems. South Africa, Israel, China, South Korea, Brazil, and even Singapore, have learnt to successfully navigate this cycle.

There is no reason why we cannot emulate their example. In our case, so far, technology transfers have taken place only to the OFB and the defence PSUs. Their experience should not become the only basis for drawing conclusions on this subject. The appetite for growth of the private sector, and its new found confidence, would undoubtedly yield different results.

A survey of the global defence market will reveal that we are currently the biggest importers of defence systems. The US and China do spend more but they mostly buy domestic. The figures of our projected purchases are being regularly quoted in thousands of crores. They do give us sufficient strength to extract terms that could be used to considerable advantage. Look at the pending procurements: some 200 helicopters, 126 advanced fighters, approximately 800-1000 artillery guns, and half a dozen submarines. Each of these would run into billions of dollars. The conclusion is obvious-buy sensibly.

With these purchases in the pipeline, if we did not get all the technologies we need, we will have only ourselves to blame. Procurement terms must state our purchase imperatives unambiguously. As a matter of fact we could consider modifying our procedures when acquiring big ticket items.

Take the case of advanced fighters. All contenders have proven comparable systems. The differences essentially stem from design philosophies and the source of sub-systems and systems that have been selected for integration.

The gaps in features are so narrow that quite often the choice can be a matter of individual predilection. The same arguments can be applied to the helicopters we want or the submarines. Selection could therefore be based on the totality of the package a vendor offers and not just the L-1 criteria after qualifying. To what extent and in what manner is technology being offered? What are the long term buy back agreements?

What kind of investments is the vendor making in India? For such high value transactions we must extract much more than what we have done hither to. We need to therefore delve deeper into the manner in which we pursue major acquisitions. There could also be a case for some coordination with say the Civil Aviation Ministry taking into account the carriers that Air India would be planning to induct. An important caveat at this point would be in order: under no circumstances should the views of the concerned service headquarter not be the ultimate deciding factor. While charting the strategy for the development of our domestic defence industry we must identify technologies that require special attention; technologies where our capabilities merit quantum upgradation. It can be assumed that the DRDO, the services headquarters, and also the CII, would have undertaken studies on this subject. Our acquisition plans must look at integrating the road map that we should have drawn for technology inflows and digestion. Electronics, optics, communications and avionics, are generally the areas that we should be focussing on. We have for a few decades depended exclusively on Bharat Electronics for all our communication requirements as also all our electro-optical products.

Today Bharat Electronics may be a profit making company but has little to offer in terms of future technologies or next generation products. The same story applies to HAL, notwithstanding the successful development of the ALH, which should have been offered at least ten years earlier.

There is therefore a strong case to encourage private sector companies to enter these fields. The logic that since the Government has made investments in creating capabilities, all orders must be confined to these companies has proven over time to be counterproductive. A change in approach is long overdue. India urgently needs an HAL/BE in the private sector. The Government must encourage and support their emergence.

The subject of exports has also been grossly neglected. There may be a Joint Secretary in the Department of Defence Production responsible for promoting exports, but he can do little under the present dispensation. Pakistan's Ordnance Factories have consistently exported more than us. No defence industry can expect to sustain itself purely on the basis of sales in the domestic market.

Our private sector, unlike our Government owned establishments, have understood this. But they need much more support. The Government and the industry have to work together in a closely coordinated manner. Witness the way in which over the past few months the Heads of Governments of Germany, UK and France have brought with them the captains of their defence industries to India. The agenda requires no amplification. Here again we must push to get our act together

If India's defence industry is today on the threshold of transformation, considerable credit must be given to the role played by the CII. FICCI has also contributed, but only marginally. We may recall the first Army-Industry Partnership Seminar conducted in the mid nineties under the aegis of the CII. Many of us sceptics murmured-'what's the point?' But CII persevered. It continued with its efforts to nudge the industry and simultaneously influence our policy makers. It has also been actively persuading the big global players to look at teaming with the Indian industry. The results though slow, in the coming times would soon be there for us to witness. Having reached thus far, the CII must not take its foot off the pedal. Much more still needs to be done. Before concluding, some of the suggestions made are listed below:

- Protection to the PSUs and the OFB from domestic players must be progressively withdrawn.
- A major overhaul of the functioning control, organisation and functioning of the OFB and the defence PSUs has been long overdue. Can we not figure out a way to move forward on this issue?
- Pressures to dilute the 'offset clause' of the DPP must be resisted. What we should be focussing on is the mechanisms for monitoring post contract implementation.
- Encourage the absorption of service officers in the defence industry. The rules of interaction with industry representatives must change. The MOD and the services headquarters should be more accessible to domestic industry. Currently doors for foreigners open up much more easily.
- Put in special efforts to promote and assist the growth of the private sector in the areas of aviation, communications, electronics and sensors (optics). There should be a comprehensive action plan for the acquisition of key technologies. The Government and the industry should work in concert on this issue.
- Re-examine our procurement policies and strategies for major purchases. Given the nature of the global market we can perhaps extract much more from our big deals.

- The growth of our defence industry can only be sustained if its business model takes into account the imperative of exports for sustenance.
- The laudable role played by the CII merits recognition. Both the Government and the industry should continue to encourage the CII to step up its activities to accelerate reforms and change.

Our vision for India in the next two decades would be flawed if it did not envisage a sizeable, vibrant and sophisticated defence industry for us that is globally competitive and has the capacity to research and develop new state of the art cutting edge technologies.

Our industry has acquired a new found confidence. All it needs is direction and support form the Government. The launch of the Nano within four years of it being conceived has been inspiring. We hope the global awe it has attracted is repeated time and again. We want Nano clones now coming out of India's defence industry stable

With increasing outsourcing opportunities, the Indian aerospace and defence industry is emerging as a key participant in the Asia Pacific aerospace and defence market. Apart from India's perceived viability as an outsourcing hub for aerospace and defence products, the overwhelming involvement of the Government in areas of supply and demand cements its advantage in the industry.

The Government's pro-active soliciting of international cooperation has seen production moving to India, generating more opportunities for the country. Export competitiveness has been given priority, hence, there has been an increased thrust towards reduced import dependency.

The Indian economy is one the fastest growing in the world, reflecting the successful reform process initiated in 1991.

The Indian Government has gradually opened its key sectors to foreign participation and foreign investment in the Indian aerospace and defence industry which currently has a 26 percent cap. Meanwhile, since two-thirds of the Indian population depends on agricultural income, reforms in this area are widely considered necessary to aid economic growth.

Development of the agriculture sector, trade, as well as capital liberalisation, and improvement in investments, are some vital areas being focused upon by the current Government. The *Frost & Sullivan* Country Industry Forecast service for the Indian aerospace and defence industry uses a macroeconomic perspective to provide a focused analysis of the industry.

This service covers an array of issues pertaining to the industry including political stances, trade policies, industry regulations, as well as their overall impact. Besides enabling decision makers to assess the impact of non-market forces, this analysis also helps in identifying new opportunities in the industry. In addition, it provides a strong base for preparing business contingency plans.

SIGNIFICANCE OF THE ARMS TRADE TREATY FOR INDIA

Despite existing legislation in India, the problem of gun violence from illicit small arms has grown instead of abating. It is thus evident that the national laws and procedures prove inadequate to control the problem. An international agreement would help by helping states to review the loopholes within respective national legislations relating to SALW marking, recording and tracing methods. In the South Asian context, there is a need for dedicated attempts by states to prevent losses from government armouries and recover illicit weapons. Security sector bureaucracies tend to assume that problems of illicit SALW will go away once the problem of insurgent movements are solved. In a way, it explains a lack of political mobilization for victims of gun violence in India; it further explains why the problem of illicit small arms manufacture has grown in the country. To assuage concerns of states that the ATT may impinge on their sovereign rights, the treaty should obligate the governance structures of the states to carry out accountability checks and stockpile verification procedures to prevent flow of illicit small arms from and across the nation's borders. This should make up for the ressistance to effective international verifiable processes for the recovery of illicit small arms or stockpile monitoring and verification. India is located in an unstable region where controls on small arms proliferation by other states in the neighbourhood are weak. Considering there is easy availability of illicit small arms from across the border, and the fact that small arms are being manufactured in illegal factories in the region, provisions for a strong ATT will converge with India's long-term security and political interests in creating a stable regional order, by helping to address the problem of illicit weapons and armed political violence. This would also have application elsewhere in the region, given that smaller countries such as Nepal and Sri Lanka have faced much stronger threats from insurgent movements, i.e., Maoists and Liberation Tigers of Tamil Elam, respectively.

In terms of India's arms exports to countries with poor human rights records, such as Myanmar and Sudan, its compliance with ATT principles could be open to question. For countries where the application of international human rights and international humanitarian law has been found wanting, continuation of such could become a problem.

If the ATT includes adequate requirements for transparency and accountability, it will benefit India in two ways: one, it will improve its own processes for security sector accountability for stockpile management; and two, it will reduce the risk of diversion to NSAsfrom arsenals in those neighbouring countries that do not have strong, democratic control of their military sectors.

Indian security concerns relating to small arms and ammunition are primarily three-fold:

- risks of diversion of such arms to NSAs by centres of domestic production;
- illicit manufactures in neighbouring countries and illegal diversion from their arsenals; and
- sales by arms-exporting countries to intermediaries which are then re-transferred to third parties without proper end-user verification or accountability.

The ATT must identify action to be taken by or against the state parties that fail to control the abovementioned risks. India should urgently engage the international community to address these concerns. And, if India continues to engage with the ATT perfunctorily, then in all likelihood the ATT will come into force without having Indian concerns on board.

According to a representative of the Indian delegation in July 2011, the ATT is indicative of India's shifting position: "...the draft paper seems somewhat vague, to my delegation, in addressing the question of the illicit trade of conventional arms." 5

Thus the question is: what have the Indian representatives done to gather informed Indian opinion and develop India's position to advance progressive solutions to our country's problem from rising illicit trade of conventional arms?

Indian officials may also be concerned that allegations of human rights violations against its armed forces operating in disturbed areas could prevent transfer of technologies required for the design and manufacture of a new generation of SALW, from being acquired by its military from international sources. A way around this would be for the Indian armed forces and para-military forces being trained in programmes to address these issues: compliance with humanitarian and human rights laws and introducing human security concerns and those of victims of gun violence as well as security sector governance reforms.

Citizen-centric Considerations for Drafting of ATT

It is an accepted norm that states have sovereign rights to acquire weapons from international sources for their territorial defence. But they also have an obligation to ensure that such weapons that are acquired by their security forces, or are in transit, are not diverted to illicit markets or put to illegitimate use against any other state. In this regard, all states should actively co-ordinate international initiatives to identify and track violations of legitimate arms trade.

In pursuit of the abovementioned obligations, weapons-exporting countries, whose weapons are found in illicit trade, must share responsibility and compensation provided to the victims of gun violence irrespective of the territory in which the crime has occurred. In that regard, states which neglect compliance with provisions of the treaty, after having joined the ATT, should be deemed to be trading in illicit weapons and, therefore, debarred from international arms trade.

In order to achieve the objectives of arms acquisition transparency and responsibility, state parties should submit comprehensive national annual reports on international transfers of all arms and ammunition covered by the treaty to an international register, which should

a) analyse the data and publish comprehensive annual report on losses, diversions or thefts from national weapons stocks and arsenals;
b) publish assessments given by the state authorities on illegal manufacture of weapons in their territories;
c) enable legislative provisions for nationalverification of weapons stockpile security; and
d) provide international support and guidance to state parties in the form of regional training programmes for production of their national reports.

It is extremely important to have an international reporting and regulatory mechanism so as to standardise weapons markings, remove ambiguity and different interpretations in state practices as far as possible. Variations in implementation of the provisions of post-manufacture and imported weapons marking must be reduced to the minimum. This could be done by acceptance of best practices related to post-manufacture and import marking technologies.

A general lack of information and capacity in developing countries could impair such states from implementing provisions of the reporting, marking and regulatory mechanisms. Considering that the need for technical assistance is met through international organisations, more developing countries could be willing to undertake practical measures to implement the ATT markings and reporting requirements. This would help to maintain national arms sales registers that record and check all small arms and weapons held in the public sector as well as those held by private individuals, and their sales and gifts. If there is pilferage from state arsenals or from the state's stocks of de-commissioned weapons, data on such illicit weapons must be recorded in national registers and made available to the neighbouring states upon formal request. In this regard, the legal sales to individuals holding weapons licences can be abused if such individuals sell weapons to non-licence holders. States should be obliged to register all transactions between private individuals. For this purpose, all state parties should maintain a national contact point.

In addition, states should organise specialised agencies to proactively trace, track and seize illicit transfers of weapons to detect and prevent illegal manufacture of weapons on their territory, and to recover weapons lost by individuals and state agencies. All states must organise specialised police bureaus dedicated to these tasks with SALW control task forces deployed in areas that have a high incidence of illicit weapons.

Such a dedicated agency could be in shape of a specially-trained constabulary to investigate, recover and destroy illicit weapons and their manufacturing facilities and prevent unauthorised sales of weapons to and from former security forces personnel. Arming of civilians in border areas and disturbed districts must be banned. The state must maintain its monopoly over use of force in its territory.

Regional Cooperation Centres for prevention of illicit weapons transfers must be created to train and build capacities for detection, seizure and reporting mechanisms within the executive branches and the national security sector. The need for this can be gauged by the fact that the problem of illicit weapons proliferation varies in scale and scope from region to region and from province to province within states. For example, in the India-Pakistan sub-region, some districts/provinces are more notorious for manufacture of illicit weapons which end up across the borders in other states, and which contribute to high incidences of gun violence and illicit weapons proliferation.

As Pakistan has been more explicit in its call to prevent, combat and eradicate the illicit trade and trafficking in conventional arms, particularly small arms and light weapons, it behoves India to join its neighbour to the west in its quest to find practical solutions to address this problem. Whenever an importing state transfers imports weapons from government stocks to another government or civilian end user for re-sale, the re-assignment marking should be reported to the Central Register to be maintained at the arsenals of the original manufacturer as well as at the ATT Secretariat.

The compliance obligation for original markings should be on the seller and not on the buyer or importer. If a weapon is re-transferred to a third party, then the marking obligation should rest with the re-exporting state. India should move from its current method of engraving markings for the weapons it manufactures to non-erasable marking technologies.

As international assistance is required to develop standardised stockpile security management and verification procedures, its absence allows theft and pilferage to remain unverified within the state's security sector. To ensure compliance, penalities must be identified against states which neglect to check transfers of illicit small arms across their borders. This practical step is important for inclusion from India's perspective as large-scale illicit small arms are being transferred to insurgent groups in India through third countries.

The ATT should have provisions for verifiable destruction of old or de-commissioned weapons as these are likely to leak out of stocks or be sold without adequate end-use control.

SALW Marking, Recording and Tracing

Considering that weapons continue to be manufactured illicitly, whether in, for example, Landi Kotal, Darra Adam Khel in Pakistan or smuggled through other countries in the region add to the burden of problems in local policing and local security. 8 Illicit manufacturing in India or in Pakistan can have as much destabilising effect within their respective territories as they would have across borders. If the states are unable to comply with their public safety obligations, there is a need for international initiatives to be mobilised to address limitations in domestic processes relating to illicit gun manufacture at small-scale industrial facilities in a large number of small towns.

Ammunition Lot Markings, Recordings and Tracing

Even though it is very difficult to assign ownership of ammunition to a stock or group when recovered at the scene of crime, ammunition markings, when combined with thorough international verification of the chain of sales contracts (even if ammunition lots are re-transferred), should be enough to launch an enquiry into the leakages in sources of illicit arms proliferation. Methods for tracing of ammunition lots must begin from markings by the original manufacturer being standardised and made mandatory. Standardised international practices must be designed and adopted to help to identify and follow ammunition lots right from the place of recovery to its original source of manufacture in order to discourage illicit trafficking.

It is important that larger countries in South Asia—India and Pakistan—should lead the way to develop national legislation that obligate the original ammunition manufacturer to mark the identity of the first export recipient of ammunition; thereafter, subsequent re-sales must be recorded in an international tracing registry. Alongwith online book keeping procedures, lot numbering will make it possible to trace the movement of ammunition.

There are two preconditions essential for tracing: (a) the ammunition has been marked according to standardised international practices, and (b) the information relating to the marked ammunition has been recorded and stored in a centralised database, thus enabling tracing to start and evidence can be collected to initiate legal proceedings against all participants insmuggling en route.

Ammunition markings are not the only means of tracing a weapon. Even a marked ammuni¬tion lot could be transferred several times after it was diverted from its original purpose. But markings, combined with thorough analysis of the sales or re-sales contracts, should be sufficient to start an enquiry into the sources of illicit proliferation.Combined with legislated obligations for national-level recording and book keeping, the state parties would be provided with a means of detecting diversions from national stocks. In countries, where surveillance of ammunition delivery personnel are weak, ammunition lot marking could be a valuable back-up method. Internationally binding and nationally-regulated management of ammunition stockpiles and SALW transfers must develop preventive and pro-active measures to check illegal di¬version. It is in India's interest to convince countries that oppose the international practice of marking of SALW and ammunition to strengthen their national stockpile management and verification practices. It is curious that the states that seem most affected by the non-regulation of ammunition also oppose any international controls measures most fiercely.

EDB Engineering , a Belgian company, has developed a process for laser-marking of ammunition. This technology is regarded as revolutionary for the efficient tracea¬bility of ammunition. The innovative technique is based on laser technology and can apply a marking after assembly, just before the cartridges are packaged and delivered to the customer. Such a procedure would be impossible with the stamping technique, which, in any case, can be defaced. The armaments industry views this technique as an effective ammunition marking process, which has since been developed for one of the world's leading ammunition manufacturers. EDB has proved that, technically, the identification of each piece of ammunition is a feasible operation and that financially too this laser process may be considered to be acceptable. However, the costs will come down once this technology gets widely spread.

SMALL ARMS AND LIGHT WEAPONS MARKINGS

As micro-stamping and laser marking technology will become widely available, it will enable manufacturers to stamp all the information needed to mark the origin, registration and tracing of am¬munition, right from the time of manufacture. The same technologies, with due modification, can used for marking and tracing of SALW.

International cooperation is required to facilitate access to state-of-the-art technology for un-erasable and unique/standardised markings. There is a need to facilitate developing countries to fully implement provisions on post-manufacture non-erasable marking of weapons to establish the place and date of manufacture of weapons as part of their production process. These non-erasable markings should be of three kinds:

- Proof marking, which should indicate links with an ATT Central Register that must be maintained at the factories of its original manufacture and at the ATT Secretariat.
- Import marking, for identification of the country and year of import.
- Weapons assignment and export marking, which should identify weapons designed for the country's armed forces, weapons designed for security forces of foreign states, or weapons assigned for sale to private individuals.

The un-erasable laser markings that are required to verify diversion of SALW should describe the year of manufacture, original manufacturer, weapon number, and the identification of the recipient of the arms. The units of armed police and the military also need to have access to facilities of markings as weapons get transferred from one unit to the other. The information must be inscribed deeply enough to prevent erasure of marking history. It should be inscribed at such places on the weapon where average wear and tear would not deface the history of re-transfers. Recording of these markings must be available in national databases and records maintained for a period of 50 years for SALW. The data should be transferable officially to the elec¬tronic register kept by the national authorities and specific querries must be responded to if formally requested by international parties to the treaty.

With these developments in standardised international marking of SALW and ammunition, it would be possible to identify leakages and trace illicit transfers as never before. It will plug loopholes in illicit transfers and reduce the burden on weapons recovery policing. In South Asia, it will release resources and increase confidence in the police system to go actively after illicit manufacture within small villages and towns of the country. Once national legislations are made and enforced, it is likely to make the technology cost-effective through a wider international spread and obligatory standardisation of weapon's marking norms.

International Traceability Instruments

Improvements in domestic legislation and controls on SALW and ammunition would help in identification of illicit delivery and smuggling networks.

In absence of a legally binding in¬ternational traceability instruments, countries that export SALW and ammunition can avoid responsibility when their arms or ammunition are seized overseas in the hands of criminal gangs or insurgent groups. Related domestic legislation, control and prevention instruments in different countries will lead to effective marking to check illicit arms transfers and smuggling.

Many states have an irrational fear of having to account in front of international jurisdictions, little realising the larger benefits to public safety in their countries.

The Indian state should actively engage to encourage promotion of international processes that obligate arms and ammunition manufacturing countries to frame their legislation on marking, recording of data, and a tracing me¬chanism based on active international cooperation and changing political habits.

These steps should be the basis of the Internatio¬nal Instrument for the traceability of SALW and lead to its effective implementation. Even though there would be a political-bureaucratic battle to build up regional consensus in South Asia to abide by regional and internatio¬nal instruments, our diplomats owe this to thousands of innocent victims of firearms in India.

Thereafter, the armed forces and armed police, as part of obligations of the state parties, must annually report losses and recoveries to their respective parliaments. This should include methods of effectiveness of management of marking, recording and tracing for verification of ammunition stocks. The report should explain responsibilities of personnel for marking (on principles of uniformity and clarity) and tracing by recording in a data base. Recording of movement of ammunition (including re-location of stocks, sales and transfers within or between stocks) and independent cross-checking of stock holdings is essential for tracing of illicit trafficking.

International Experience

There are useful examples of counter-measures against illicit proliferation of SALW from Brazil, where a compulsory electronic connection between the databases of the armed force establishments is required with the offices controlling manufacture, imports and exports of weapons and the Brazilian Federal Police, which maintain a centralised information and data on confiscated weapons and ammunition.

Previously, a lack of communication and information exchange between these institutions prevented efficient action against diversion and trafficking. The new law also provides for a centralised ballistic information system run by the Brazilian Federal Police, which contain samples of bullets fired from each small arm and light weapon manufactured in Brazil. This should make it possible to identify light weapons used during crimes as well as identifying the origin of ammunition which was legally transferred but since been diverted to the illicit market.

The new Brazilian law on ammunition makes it obiligatory for the police and the armed forces to have their stampings on bullets and cartridges to be included in their lot numbers. This measure should improve the security of military and police stockpiles, and would enable the police to identify the leakages of ammunition from each of the two institutions towards organised crime. The penalties provided in the law should be sufficiently dissuasive towards arms trafficking, diversion of ammunition, theft and illicit stockpiling of ammunition, illicit manufacture and trading in firearms, and activities related to international arms trafficking.

Recommendations

India needs to take a progressive approach to address the problem of illicit small arms which takes into account humanitarian concerns. This approach aims to provide state parties with a means of detecting diversions from national stocks or from points in transit. In states where the control and surveillance of ammunition-handling personnel are inadequate, ammunition lot markings could also serve as a valuable tool for back-up surveillance against diversion or theft.

In addition, if in due course of time, all countries are obliged to have electronically connect their weapons database and ammunition manufacturing entities, the details of losses by units under their Minstries of Defence and the armed police units under the Ministry of Home Affairs; traceability of diverted weapons will then be easier. But the Indian paper is conspicuously silent on much needed aspects of public safety. Fortunately, there is a view that advocates ATT to take humanitarian concerns into account. The least Indian diplomats can do in New York is not to obstruct such advocacy and abstain from criticising progressive ideas, as the Indian public certainly does not want a still-born or an ineffective arms trade treaty.

INDIA ABSTAINS AND EXPOSES THE ARMS TRADE TREATY

Once again India has been forced to abstain from voting in favour of a discriminatory global Arms Trade Treaty (ATT) – after its unpleasant experience with the NPT and the CTBT in the past. The treaty, aimed at laying down common international standards and limiting the illicit sale of conventional arms, was passed by the UN General Assembly with an overwhelming majority of 154 votes on April 3, 2013. Iran, North Korea and Syria voted against the treaty while China, India and Russia abstained.

As the largest importer of arms in the world, India objects to the ATT on several counts. First and foremost, India finds it difficult to accept that the treaty will enable arms exporting countries to impose unilateral conditions on the countries that import arms. The treaty has failed to address Indian concerns about the illegal transfer of arms to terrorist organisations, insurgent groups and other non-state actors who oppose democratically elected governments. The treaty also does not ensure a "balance of obligations" between arms exporting states and the importers of arms.

As a country with a pacifist strategic culture, India has traditionally abhorred the export of arms and itself refrained from doing so for several decades after independence. India has 39 Ordnance factories, which are wholly government owned, and eight Defence Public Sector Undertakings (DPSUs). India's defence exports are less than two per cent of the total production of weapons and equipment and were valued at USD 191 million (Rs 859.60 crore) in 2008-09. These are mainly indigenously produced surplus small arms and light weapons that have been supplied to some of India's neighbours as a goodwill gesture. However, the new Defence Procurement Policy (DPP) and the new Defence Production Policy (DPrP) are encouraging the formation of joint ventures with 26 per cent foreign direct investment (FDI). This is expected to go up to 49 per cent, gradually resulting in an increase in arms exports as MNCs will begin to use their Indian joint ventures as hubs for sourcing weapons and equipment components for their factories abroad.

India is likely to spend approximately USD 100 billion for the import of weapons and defence equipment over the next 10 years. The DPP stipulates an offsets commitment of 30 per cent of the total value of a contract if it exceeds USD 66 million (Rs 300.00 crore). In fact, the offsets obligation specified for the multi-mission, medium-range combat aircraft (MMRCA) is 50 per cent of the total value, which is estimated to exceed USD 12 billion. Assuming that 60 to 70 per cent of the import contracts will exceed USD 66 million, defence MNCs exporting to India will be required to procure items worth approximately USD 18 to 21 billion from Indian companies over the next 10 years by way of direct and indirect offsets. Even though the items that may be exported by these MNCs and joint ventures will be mainly components and not fully assembled weapons system, India needs to ensure that the stipulations of the ATT do not bar such exports.

South Asia is arguably the second most dangerous global hotspot after West Asia and radical extremism in the Af-Pak area is making the region further dangerous. One of the major reasons for this is the large-scale proliferation and easy availability of small arms and light weapons (SALW). India has witnessed around 152 militant movements since independence, of which 65 are believed to be still active in one form or the other. Pakistan is still the primary source of small arms that are India bound. It uses SALW as political and military tools against New Delhi and facilitates smuggling of SALW both through sea and land routes to ISI-supported terrorist organisations and sleeper cells across India. Funding for SALW proliferation can be accredited to money laundering and safe havens abroad organised through hawala channels. The transfer of small arms takes place mostly through clandestine routes and the grey market.

The Chinese angle to SALW proliferation in South Asia also cannot be ignored. Chinese weapons gained immense popularity among the insurgent groups in the region as they were competitively priced and low-level officials offered counter-trade agreements. The Chinese weapons pipeline soon permeated into Myanmar's underground markets along the Thai border. Beginning with the Type 56 rifle, China produced and offered for sale five different varieties of rifles (Type 56, 68, 79, 81 and 5.56 Type CQ), allied light machine guns and sub-machine guns. China also became the prime official supplier to Sri Lanka, Myanmar and Pakistan (including anti-aircraft and anti-tank weapons). Significantly, large numbers of weapons of Chinese origin have been seized in Cox's Bazaar in Bangladesh.

The Chinese supplied small arms to Indian insurgent groups in Manipur, Mizoram, Nagaland and Tripura for many years up to the late-1970s. In a statement with far reaching consequences, India's Home Secretary, G K Pillai, said on November 9, 2009, that the Maoists in India were receiving small arms from China, "Chinese are big suppliers of small arms..." Earlier, then Union Home Minister P Chidambaram had said in an interview in October 2009 that the Maoists were acquiring weapons through Bangladesh, Myanmar and possibly Nepal since the Indo-Nepal border is a porous border.

Since 1989-90, Indian security forces have seized huge stocks of arms and ammunition along the LoC in J&K alone. It has been documented that between 1990 and 2005, as many as 28,000 assault rifles of the AK-47 series; 1,300 machine guns; 2,000 rocket launchers; 365 sniper rifles; 10,000 assorted pistols; 63,000 hand grenades; seven million rounds of ammunition; 6,200 land mines and IEDs and 37,000 kg of explosives were recovered from various hideouts in J&K during counter-proxy war operations. Large-scale recoveries are still being made. Large numbers of illegal arms also comes into the country through the north-east and from the Khyber-Pakhtoonkhwa province (NWFP) on Pakistan's Afghan border. India finds itself at the centre of two major international weapons warehouses—the NWFP and the Southeast Asian arms market comprising Thailand, Cambodia and Myanmar, with approximately 13 identified gun-running routes close to India's north-eastern border areas and the Chittagong hill tracts.

Countries exporting arms have a responsibility to ensure that they do not provide weapons without strict end user verification or else SALW may be diverted to wage intra-state conflict by non-state actors. The ATT should have refrained from imposing new norms; it should have reinforced the existing obligations and responsibilities of all countries under international law and should have provided a mechanism for their effective application to the trade in SALW.

The present treaty is also deficient on monitoring and verification. While initially monitoring may have to rely on the good practices of the member states, viable technical means need to be developed over time. Subsequently, the treaty must make provisions for intrusive international monitoring of sources, means of transportation of weapons and, where possible, their end use based on formal complaints being launched by affected state parties. Such a system can only be implemented by constituting an international body like the IAEA.

India accords immense importance to compliance with arms control, non-proliferation and export control regimes, even though India is not a signatory to some of them. Hence, an initiative like the ATT, that seeks to establish a global benchmark, would under normal circumstances have been welcomed and supported, but the treaty has turned out to be discriminatory.

The government of India has instituted stringent controls for the export of arms, including the requirement of an end-user certificate from the country to which SALW are to be exported. Each request is thoroughly vetted before an arms export license is cleared by the government.

India ensures that no arms are exported to countries that are involved in conflict, or to non-state actors engaged in intra-state conflict. In fact, most arms exports out of India so far have been those of goodwill gestures towards friendly countries in India's neighbourhood. Despite repeated requests from Sri Lanka and at the risk of driving it into Chinese or Pakistani arms, India had steadfastly refused to supply offensive weapons when the Sir Lankan armed forces were engaged in fighting the LTTE. Only non-offensive equipment like air defence guns and radars were supplied.

Elaborating on the complexity of small arms proliferation, former UN Secretary General, Kofi Annan had stated perceptively, "Small arms proliferation is not merely a security issue; it is also an issue of human rights and of development." The moral argument for an ATT, one that underpins human security, social and economic development is overwhelming. However, if it is viewed through the prism of disarmament or arms control instrument, it will not find much support. While India has not voted in favour of the ATT, it will undoubtedly adhere to all its provisions, much as it has done in respect of the NPT and the CTBT.

Bibliography

Ahmad, Imtiaz: *State and Foreign Policy: India's Role in South Asia*, New Delhi, Vikas, 1993.

Ajey Lele: *Strategic Technologies for the Military : Breaking New Frontiers*, Sage, Delhi, 2009.

Allison, Graham, *Nuclear Terrorism: The Ultimate Preventable Catastrophe*, New York: Times Books, 2004.

Appleby, Paul H.: *Policy and Administration*, Birmingham, AL: University of Alabama Press, 1949.

Barber B.R.: *Strong Democracy. Participatory Politics for a New Age*. Berkeley, University of California Press, 1984.

Bhat, T.P. : *India and China : Trade Complementarities and Competitiveness*, Bookwell, Delhi, 2008.

Chandra, R.: *Judicial System in Mechanical Warfare*, Lucknow, Print House (India), 1992.

Chitkara, M.G. : *Indo-Pak Relations Challenges Before New Millennium*, APH, Delhi, 2001.

Conway, G. 1992. *Sustainable Rural Livelihoods: Practical Concepts for 21st Century*. Sussex: Institute of Development Studies.

Deepak, B R : *India and China : 1904-2004 : A Century of Peace and Conflict*, Manak, Delhi, 2005.

Dixit, A.K. : *Military Wars and Rescue Techniques*, Cyber Tech Pub, Delhi, 2010.

Freedman, Lawrence. *The Evolution of Nuclear Strategy*. Studies in International Security, #20. New York: St. Martin's Press, 1981.

Goel, Suresh : *Military, Security and Intelligence Agencies*, MD Publications, Delhi, 2009.

Jha, Prem Shankar : *India and China : The Battle Between Soft and Hard Power*, Penguin Books India, Delhi, 2010.

Kaufmann, Albert R. *Nuclear Reactor Fuel Elements: Metallurgy and Fabrication*. New York: Interscience Publishers, Inc., 1962.

Keane J.: *Democracy and Civil Liberty*, London, Verso, 1988.

Kumar, Raj : *Weapons and Military Technology*, Sumit Enterprises, Delhi, 2009.

Kunju, N. : *Indo-Pak : Nuclear Cold War*, Reliance, Delhi, 2002.

Leena Parmar: *Military Sociology : Global Perspectives*, Rawat, Delhi, 1999.

Mary, W.: *Asian Power and Politics: the Cultural Dimensions of Authority*, Cambridge, Belknap Press, 1985.

McPhee, John. *The Curve of Binding Energy*. New York: The Noonday Press, 1992.

Moseley, Philip E.: *Russian Diplomacy and the Opening of the Eastern Question*, Cambridge, Harvard University Press, 1934.

Nayyar, K K : *National Security : Military Aspects*, Rupa, Delhi, 2003.

Peter Van Der Veer: *Patterns of Middle Class Consumption in India and China*, Sage, Delhi, 2008.

Posen, B.R.: *The Sources of Military Doctrine*, Ithaca, 1984, Cornell Univ. Press.

Prasad, Lal Bahadur : *Indian Political System and Law*, New Delhi, Shree, 2005.

Puryear, V. J.: *International Economics and Diplomacy in the Near East*, London, Oxford University, 1935.

Randall Forsberg: *The Arms Production Dilemma: Contraction and Restraint in the World Combat Aircraft Industry*, Cambridge, Massachusetts: MIT Press, 1994.

Robert M Cassidy: *Counterinsurgency and the Global War on Terror : Military Culture and Irregular War*, Pentagon Press, Delhi, 2008.

Samuel P. Huntington: *The Soldier and the State : The Theory and Politics of Civil-Military Relations*, Natraj Pub, Delhi, 2005.

Shaun Narine, *Explaining ASEAN: Regionalism in Southeast Asia*, Boulder, CO: Lynne Rienner Publishers, 2002.

Singh, R.S.N. : *Asian Strategic and Military Perspective*, Lancer, Delhi, 2005.

Singhal, D. P.: *India and Afghanistan: 1876-1907. A Study in Diplomatic Relations*, St. Lucia, University of Queensland, 1963.

Thampi, Madhavi : *India and China in the Colonial World*, Social Science Press, Delhi, 2010.